Punctuated Equilibria and Sino-American Relations

In many areas of the natural and physical world, long periods of seeming stasis or small incremental changes are interrupted by large, sudden leaps. This book illustrates how similar processes characterize international relations. It points to such occurrences as the collapse of the USSR, the unraveling of Napoleon's wartime alliance, and the possible future status of the US dollar; and it illustrates in greater detail the admission of China to the United Nations, the history of economic development of various countries, and the possible formation of a countervailing coalition against US primacy. Steve Chan investigates these instances and explains the dynamics governing these processes of lulls and lurches and illuminates how qualitative research can apply the Boolean logic to study systematically the danger of a possible future Sino-American conflict based on past episodes.

STEVE CHAN'S other recent books include *Mobilizing the Past* (Stanford, 2025); *Fuses, Chains and Backlashes* (Oxford, 2025); *Geography and International Conflict* (Routledge, 2025) with Weixing Hu; *Taiwan and the Danger of a Sino-American War* (Cambridge, 2024) and *Culture, Economic Growth, and Interstate Power Shift* (Cambridge, 2024).

Punctuated Equilibria and Sino-American Relations

Lulls and Lurches across the Pacific

STEVE CHAN
University of Colorado Boulder

CAMBRIDGE
UNIVERSITY PRESS

CAMBRIDGE
UNIVERSITY PRESS

Shaftesbury Road, Cambridge CB2 8EA, United Kingdom

One Liberty Plaza, 20th Floor, New York, NY 10006, USA

477 Williamstown Road, Port Melbourne, VIC 3207, Australia

314–321, 3rd Floor, Plot 3, Splendor Forum, Jasola District Centre, New Delhi – 110025, India

103 Penang Road, #05-06/07, Visioncrest Commercial, Singapore 238467

Cambridge University Press is part of Cambridge University Press & Assessment, a department of the University of Cambridge.

We share the University's mission to contribute to society through the pursuit of education, learning and research at the highest international levels of excellence.

www.cambridge.org
Information on this title: www.cambridge.org/9781009634489

DOI: 10.1017/9781009634502

First published 2025

Cover image: Stars and stripes / simon2579 / DigitalVision Vectors / Getty Images

A catalogue record for this publication is available from the British Library

Library of Congress Cataloging-in-Publication Data
Names: Chan, Steve author
Title: Punctuated equilibria and Sino-American relations : lulls and lurches across the Pacific / Steve Chan, University of Colorado, Boulder.
Other titles: Lulls and lurches across the Pacific
Description: Cambridge, United Kingdom ; New York, NY : Cambridge University Press, 2025. | Includes bibliographical references.
Identifiers: LCCN 2025006320 (print) | LCCN 2025006321 (ebook) | ISBN 9781009634489 hardback | ISBN 9781009634465 paperback | ISBN 9781009634502 epub
Subjects: LCSH: United States–Relations–China | China–Relations–United States | Equilibrium
Classification: LCC E183.8.C5 C3888 2025 (print) | LCC E183.8.C5 (ebook)
LC record available at https://lccn.loc.gov/2025006320
LC ebook record available at https://lccn.loc.gov/2025006321

ISBN 978-1-009-63448-9 Hardback
ISBN 978-1-009-63446-5 Paperback

Contents

Contents

Preface

Change is a common feature of our social and physical world. Some people may even argue that it is an inevitable part of life. Yet, in my discipline of political science and, more specifically, the field of international relations, change has not been a central research concern. Although it is by no means absent in our research agendas, the dynamics that initiate and characterize change have not been at the forefront of our collective enterprise. Thus, for example, although power-transition theory (Organski and Kugler 1980) and its more recent rendition as Thucydides' Trap (Allison 2017) obviously stress power shifts between major states as a source of war, analysts have not generally sought to understand the sources and nature of such changes in altering relations between the pertinent states. Our typical mode of analysis involves linear extrapolation of existing trends, and thus assumes inertia and continuity. Questions concerning velocity, cyclicality, periodicity, reversibility, and sudden surges or plunges rarely attract our collective attention.

Just as with change, stability or stationarity is ubiquitous or appears to be so – until some disturbance occurs to disrupt stasis and initiate change. For example, a ruling elite may be able to perpetuate its power for a long time until social pressure reaches a critical point to produce a revolution replacing it with a new regime with a very different ideology and policy agenda. This political change can be massive and occur abruptly. Thus, we need a theory or at least a perspective that would be able to capture and hopefully explain both persistence and transformation. Frank Baumgartner and Bryan Jones ([1993] 2009) addressed this need in their influential book on the making of public policies in the United States. Whereas previous scholarship has emphasized incrementalism, gradualism, or seeming stasis as the dominant feature of American policy processes and their output, these authors showed that public policy can also occasionally exhibit sharp departures from the routine when a confluence of favorable conditions exists (Kingdon

1984). Stasis and change are both present in policy processes, giving them the appearance of long periods of quiescence followed by brief interludes of sudden bursts of innovation.

Baumgartner and Jones drew their inspiration from evolutionary biology and the concept of punctuated equilibrium popularized by Niles Eldredge and Stephen J. Gould (1972) to describe long periods of species stability that is sometimes interrupted by rapid, localized leaps in a relatively short (geologically speaking) time. Contrary to the then prevailing Darwinian view which saw biological evolution as a gradual process consisting of incremental changes occurring over a very long time, they contended that it was characterized by protracted periods of stasis *and* short, sudden bursts of transformation. Fossil records show both continuity and discontinuity. Stasis and change are two sides of the same coin; they are mutually constitutive.

This book applies this new (for most analysts of international relations) and exciting perspective to study Sino-American relations, such as in establishing landmark events that represented critical turning points in successive "epochs" in the history of relations between China and the United States, such as Mao Zedong's decision to intervene in the Korean War in 1950 (Chen 1994; Whiting 1960) and Richard Nixon's decision to visit Beijing in 1972 (Shambaugh and Sutter 2022). It seeks to explain the culmination of a long process in the United Nations that in October 1971 finally punctured the previous deadlock that had kept Beijing out of this world organization, applies the "garbage can" model of policymaking and its conjunctive logic to discern the probability of US military intervention in a conflict with China over Taiwan's status, and illuminates the dyssynchronous timing and phases of economic development (such as shown by Walt Rostow's 1971 stages-of-growth model) and their effects on interstate power shifts and frictions that may presage war (such as in Graham Allison's 2017 rendition of Thucydides' Trap).

The processes involved in these phenomena are characterized by protracted periods of dormancy followed by sharp and sudden discontinuities or ruptures which we also see in the natural world, such as those shown by the dynamics producing earthquakes, avalanches, landslides, and volcano eruptions. In international relations, similar processes have characterized the sudden defection of Napoleon and Hitler's wartime allies, the rapid abandonment of communism by Eastern European regimes in quick succession in the final days of the

Cold War, the precipitous decline and sudden collapse of the USSR after over seventy years of communist rule, and the acceleration of "unraveling" near the end of US involvement in the Vietnam and Afghanistan wars.

The future status of the US dollar in international trade and finance, Washington's mounting costs in financing its budgetary deficit and national debt, the danger of overreaching in the formulation and conduct of its foreign policy as explained by Paul Kennedy's (1987) warning about imperial overstretch, and the emergence of a possible anti-US coalition from incipient coalitions such as the Shanghai Cooperation Organization and the BRICS (Brazil, Russia, India, China, and South Africa) group may also show similar processes of seeming stasis for a long time only to be disrupted by a major, dramatic breakthrough. With respect to the possibility of an anti-US coalition, it either will not form or will form very quickly for reasons that should become evident from my analysis in this book. For a variety of psychological, bureaucratic, and political reasons, major policy changes are rare. But when they happen, they tend to be big and sudden, and "fast and furious." These illustrations point to the buildup of cumulative pressure eventually producing a sharp disruption, because the forces favoring the status quo have held change at bay for too long. The looming insolvency of the US social security program comes to mind. Delay in addressing this issue makes a future attempt to fix it more challenging and potentially requiring more drastic action.

These illustrations also suggest that linear extrapolations of recent trends, especially if they are based on a few observations, can be highly misleading. Thus, just as a dramatic transformation can occur after a long period of quiescence, this development does not continue forever. In other words, stagnation can follow in the wake of a punctuation which leads to a new equilibrium and thus another prolonged period of "normalcy." For example, the meteoric rise of China's economy, which has caused consternation and even alarm in Western circles, cannot continue forever. As the German saying goes, trees do not grow to the sky. At the same time, even when conditions may appear to be calm and stable just a short while ago, an imminent danger can materialize suddenly such as a gathering storm threatening seafarers. Moreover, path dependency, accelerating momentum, and cumulative pressure can conspire to produce the onset of a state's rapid ascent or precipitous decline.

This book represents the latest contribution to my research program on Sino-American relations. This program has been motivated by a general concern with a possible conflict between the world's two most powerful states and thus the most important interstate relationship barring none. My previous books have dealt with different aspects pertinent to this concern, such as the ongoing power shifts between these two countries, their respective culture and economic performance affecting these shifts, their policy outlook and revisionist tendencies, their geopolitical circumstances, the domestic sources of their foreign policy, and their respective alliance ties that can engulf them in a clash that originates from a dispute involving a third party.

More than any of my previous books, research on this one has encouraged me to leave the comfort zone provided by a familiar disciplinary niche to venture into fields afar. This intellectual journey has brought me into contact with topics that I had known little or nothing about, such as those that have engaged the attention of colleagues working in the fields of public administration and policy, budgetary processes, international environmental regimes, fuzzy logic, earth sciences, and even paleontology. This foray has broadened my intellectual horizon.

Three themes have run through my previous research, and they continue to characterize this book's orientation and premise. First, I emphasize the importance of situating Sino-American relations in a comparative context, applying insights from international relations scholarship in general to study this dyad rather than treating it as sui generis. The reader will see frequent instances when I draw on theoretical insights and historical analyses of other countries' experiences to inform our understanding of this dyad. Second, I argue that monocausal explanations are rarely adequate for explaining complex phenomena such as war and peace. Rather, it is more fruitful and valid to direct our attention to a confluence of conditions, or the conjunctive influence of several factors, and their interactive effects in affecting the evolution of interstate relations. Finally, we need to attend to both change and stability – and the causes for both. Reasoning based on linear extrapolation from current or recent conditions can be seriously misleading and dispose us to overlook signs of significant changes lying ahead. These themes continue to be relevant and important for this book.

Many colleagues working in the field of China studies or Sino-American relations have invested heavily in learning the Chinese language and spending time on fieldwork in China. Therefore, they have less time and energy devoted to catching up on social science methods and theories in general. They publish in country- or area-specific journals like the *China Quarterly* and *Asian Survey*, addressing a readership consisting primarily of other country or regional experts like themselves. Their studies tend to be Sino-centric and often offer rich, descriptive narratives. These scholars are generally detached from the field of international relations as reflected in research published in journals like *International Security*, *International Studies Quarterly*, *Journal of Conflict Resolution*, and *International Organization*. Conversely, scholars of international relations, such as those who specialize in the study of war and peace and publish in those journals just mentioned, often lack deep knowledge of specific countries such as China and their historical background. Their work often utilizes large datasets and statistical methods. While their work is useful for showing broad empirical patterns, this work by its very nature is usually not informed by knowledge about specific cases or contexts. There are also colleagues who have worked in government and thus participated personally in policymaking. They write for journals such as *Foreign Affairs* and *Foreign Policy*. These colleagues have valuable policy experience, and their work has timely relevance for public policy. They are, however, usually uninterested in pursuing the rigor of empirical research or the development of theory. Each of the above scholarly communities makes a valuable contribution in its own way, but it does not usually interact or communicate with the others – even though there are certainly examples of those who have navigated successfully across these boundaries and established a well-deserved reputation and impressive credentials in all these communities. My own work shows this "tribalism." In this book, however, "I let myself go a little" as Albert Hirschman (1970) has reportedly said about writing his influential book, *Exit, Voice, and Loyalty*. As mentioned already, I have ventured into unfamiliar topical areas, an intellectual journey that is of course exciting but also risky. I hope that the result is not disappointing.

1 Introduction

The Perspective of Punctuated Equilibrium

This study is about change, a particular kind of change in international relations. In the realm of social, economic, and political affairs, we often observe seemingly sudden, major changes after long periods of stagnation. Stocks can trade sideways for a long time only to have their share prices surge or fall precipitously in a matter of days, even hours. We also sometimes gain the impression that state governments in the United States can change their policies, such as on the legalization of marijuana, gambling, and same-sex marriage or the settlement of class action lawsuits with large corporations in quick succession or en masse after a protracted period of relative inactivity. In economic development, we also often encounter prolonged periods of stagnation to be followed by sudden growth spurts or brief intervals of "efflorescence" (Goldstone 2002).

In the natural world, volcanoes can erupt violently, and massive earthquakes can wreak havoc after long periods of dormancy. An avalanche can be set off suddenly when a new layer of snow is added to an already overloaded snowpack, and when vibration or movement triggers it to slide. Similarly, rain-soaked soil is prone to sudden, even massive, land- or rockslides. Fossil evidence from plants and animals suggests extended periods of stasis followed by abrupt (in terms of geological time) spurts of species transformation. This evidence suggests that instead of a constant rate of incremental adaptation, evolution appears to be characterized by sharp discontinuities. Niles Eldredge and Stephen J. Gould (1972) describe this phenomenon as punctuated equilibrium whereby long periods of species stability are followed by rapid, localized bursts of change, which can in turn lead to another era of stasis or in many cases, extinction. Instead of small, gradual changes over many millions of years due to natural selection, the evolution of species appears sometimes to be characterized by abrupt leaps. These paleontologists argue that the fossil evidence necessary to support Charles Darwin's (1859) theory of evolution

1

based on gradualism is virtually nonexistent, and that the history of species tends to be instead characterized by long periods of stasis interrupted by short surges of transformation. They state their thesis in these words:

We believe that punctuational change dominates the history of life: evolution is concentrated in very rapid events of speciation (geologically instantaneous, even if tolerably continuous in ecological time). Most species, during their geological history, either do not change in any appreciable way, or else they fluctuate mildly in morphology, with no apparent direction. Phyletic grad-ualism is very rare and too slow, in any case, to produce the major events of evolution. Evolutionary trends are not the product of slow, directional transformation within lineages. (Gould and Eldredge 1977: 115)

In Gould and Eldredge's view, paleontologists have for too long accepted as an article of faith the assertion that evolution is a smooth, gradual, incremental process. Instead of considering the lack of fossil evidence supporting this assertion as meaningful data, they have dis-missed its significance by treating this phenomenon as a problem of missing data or "no data" – or, in other words, imperfection in the data thus far collected. Yet, an absence of evidence showing change is itself important and meaningful data. Accumulated evidence on speci-ation points to long periods of continuity that are interrupted by sudden, major transformation without intermediate stages of change. Gould and Eldredge (1977: 116, italics in original) argue, "morpho-logical breaks in the stratigraphic record may be real, and that *stasis is data* – that each case of stasis has as much meaning for evolutionary theory as each example of change."

These same authors remind their readers that Western liberal thoughts have a proclivity to favor perspectives emphasizing incremen-tal processes producing gradual but ineluctable progress. The idea that cumulative quantitative changes can erupt suddenly to produce a qualitative – revolutionary – transformation tends to be more alien to these thoughts. This idea, however, is more popular in other belief systems. Gould and Eldredge (1977: 146) quote from the anonymous writer(s) of an official Soviet handbook on Marxism and Leninism:

The transition of a thing, through the accumulation of quantitative modifi-cations, from one qualitative state to a different, new state, is a leap in development ... It is the transition to a new quality and signalizes a sharp turn, a radical change in development ... We often describe modern

Darwinism as a theory of the evolution of the organic world, implying that this evolution covers both qualitative and quantitative changes. Leap-like qualitative changes in social life are designated by the concept of revolution ... The evolutionary development of society is inevitably consummated by leap-like qualitative transformation, by revolutions.

The world view or belief system of Chinese Communists shares this understanding of the nature of change:

"Quantitative changes" (incremental changes in actor attributes) can over time lead to "qualitative changes" (step-level leaps); the occurrence of a "qualitative change" indicates that a structural transformation in actor relationships has taken place. (Bobrow et al. (1979: 56)

There can be long periods of stability with barely discernible signs of change, but less visible processes can be unfolding beneath the surface such that their cumulative effects can suddenly accelerate momentum to culminate in a drastic transformation of the status quo. Protracted stasis followed by large change can indeed be two sides of the same coin. Resistance to change produces increasing pressure over time so that when change occurs, it is more sudden and massive. The analogy of a coiled spring comes to mind.

The Genesis of Punctuated Equilibria in Political Science

This book is interested in the possible occurrence of such step-level change in international relations, especially as it pertains to Sino-American relations. Our accustomed ways of thinking and our usual methods of analysis (based on linear extrapolation) are not equipped to address such phenomena. In the realm of social sciences and human behavior, Stephen Gould (2002: 957) observes that "plateaus of stagnation and bursts of achievement might express a standard pattern for human learning," and that "important changes in our lives occur more often by rapid transition than by gradual accretion." Birth and death, marriage and divorce, career changes, and for academics, degree conferral and tenure decisions mark life's turning points.

In their influential book on agenda setting, Frank Baumgartner and Bryan Jones ([1993] 2009: xvi) conclude that "the course of public policy in the United States is not gradual and incremental, but rather is disjoint and episodic." They go on to remark that it is characterized by "long periods of relative stability or incrementalism interrupted by short bursts of dramatic change," giving the impression that "the American political system lurches from one point of apparent equilibrium to another" (Baumgartner and Jones [1993] 2009: 10, 12). Their book can be traced to a distinguished intellectual pedigree in the study of American politics and policymaking.

This tradition includes Walter Burnham's (1999) work to frame the study of US elections following V.O. Key's (1955) pathbreaking analysis of the history of elections in terms of punctuated equilibrium – that is, a series of "normal" elections followed by occasional "critical" elections that realign voters' allegiance to the political parties, thus introducing fundamental changes to the political landscape. It was, however, the publication of *Agendas and Instability in American Politics* in 1993 by Baumgartner and Jones that popularized this concept among political scientists. Its popularity has produced a rapidly expanding literature that has become quite challenging for scholars to keep track of. Although there are studies showing that this idea does not correspond to some areas of policymaking such as forestry management by the US federal government and the regulation of tobacco smoking at the state level (e.g., Cashore and Howlett 2007; Givel 2006; Givel and Glantz 2001), there are many more studies reporting supportive evidence, suggesting that just as in the natural world, changes in human institutions and public policies can be characterized by long periods of stasis or stability punctuated occasionally by the onset of disruptive dynamics that produce profound changes in existing organizations, outlooks, and policies.

Baumgartner and Jones' ([1993] 2009) book built on the intellectual foundation of another influential book by John Kingdon (1984) on agenda setting. Kingdon's work points to the role of crises and shocks creating windows of opportunity for major policy change to occur and the role of political entrepreneurs in seizing such occasions to promote new ideas and solutions that make this change possible. Epistemic communities and mobilization of previously uninvolved interest groups also have a role in enabling this change. Kingdon argues that major and abrupt policy changes can occur when there is such a confluence of facilitative conditions. This combination usually consists of (1) a perceived problem, (2) a receptive policy venue, (3) a new understanding of the problem and a way to solve it, and (4) an effective coalition with the power to override institutional resistance (Goertz 2003).

The idea that policies can occasionally undergo sharp alterations highlights a reaction to the established and widely shared views about organizational behavior and budgetary processes. The traditional views emphasize human beings' bounded rationality, their susceptibility to information overload and cognitive rigidity, their proclivity to follow precedents and make incremental adjustments, and the forces of bureaucratic inertia and the power of vested interests, all of which tend to enhance the defense of existing institutions and the continuation of existing policies. These precepts were introduced by the seminal works of Charles Lindblom (1959), Otto Davis et al. (1966, 1974), Herbert Simon (1957, 1977, 1983), and Aaron Wildavsky (1964, 1975, 1992). The new perspective introduced by punctuated equilibrium did not so much supplant the old insights provided by these classic studies as to complement them. Indeed, as explained below, protracted stasis and abrupt change can both be true, constituting the two sides of the same coin.

Bureaucratic inertia, vested interests, entrenched organizational routines, and the tendency to make incremental adjustments and marginal policy changes reflecting bounded rationality, satisficing reasoning, and "muddling through" can explain long periods of apparent stasis or stationarity in government policies and political institutions. The general idea behind these views is that policymaking is more focused on avoiding disasters and mitigating errors rather than maximizing gains. Political institutions, policy agendas, and bureaucratic practices are therefore usually "sticky." They tend to resist change and work to perpetuate themselves. Tensions and pressures, however, can accumulate over time, making the status quo more vulnerable to shocks that trigger dramatic, even revolutionary, transformation. Such transformation is often preceded and facilitated by the mobilization of groups that were previously uninvolved or marginalized by the existing institutions.

Challenges to the status quo also often require a basic alteration in our cognition – that is, our understanding or perception of a policy problem – to galvanize action. Policy action requires the perception that a problem exists and that there is a need to address it. How urgent is the need and what is the proper solution to resolve it hinge on problem definition (Baumgartner and Jones 2015). That problems sometimes go unrecognized for a long time can indicate people's cognitive rigidity, but this phenomenon can also reflect societal consensus. Poverty has long existed, but it used to be seen as a private matter of individual misfortune. It did not become an issue for public policy until people began to see it as a social problem for which the government has a responsibility to address. Of course, before the advent of modern welfare states, governments lacked the wherewithal in material resources or political capability to take on this responsibility. As already mentioned briefly, changes in public policy occur when there is not only the recognition of a problem, but also the realization of available solutions to address it – with energetic entrepreneurs bringing them together when a window of opportunity for change presents itself. In the words of Frank Baumgartner and Bryan Jones (2009: xxvii):

Policy change is disjoint and episodic; much major policy change occurs outside the course of electoral politics; resistance to change is not solely a function of conservative rules of the game and the resources of the actors; it has its roots in the cognitive and emotional architectures of people.

In a book review in 1984, Stephen Krasner (1984) introduced briefly the ideas of punctuated equilibrium and path dependency in the evolution of state formation and development. Punctuated equilibrium subsequently "caught fire" (to borrow a phrase often used to describe the phenomenon when an issue gains popular and elite attention and moves up the policy agenda) in the wake of Baumgartner and Jones' ([1993] 2009) book. This work on the life cycles of public policies has been hugely successful in inspiring other similar studies and in establishing an expanding research program as the literature review in Chapter 2 will show. It has inspired a vast and still expanding literature on public policy (Cairney 2012; Green-Pederson and Princen 2016). International relations scholars, such as Claudio Cioffi-Revilla (1998b), James Colgan et al. (2012), Paul Diehl and Charlotte Ku (2010), Gary Goertz (2003), Weixing Hu (2012), James True et al. (2007), and Oran Young (2010) have also adopted the idea of punctuated equilibrium in their study of a variety of topics, including the evolution of international legal and political norms, international environmental and energy regimes, and the histories of budgetary decisions, interstate conflicts, and relations across the Taiwan Strait. Diehl (1998), Diehl and Goertz (2000), and Durant and Diehl (1989) have also sought to apply the insights from punctuated equilibrium in paleobiology, John Kingdon's (1984) study of agenda setting, and the "garbage can model" of decision-making (Cohen et al. 1972) to the analysis of interstate rivalries and foreign policy. I will discuss these studies in more detail in Chapter 2.

Borrowing methods and perspectives from another discipline can often be problematic (Givel 2010; Prindle 2012). Even analogies from the same field of study can be misapplied and thus produce misleading conclusions (Khong 1992). This said, concepts imported from a different field can also provide fruitful avenues for new research approaches (Prindle 2012). Insights learned from the natural sciences can offer a novel and refreshing way to inform social scientists' analysis of old enduring topics. I am far from the first person to introduce potentially useful ideas from other fields. In addition to Baumgartner and Jones, others such as Robert Axelrod (1984), Randall Schweller (2014), and Shiping Tang (2013, 2020) have shown powerful insights that can be gained from archaeology, anthropology, evolutionary biology, and theoretical physics. Naturally, unlike biological processes such as natural selection, social scientists are interested in the study of human behavior and the institutions created by people. Unlike natural phenomenon, people have will, volition, and often an ability to shape their circumstances and thus influence the course of events. Social scientists must therefore attend to the motivations for this behavior and the circumstances that shape people's judgments, capabilities, and conduct.

Thus, for example, Colgan et al. (2012) argue that intense dissatisfaction on the part of powerful actors gives impetus to major, de novo institutional change in the energy regime complex when these actors have heterogeneous preferences. When these actors have homogeneous preferences, they are more likely to undertake path-dependent reform largely within the existing institutional context. Stasis is the default situation in this example, unless there are actors who are seriously dissatisfied and who also have the wherewithal to act on their demand for change. In addition, political entrepreneurship is necessary to bring about change. In a similar vein, Baumgartner and Jones ([1993] 2009) see the evolution of public policy to result from political struggles to define policy problems (or what they call "policy images") and to control the institutional forum for policymaking ("policy venue"). Human agency and the policy environment – or what Benjamin Most and Harvey Starr (1989) have called "willingness" and "opportunity" – both matter when we study political behavior. John Kingdon

(1984) expresses the same idea when he says change becomes possible when there is a confluence of three critical factors: There are a problem, a solution, and a political entrepreneur. In the absence of these concurrent conditions, the strong vested interests of "policy monopolies" and institutional inertia sustain prolonged periods of stasis or "business as usual."

Relevance Potential for International Relations

For scholars of international relations, the idea of punctuated equilibrium invites us to see in a new light ongoing power shifts among states. This idea cautions us against linear extrapolation of the recent economic growth of countries to infer their relative position in the interstate hierarchy and the distribution of power among the elite group of great powers in the coming years. The trajectories of interstate power shifts can reflect disjointed, nonlinear changes rather than gradual, smooth transitions. Some countries can experience sharp ascent while others can suffer precipitous decline. As other examples, the idea of punctuate equilibrium directs our attention to study more closely such processes as those that have led to the sudden collapse of governments (including the rapid demise of the former USSR, an event that practically no one had foreseen; e.g., Wohlforth 2003) and the abrupt disintegration of alliances (such as that of the Warsaw Pact and the wartime coalitions led by Napoleon in his successive campaigns until his military debacle in Russia and defeat at Waterloo; e.g., Schroeder 1994). Indications of increasing pressure on a policy or political system may be barely discernible to a casual observer, but the strains brought about by its cumulative effect over time can produce a sudden upheaval and fundamental transformation.

On the eve of World War I, the distribution of power in Europe was delicately balanced between the Triple Alliance and the Triple Entente. There were recurrent crises prior to July 1914 but war was averted on each occasion. Europe, however, was a tinder box created by a confluence of developments such as armament races (especially the Anglo-German naval competition), tightening alliances (the Triple Alliance versus the Triple Entente), intense political rivalry and commercial competition, ongoing power shifts (not just Germany's rise, but also the decline of Austria-Hungary and the Ottoman Empire and a Russia on the cusp of "taking off"), and changes in the German, Austrian, and Russian leaders' gestalt outlook (e.g., Lebow 2000/2001, 2003; Thompson 2003). These conditions made it possible for the assassination of Archduke Franz Ferdinand and his wife to trigger a large conflagration. Some scholars have argued that given this constellation of factors, even if Sarajevo had not happened, some other incident could or would have resulted in the eruption of this horrific conflict because Europe was "ripe for war."

War in this case was the punctuation that disrupted and, indeed in some important ways seen retrospectively, overthrew the preexisting state of interstate affairs in Europe. In this case, the punctuation came, both figuratively and literally, as an explosive change. Some historians (e.g., Carr 1946), of course, saw both world wars as a single, protracted struggle – albeit interrupted by a brief interlude of peace or ceasefire in the 1920s and 1930s – that transformed fundamentally not just the European interstate system, but also the entire interstate system that was previously centered on Europe, moving its center of gravity to the United States and to a much less extent, the Soviet Union after 1945.

Recent financial crises remind us about the powerful forces of disruptive dynamics. Foreign capital rushed in to invest in the newly industrializing countries in East Asia in the 1980s and 1990s. This inflow of money inflated local asset prices, including the currency values of countries such as Thailand, South Korea, Malaysia, and Indonesia. This development in turn caused these economies to overheat, and eventually brought about a market crash when these same foreign investors acted on their herd instinct in their collective rush to withdraw their money from these countries, thus compounding the gravity of the situation in a cascading financial crisis dubbed the "Asian flu" in 1997. Runs on banks share this disruptive dynamic, and the effects of accelerating contagion are again evident in the US recession in 2008–2009 brought about by the housing bubble.

Other timely and important topics pertaining to the process of punctuated equilibrium abound in contemporary issues and ongoing developments. What are the implications of the increasing gap between Washington's foreign commitments and its declining resources to finance these commitments? Paul Kennedy (1987: 515) has warned about the danger of imperial overstretch ensuing from this gap, remarking that:

the United States now runs the risk, so familiar to historians of the rise and fall of previous Great Powers, of what might be called "imperial over-stretch": that is to say, decision-makers in Washington must face the awkward and enduring fact that the sum total of the United States' global interests and obligations is nowadays far larger than the country's power to defend them all simultaneously.

Although a state may be able to manage a resource shortfall in the short run, in the long run the cumulative costs of its imperial burden will overwhelm it. Analysts have investigated the so-called defense-growth trade-off about the opportunity costs of military expenditures, most particularly whether this spending comes at the expense of future economic growth (e.g., Rooney et al. 2021; Russett 1970). Naturally, these opportunity costs may not be evident in the short run – just as the ill effects of smoking may only become manifest over time. The long-term cumulative effects, however, can be devastating. The USSR's crushing defense burden and its ruinous consequences on its economy are just one more recent dramatic example.

What does Washington's frequent resort to financial sanctions against other countries augur for the dollar's status in the coming years? Presumably, those who have been subjected to such economic coercion would want to reduce their vulnerability to this pressure again in the future. Even onlookers who worry about becoming potential targets of this coercion would want to make anticipatory adjustments, such as by lessening their reliance on the dollar and diversifying their commercial and financial relations away from the United States. Thus, the increasing incidence of sanctions should be correlated with their diminishing effectiveness over time. Moreover, Washington's fiscal extravagances have caused its budgetary deficits to rise and the concomitant imperative to borrow increasing amounts of money to finance this chronic shortfall. This practice has the effect of exporting US inflationary pressure and depreciating the dollar as a store of value. Even though the dollar may appear to be invulnerable today, there will be a tipping point at which its heretofore unassailable position will be undermined.

This challenge may come from the BRICS group (Brazil, Russia, India, China, and South Africa) whose membership expanded in 2024 by an additional four countries (Egypt, Ethiopia, Iran, the United Arab Emirates – Argentina, which was also invited to join this group, has since declined after the election of a conservative president,

Javier Milei, and Saudi Arabia participates in its activities although it is unclear whether it has joined this group officially; Turkey is among those states that have applied for membership). This expansion represents one of several incipient developments portending a possible anti-Western or anti-US coalition. It can be dangerous for a country to mount an overt, direct challenge against the USA. The fates of Saddam Hussein, Muammar Qaddafi, and Manuel Noriega warn other leaders about what can happen to them and to a small, even middle-ranked, country if they come into Washington's strategic crosshairs. The well-known impediments to collective action (Olson 1965, 1982) and the resulting phenomenon of free-riding and buck-passing (Christensen and Snyder 1990) have had the effect of forestalling thus far the formation of an anti-US coalition. An overt countervailing coalition against the preponderant USA is difficult to organize. Individual "troublemakers" can be picked off quickly and easily by the USA before such a coalition has a chance to form. But should this coalition come to pass, it will develop quickly – a prospect that again augurs a sudden and fundamental transformation of the international system as we know it today.

We are seeing some incipient signs of such a development. Lawrence Broz et al. (2020) presented evidence on high-level delegations sent by other countries to attend China's Belt and Road Initiative summit in Beijing in 2017, and Jing Qian et al. (2023) looked at the founding members of the AIIB (the Asian Infrastructure Investment Bank initiated by China) who have appeared to turn away from the World Bank for loans to develop their infrastructure. Both of these studies showed high-cost signals indicating an increasing number of countries' dissatisfaction with the current international order, and thus indications pointing to the possible eventual displacement of existing international organizations created and sponsored by the United States after World War II.

Finally, the world's chronic trouble spots may remain quiescent for some considerable length of time, but the underlying tension can build up gradually to cause another outburst of violence such as shown by the recent armed conflict between Israel and Hamas with the potential to involve other parties such as the Hezbollah, Iran, Yemen's Houthis, and the United States. Relations across the Taiwan Strait have experienced crosscurrents since the last crisis in 1995–1996. Taiwan has become highly dependent economically on the Chinese mainland, while its people have increasingly identified themselves as Taiwanese rather than Chinese. These developments have reached a plateau and have remained so in the past three decades or so. In the meantime, China's military modernization has shifted the balance of power across the Taiwan Strait and between Beijing and Washington. Steady, if not entirely amicable, Sino-American relations had provided a ballast against turbulence relating to Taiwan's unresolved status, but the recent deterioration in this relationship and intensified Sino-American competition have removed this important source of stability. The uneasy balance of offsetting forces that has kept peace across the Taiwan Strait in the past is in danger of being upset by more recent developments. Thus, it has become questionable whether the seeming stasis that has characterized relations among the three sides (Beijing, Taipei, and Washington) will continue to hold. Whereas the continuation of status quo – namely, Taiwan's de facto, but not de jure, independence – may be acceptable to Taipei and Washington, Beijing may not have infinite patience to accept the perpetuation of this situation which means putting up with the continuation of a divided nation perhaps forever from its perspective. In short, the incompatibilities in the pertinent parties' objectives and recent developments threaten to shatter the fragile compromises that have thus far prevented simmering tension from boiling over.

This Book's Purpose and Rationale

The examples mentioned in the preceding paragraphs are suggestive; they refer to the possibilities of unfolding processes that can produce a sudden transformation rather than predictions that such outcomes will come to pass. In some respects, my analysis in this book shares with other studies that have sought to explain changes that have already occurred, such as Colgan et al.'s (2012) study of the history of energy regime complex and Baumgartner and Jones' ([1993] 2009) analysis of public policies regarding nuclear energy, tobacco smoking, pesticide, and automobile safety in the United States. For example, I have included in the following discussion case studies such as Beijing's admission to the United Nations and the critical turning points in Sino-American relations initiated by Mao Zedong's decision to intervene in the Korean War and Richard Nixon's decision to visit China in 1972. In other respects, this book's analysis is more prospective than retrospective, such as my discussion of the prospects of US military intervention in a crisis over Taiwan's unresolved status and the ongoing and possible future power shifts between Beijing and Washington. It does not claim that the denouements being studied are inevitable or even necessarily probable. Nor does it deny that international relations or socio-political phenomena in general can evolve gradually. Rather, my analysis seeks to introduce a particular perspective suggesting that long periods of gestation and small adjustments can be interrupted by a sharp break or discontinuity, introducing a qualitative transformation of relations.

Therefore, to be clear but at the risk of being repetitive, I do not claim that punctuated equilibrium applies to all policy issues. As already mentioned, several studies have shown that it does not correspond to the processes involved in the US federal government's management of forestry and the regulation of tobacco smoking at the state level (e.g., Cashore and Howlett 2007; Givel 2006; Givel and Glantz 2001), The extent to which various issue areas are susceptible to the process of punctuated equilibrium is in itself an important topic for inquiry but it is not the purpose of this book, which is to introduce this relatively novel perspective to international relations scholarship. Nor does this book aim to confirm or disconfirm propositions regarding punctuated equilibrium. It is more akin to Graham Allison's (1971) classic study of the Cuban Missile Crisis, seeking to introduce different perspectives or models on policymaking. Each of Allison's perspectives or models is not meant to assert how the world of foreign policy "really" operates to the exclusion of other perspectives or models. Finally, studies on punctuated equilibrium have been mostly retrospective analyses. Due to the very nature of policymaking which tends to be often serendipitous, it is difficult to make falsifiable predictions about it. Even when researchers have a reasonable grasp of the process at work, accurate forecasting can still elude them such as with respect to the timing of earthquakes and volcano eruptions and the progression of various kinds of cancer. Perhaps with the introduction of artificial intelligence, there will be revolutionary changes in these and other fields bringing about a fundamental transformation in our knowledge about these matters. If so, this will constitute another example of punctuated equilibrium. Between such punctuations, researchers practice in the realm of "normal science" or within the boundaries of an existing paradigm. Scientific revolutions are triggered by paradigmatic changes altering people's basic understanding of their subject matter (Kuhn 1970). Finally, and as already mentioned, gradualism and punctuation are not mutually exclusive but are rather two sides of the same coin.

My discussion in the rest of the book turns to those aspects of evolving international relations that can be informed by the perspective of punctuated equilibrium – processes for which our customary reasoning based on linear extrapolation and incremental adjustment is ill-suited. This is an important point, reflecting the original way in which Eldredge and Gould deployed the concept of punctuated equilibrium. As David Prindle (2012: 35) has pointed out, "the notion of 'punctuated equilibrium,' as elaborated by Eldredge and Gould, is a *descriptive*, not a *causal* concept. It does not reject the possibility of causality but assumes a prior causal theory, that of Darwinian natural selection. PE is instead an alternate characterization of the pace and structure of the development of life that is created by the Darwinian causal mechanism" (italics in original).

A skeptical reader may ask "what is then the big deal, since you cannot make predictions or for some issues and situations, even say how likely an outcome will be?" As suggested in the preceding discussion, the very introduction of the idea that public policymaking is characterized by both lulls and lurches is a huge revolutionary idea that has transformed our basic understanding of agenda setting and decision processes in policymaking, one based on the previous conventional wisdom and consensus that they are dominated by inertia, incrementalism, and bounded rationality. Scientific revolutions have followed such paradigm shifts resulting from a recognition of anomalies that cannot be accommodated by existing understanding (Kuhn 1970).

Unfortunately, social scientists grapple with phenomena that are fundamentally more difficult to predict than the subject matter for those who work in the natural and physical sciences. Moreover, predictions and even looser forecasts still elude many experts in the latter fields. Although they continue to make progress, oncologists are still limited in their ability to provide specific prognosis about individual cancer patients or the efficacy of specific medical treatments for their patients. Their prognoses depend heavily on statistical inferences from a pool of past cases, which are sometimes limited in their number of observations. We encounter a similar situation with respect to avalanches and earthquakes. Although the pertinent experts are knowledgeable about the general conditions or dynamics that bring about these occurrences, they cannot make specific predictions about the timing and location of avalanches or earthquakes. This comment of course does not deny that progress is being made constantly so that such predictions may increasingly become a reality in coming days. Policy punctuations are inherently unpredictable because the confluence of conditions necessary for them to occur tends to be characterized by randomness. This point will become clearer when I discuss later in more detail the "garbage can" model of policymaking. I realize that these comments are redundant, but I repeat them to respond to possible misunderstanding as implied in the reviewers' feedback I have received for this book.

Having conceded that the application of punctuated equilibrium to study international relations does not promise to produce point predictions does not mean, however, that this work is not important or useful. None of the studies on public policy to be reviewed in the next chapter claims to be predictive in this sense. All these studies seek to show past patterns that corresponded (or not) with the expectations of punctuated equilibrium. As will be explained later, the logic motivating my empirical analysis, such as the prospects of US intervention in a conflict involving Taiwan, seeks to determine which combination of factors is necessary, perhaps even sufficient, for an event to happen. When one or more of these factors is missing, one may argue that the event in question is unlikely to happen. When all the relevant factors are present, the probability of this occurrence becomes very high – even though we can never be certain. As my empirical studies will show, this approach to inquiry may be handicapped by the small number of historical cases available for a more comprehensive and thus convincing study and by the lack of sufficient variation among them to reach strong conclusions about the questions we seek to answer. This may be disappointing, but the pertinent logic and perspective are still valuable. Until we have better data, we try our best with what we have available now. Moreover, humility in the face of empirical uncertainty is in my view a virtue, not an admission of defeat.

A Brief Preview of the Rest of the Book

In Chapter 2, I undertake an extensive review of the burgeoning literature on punctuated equilibrium in political science. It also presents the logic behind this perspective and the evidence developed thus far about it. This review is followed by Chapter 3 which provides an overview of the recent relationship between China and the United States. This review shows that this relationship features lulls and lurches as predicted by the perspective of punctuated equilibrium. Its history has been marked by two epochal punctuations – China's decision to intervene in the Korean War and Richard Nixon's visit to Beijing – followed by a prolonged period of relative stability. However, the most recent deterioration in this relationship cannot be traced to any specific event or cause (a phenomenon that does not necessarily contradict the idea of punctuated equilibrium, which does not rule out gradualism such as in some instances of evolutionary biology). The collapse and dissolution of the USSR and the 2008–2009 recession set off by the housing bubble in the United States, however, represented two other watershed events suggesting major turning points in Sino-American relations albeit without triggering an immediate and direct punctuation in these relations or precipitating major new foreign policies by these countries. Chapter 2 also introduces an example from the United Nations General Assembly's rollcall votes on the resolution to recognize the Beijing government as the legitimate representative of China that was finally passed in 1971 following years of failure due to the opposition led by the United States. It illustrates the maturation of a process, gathering momentum, and snowball effect stemming from the psychology of "going with the winner."

In Chapter 4, I will explore the prospects of US military intervention to assist Taiwan, thereby bringing it into a direct armed conflict with China. Large, devastating wars in the past have often originated from such intervention by a great power to protect or bolster its protégé in a local conflict. The chain of events set off by the assassination of Archduke Franz Ferdinand in July 1914 comes to mind. It led to a showdown between Austria-Hungary and Serbia, which in turn brought Russia (Serbia's patron) and Germany (Austria-Hungary's ally) into the conflict, changing it into a multilateral affair. Similarly, Britain and France's pledge to defend Poland was the proximate cause for World War II in the European theater. China and the United States do not have territorial or ideological disputes (Washington of course argues that there are important differences in its values and Beijing's, and China proclaims its communist ideology that is anathema to the

USA, but China does not seek to promote or export its values or model of government). Washington's involvement in a contingency involving Taiwan would be the most likely scenario for starting a direct armed confrontation between them. I will introduce Boolean logic to past instances of US interventions and noninterventions in conflict episodes involving China and the USSR/Russia to determine the combination of factors that is likely to affect Washington's decision calculus. This Boolean analysis follows up on the idea, introduced earlier in Chapter 2, that policies are the outcome of a confluence of independent streams of problems, solutions, participants, and choice opportunities – a situation in which timing is critical, an observation which in turn recognizes the influence of serendipity or randomness in policymaking. This perspective argues that policies are the result of a conjunction of factors, and it naturally disagrees with monocausal explanations of political phenomena, such as the proposition advanced by Thucydides' Trap that interstate power shifts cause war (Allison 2015, 2017).

In Chapter 5, I turn to a discussion of China's economic growth. China has maintained an average annual growth rate of about 10 percent for about thirty years since Deng Xiaoping's economic reforms initiated in the late 1970s. It has consequently managed to lift the largest number of people (estimated to be over 700 million) out of poverty in the shortest amount of time in human history. Concomitant with its economic growth, China has enlarged its political footprint in international affairs, and it has also improved its military capabilities. Much of the West's recent concern about the threat posed by a rising China reflects Beijing's relative power gain at the expense of the established major powers, especially the United States. Such concern, based on a shifting interstate balance of power, has been the leitmotif behind a resurgent interest in the power-transition theory on international peace and war (Organski and Kugler 1980) and its more recent rendition in the popular narrative of Thucydides' Trap (Allison 2015, 2017).

But as the German saying goes, "Trees don't grow to the sky." More specifically, economic growth tends to unfold in stages with long periods of gestation, even stagnation, to be followed by short spurts of rapid growth, which are in turn followed by a return to "normalcy" whereby the rate of economic growth fluctuates around a lower "new normal." In Chapter 5, I introduce Walt Rostow's (1971) stages-to-growth model, which corresponds in its general outline to the conception of change presented by punctuated equilibrium. The discussion in Chapter 5 calls attention to this dynamic, and it warns about the tendency for people to sometimes make linear extrapolation from a small number of observations, thereby to overlook the possibility of deceleration in recent trajectory and even perhaps a reversal in its direction.

As suggested already, political entrepreneurship is very much an important part of the story explaining policy stasis as well as change. Political actors seek to promote their definition of a policy problem and their proposed solution to it. They try to control agenda setting, frame policy discourse, and shape popular narrative and understanding. Their construction of reality has a dynamic of its own, thus affecting the course of foreign policy. In Chapter 6, I turn to the evolving representation of Sino-American relations, especially that which is being propagated in Washington. I argue that some of the popular reasons being given for the deterioration of Sino-American relations are not very persuasive. I suggest that changing perceptions of this relationship – or policy image – reflects more the shifting balance of power between the United States and China than other plausible explanations. Power shift, problem shift, and policy shift tend to influence and reinforce one another (Chan 2024a). Whether power shifts are translated into threat perceptions depends on identity, that is, whether the other country is judged to be one of "us" or "them" (Rousseau 2006). Political entrepreneurs play an important role in fostering particular images of the "Other," but scholars are also involved in this construction. Americans' perception of Wilhelmine Germany changed from admiration to hostility as World War I approached, and their images of China and Japan from World War II to the Korean War also underwent massive transformation in a short time (Oren 2003). A similar change occurred in their perception of Iran after religious clerics led by Ayatollah Khomeini came to power even though that country was also repressive under the Shah, a US ally whose regime was perceived in a much more positive light.

Chapter 7 concludes the book, summarizing its main arguments and policy implications. Although I do not expect an armed conflict between the United States and China, I argue that their relationship has regressed and entered into a new era of cold war. As suggested by the perspective of punctuated equilibrium, this new era can persist for some time. The proposition that major transformations come from an

unusual and thus rare combination of conditions suggests this pessim-
istic view. The default for most situations – as suggested by the insights
offered by earlier intellectual giants who have studied policymaking,
such as Lindblom, Simon, and Wildavsky – is business as usual or the
perpetuation of the status quo. It takes time, energy, entrepreneurial
skill, and especially political capital and courage to break through a
policy deadlock. Moreover, the window for promoting and accepting
change must be open simultaneously on both sides of a relationship.
That is, timing must be right for both Beijing and Washington to
incentivize and also enable their respective leaders to make changes
to improve their countries' relations. These considerations explain
both why inertia tends to prevail most of the time and why it is difficult
to undertake major course corrections.

Looking beyond Sino-American relations, Chapter 7 also takes a
step back and asks what do the discussions in the preceding chapters
offer in helping us to think about the "big picture" – meaning their
implications for policymaking and policy challenges in a global context. In these discussions, some ideas have appeared repeatedly, such as
time, momentum, cumulative pressure, trigger, conjunction, problem
images, policy attention and agenda, shocks and punctuations, and
finally, political entrepreneurship and political construction. What do
these ideas add up to in informing us about the larger issues and
broader concerns pertaining to the unfolding processes in international
relations? As the world's reigning hegemon, how these factors influence domestic politics in the United States will have an important
influence in shaping these relations.

2 | *Punctuated Equilibria*
A Review of Political Science Literature

This chapter reviews the literature on punctuated equilibrium in political science. It also provides a more detailed account of the rationale behind this perspective and the available evidence pertaining to it. As already mentioned, the idea of punctuated equilibrium came initially from the field of paleobiology, more specifically, from a seminal paper published by Niles Eldredge and Stephen J. Gould in 1972 on the nature of biological evolution. These scientists argue that, contrary to the prevailing Darwinian belief that species evolve gradually, fossil evidence points to a process whereby protracted periods of stasis are interrupted by brief bursts of change.

Charles Darwin (1859) in his landmark study, *On the Origin of Species*, had written about evolution as a slow and steady process bringing about gradual change over a very long time. Some members of a species can better adapt to and thus survive and even thrive in a specific environment because of variations in their genes, which are passed on to their offspring. The accumulation of these genetic variations in isolated places eventually gives rise to new species. Darwin did his fieldwork on the Galapagos Islands, observing various species such as finches and tortoises.

In contrast to Darwin's theory, Eldredge and Gould (1972: 108) propose that the history of life is "characterized by rapid evolutionary events punctuating a history of stasis." This view of evolution as a process of punctuated equilibrium offers an alternative interpretation of the evolutionary process. It contests the traditional view of phyletic gradualism, which sees evolution as a process of slow and gradual transformation. Rather than showing a long, graded chain of intermediate forms linking one species to another, the available fossil record points to "the sudden appearance of all or most species, which then persisted relatively unchanged for their entire existence, and at some point became extinct" (Prindle 2012: 24).

Eldredge and Gould built their proposition of punctuated equilibrium on the prior work by I. Michael Lerner (1954) and Ernst Mayr (1958, 1963) on genetic homeostasis and geographic speciation, respectively. Genetic homeostasis suggests an equilibrium condition whereby a gene pool does not change in frequency across generations. Geographic speciation suggests that physical isolation and separation lead to genetic divergence over time. Mayr (1958) has argued that mutation and natural selection introduce rapid evolution in isolated populations.

As noted earlier, Gould and Eldredge (1977: 146) argue that the idea of punctuated equilibrium can also be relevant to social and political phenomena. They state:

One law, particularly emphasized by [Friedrich] Engels, holds that a new quality emerges in a leap as the slow accumulation of quantitative changes, long resisted by a stable system, finally forces it rapidly from one state to another (law of the transformation of quantity into quality). Heat water slowly and it eventually transforms to steam; oppress the proletariat more and more, and guarantee the revolution.

Since its introduction by Eldredge and Gould, this idea of punctuated equilibrium has caught the attention of scholars working in different fields, including "human learning, organizational dynamics, technological development, fractal geometry, chaos theory, nonlinear dynamics, complexity theory, economics" (Prindle 2012: 25). It has also been used to study agricultural revolutions, technology cycles, language changes, and stock prices.

In the realm of public policy, Michael Givel (2010) reports that researchers have applied the perspective of punctuated equilibrium to a variety of policy niches. For example, Baumgartner and Jones ([1993] 2009) have studied policy processes pertaining to nuclear energy, pesticides, substance abuse, urban affairs, automobile safety, social security, and budgeting decisions. Punctuated equilibrium has also been used by these and other researchers to study the dynamics of other policy issues such as environmental protection (Baumgartner 2006; Repetto 2006), forestry management (Cashore and Howlett 2007; Salka 2004; Wood 2006a), tobacco smoking (Baumgartner and Jones [1993] 2009; Givel 2006; Givel and Glantz 2001; Wood 2006b), social security (True 1999), gun control (True and Utter 2002), alcohol prohibition and repeal (Schrad 2007), drug review and approval (Ceccoli 2003), wildfire management (Busenberg 2004), convict imprisonment (Schneider 2006), school financing and higher education (Manna 2006; McLendon 2003; Robinson 2004), same-sex marriage (Dziengel 2010), welfare programs (Jensen 2009), automobile fuel efficiency (Perl and Dunn 2007), election results (Jones et al. 2003), media coverage (Walgrave and Vliegenthart 2010), foreign aid allocation (Joly and Richter 2019), troop deployments abroad (Joly and Richter 2023), defense spending (Sharp 2019), responses to natural and human disasters (Cho and Jung 2019; Fagan 2023), the development of regulatory regimes (e.g., flood control, fire code, hospital fees, McDonough 1998; Niles 2011), bureaucratic autonomy in city governments (Park and Sapotichne 2020), and budgeting for public programs (Breunig and Koski 2006; Jones and Breunig 2007; Jones et al. 2003; Jordan 2003; Robinson and Caver 2006; Robinson et al. 2007; Ryu 2009), and a host of other topics. This incomplete list shows that punctuated equilibrium as a research topic has truly taken off. As the reader may also have inferred from these references, the largest portion of empirical research has dealt with budgetary allocations for which we have large datasets covering many years.

Mathieu Jolicoeur (2018) reports that the perspective of punctuated equilibrium has also been applied to studies on public health, such as in the management of infectious diseases (Shiffman et al. 2002) and the evolution of Israel's health system (Feder-Bubis and Chinitz 2010). A volume coedited by Baumgartner and Jones (2002a) featured chapters addressing policymaking in telecommunications (MacLeod 2002), immigration reform (Hunt 2002), health care reform (Hardin 2002), science and technology policy (Feeley 2002), and national security policy (True 2002) in the United States. Connie Gersick (1988, 1991) has even used the punctuated equilibrium perspective to study group development in human organizations. She claims that the processes observed in this setting are similar to those characterizing patterns in the natural sciences. I will, however, limit the scope of this literature so as not to venture too far from my home turf.

What is the cumulative verdict of the expanding body of studies on punctuated equilibrium? These studies offer overwhelming support for the view that punctuated equilibrium is operating in different spheres of human activity. As Michael Givel (2010: 189) states succinctly, "The major syllogistic premise of punctuated equilibrium in public policy is that there is long-term and relatively incremental policy change followed by an exogenous shock to a policy monopoly resulting in a tipping point oriented toward sharp and explosive policy change." Existing studies offer an abundance of evidence supporting this proposition.

The Logic of Punctuated Equilibrium

As already remarked, the proliferation of studies on policymaking was inspired by an influential book originally published in 1993 by political scientists Frank Baumgartner and Bryan Jones. In this book, Baumgartner and Jones ([1993] 2009) introduced the idea of punctuated equilibrium to the analysis of public policy. They showed that agenda setting in a variety of policy areas, such as government regulations of nuclear energy, pesticide, automobile safety, and tobacco smoking, has followed a common pattern of long periods of stasis that are occasionally interrupted by brief bursts of change. Prior to their book, the predominant view held that policymaking tends to be characterized by stability or incremental adjustment. This latter view reflected the seminal writings of Charles Lindblom (1959), Herbert Simon (1957, 1977, 1983), and Aaron Wildavsky (1964, 1975, 1992).

Lindblom, Simon, and Wildavsky have contributed key insights that are now familiar to students of policymaking. These scholars point to people's bounded rationality and thus limits to their ability to process information (hence the tendency to attend sequentially to problems and "muddle through" in policymaking), the reliance by large organizations on their standard operating procedures to ensure predictable behavior, and the power of vested interests to sustain the status quo. These features produce organizational rigidity, institutional stickiness, and slow and incremental policy change. Budgetary processes have provided the prime exhibit for these ideas, demonstrating the effects of these tendencies to maintain the status quo and limit the extent of change.

The influential case study on US decision processes during the Cuban Missile Crisis by Graham Allison (1971) captured these insights on bureaucratic inertia in the adage for the organizational processes model: What happens at t is a function of t-1. That is, what happens today is a function of what happened yesterday; and similarly, what will happen tomorrow reflects what happens today. Thus, institutional inertia and policy conservatism (what James Thomson (1973) has described as bureaucrats' "curator mentality") tend to prevail most of the time. There are sound reasons for this tendency. As Baumgartner and Jones (2009: 9) observe, "Models of policymaking are generally based on the twin principles of incrementalism and negative feedback." They account for a self-correcting system, reflecting the effects of gradual, marginal adjustments to existing policies and the political countermobilization of forces that oppose change.

The idea of countermobilization is naturally related to and stems from that of mobilization. Baumgartner and Jones attribute these ideas to two influential figures in the study of American politics. Anthony Downs' (1972) work is associated with the mobilization of enthusiasm which creates institutional structures in a previous policy vacuum, whereas E. E. Schattschneider (1960) is credited with the idea of countermobilization by dissenters and critics who are disenchanted with the existing policy monopolies and seek their overthrow. In his classic study of American politics, Schattschneider (1960: 71) has quipped that "organization is the mobilization of bias." The processes of mobilization and countermobilization described by Downs and Schattschneider show how these political processes can produce stasis and change respectively in policymaking.

Whereas negative feedback dampens change and fosters system stability (due to incrementalism and countermobilization as just mentioned), positive feedback (sometimes described as "bandwagon effect" or "feeding frenzy," True et al. 2007: 160) amplifies and cascades to produce rapid and major change (the environmental movement offers an example; Baumgartner and Jones 2002b). "The interaction between changing images and venues of public policies leads ... to ... positive feedback ... as the cause of disequilibrium politics" (Baumgartner and Jones 2009: 24). Negative feedback operates like a thermostat that works to offset environmental change and thus to maintain, say, a room's temperature at a constant level.

Negative feedback prevails most of the time, like the thermostat and other self-correcting mechanisms that maintain the status quo. In politics and policymaking, the maintenance of the status quo comes from a combination of factors, including vested interests, organizational inertia, a settled definition of a problem, cozy relations between bureaucrats and their congressional overseers and outside experts, and restricted access to institutional venues and rigged rules of the game in favor of existing stakeholders. But sometimes, positive feedback takes hold, due to a confluence of a new problem definition, newly mobilized participants, new policy venues, and increased media attention; these are occasions that open the window of opportunity for major changes and transformations.

In the case of the United States, the operation of positive and negative feedback appears to be associated with the shifting power balance between the federal government on the one hand and the local and state governments on the other hand. Periods of nationalization or power concentration tend to tighten linkages among policy venues, whereas periods of devolution or deconcentration of power tend to decouple them. These tendencies in turn amplify the dynamics of positive and negative feedback respectively (Baumgartner and Jones 2009: 220). The existence of multiple policymaking venues in a federal system provides greater opportunities for change in specific issue areas. Yet, a federal system can also create many policy niches that resist and hold out against change, thus favoring the forces of status quo (Repetto 2006). New ideas can diffuse and spread more quickly in positive feedback among tightly coupled or linked venues in a unitary or centralized government.

Policy stasis can thus reflect the influence of separate, independent arenas or policy silos – in other words, policy monopolies insulated from the outside world. These monopolies – sometimes described as iron triangles – feature established coalitions of administrators, legislators, and experts in different issue domains that work to protect their political jurisdiction, organization mission, access to information, and claim to expertise and authority in providing problem definitions and supplying appropriate solutions. Thus, Baumgartner and Jones (2009: 14) also observe, "The system of American governance looked more like mutual noninterference than group struggle. Political stability, then, could not be found in the balancing of interests, although it might be found in a system of noninterfering policy monopolies." Mutual noninterference and policy silos of course favor the maintenance of established policies and enhance those forces that resist change.

The forces favoring the status quo come from two main sources. "Participation in a policy monopoly is structured by two things: the formal and informal rules of access discourage participation of 'outsiders,' and the prevalent understandings of the policy are so positive that they evoke only support or indifference by those not involved (thereby insuring their continued noninvolvement)" (Baumgartner and Jones 2009: 7). The rules of the game instituted by the existing policy venues, and the maintenance of an established image of a problem thus both contribute to the continuation of the status quo. This view also implies the converse – when those seeking to introduce change succeed in developing a new policy venue, gaining wide acceptance of a new understanding or definition of an existing problem, and mobilizing actors who have been heretofore sidelined, policy change is more likely to ensue. As just described, the "stars must be aligned" for change to occur. That this confluence of necessary conditions usually does not happen in turn explains long periods of policy stasis. A new policy venue, a new policy image, and new entrants to participate in the policymaking process are often all present in initiating change (True et al. 2007). The perspective just presented therefore explains both stasis and change:

The tight connection between institution and idea provides powerful support for the prevailing distribution of political advantage. But this stability cannot provide general equilibrium, because a change in issue definition can lead to destabilization and rapid change away from the old point of stability. This happens when issues are redefined to bring in new participants ... Issue definition, then, is the driving force in both stability and instability, primarily because issue definition has the potential for mobilizing the previously disinterested. The structure of political institutions offers more or fewer arenas for raising new issues or redefining old ones – opportunities to change understandings of political conflict. Issue definition and institutional control combine to make possible the alternation between stability and rapid change that characterize political systems. (Baumgartner and Jones 2009: 16)

"How a policy is understood and discussed is its *policy image*," and "...[issue] definition is at the heart of the political battle" (Baumgartner and Jones 2009: 25, 29, italics in original). An example of issue redefinition is provided by the debate over nuclear power, which was presented initially as a cheap source of energy to the public but then shifted to safety concerns about the disposal of nuclear waste and the danger of catastrophic accidents after the mishaps at Three Mile Island and Chernobyl. Disagreement among scientists and engineers contributed to fracturing the consensus about nuclear power that had prevailed earlier. A new policy image, a new policy venue (the Atomic Energy Commission), and newly mobilized activists eventually caused this industry to shut down.

Tobacco smoking presents another example. Long-standing views on this issue as a matter of government support for agriculture and a source of foreign revenue were shattered when opponents successfully changed it into a matter of public health. Still another example comes from the public's understanding and perception of poverty, which shifted from one of private misfortune to public responsibility, thereby giving impetus to the proliferation of welfare programs since World War II and especially after President Lyndon Johnson's inauguration of Great Society. Gary Goertz (2003: 174) stresses "many problems arise because of changing technology, changing domestic policy, changing economics, and changing values." Therefore, as I will discuss later in further detail, what is important is the confluence or combination of conditions or factors that interact to present an opportunity for policymaking and to shape the output of policymaking process.

As Goertz (2003) has also observed, there is often no common agreement on what constitutes a problem, the definition and even acknowledgment of which evolves over time, varies across people, reflects some actor's (hegemonic) power over ideas, the relevant social context and technological feasibility, and the pertinent scientific knowledge. Therefore, pollution and global warming become problems when there are influential lobby groups, widening epistemic communities, and mobilized public awareness made possible by an emergent consensus based on scientific knowledge. I will pick up again later in Chapter 6 the topic of "power over ideas" or control and influence in shaping a dominant narrative in Sino-American relations – or if you will, the ability to construct and propagate a particular version of reality for the purpose of influencing policymakers and swaying public opinion.

One explanation for long periods of policy stasis is that in addition to institutional stickiness, people's ideas are also resistant to change. In order to recruit and forge support for a new policy, political entrepreneurs have to "sell" it to the relevant elite and public. Indeed, as suggested by the "garbage can" model of policymaking (Cohen et al. 1972) to be discussed in more detail in Chapter 3, not only do problems look for solutions, but the reverse can also be true; that is, solutions can also chase after problems. "Often the solution has been around long before the problem arises or is recognized" (Goertz 2003: 174). The chronological order between problem and solution can go in both directions. Political entrepreneurs with a preferred solution in mind are constantly seeking to present a new problem or redefine an old one to promote their political agenda. There is of course the joke about the "law of the hammer," such that as the tale goes, if you give a small child a hammer, she will use it for many purposes other than the original one for which the hammer was intended for.

Issue redefinition is important because it provides a way to engage and mobilize previously uninvolved supporters. It is also important because it extends to ambitious politicians an opportunity to claim a new jurisdiction. In this way, policy images and policy venues tend to coevolve in a process that matches perceived problems, preferred solutions, and sympathetic participants. "As issues are redefined over time, different groups within the Congress are able to claim jurisdiction over them. Policy changes within Congress stem often from these changes in jurisdictional authority" (Baumgartner and Jones 2009: 214).

To overturn the status quo, activists agitating for change must mobilize those who were previously disinterested or disengaged. This mobilization usually follows the redefinition of an issue by those opposed to the status quo in their effort to enlarge the arena for political contest.

Because the definition of issues is so central to political processes in disequilibrium, this book is devoted to the understanding of the issue definition process ... Because policy entrepreneurs want government to do something (or to refrain from doing something), issue definition is intimately related to agenda processes. So any study of issue definition must also be a study of agenda control and access. (Baumgartner and Jones 2009: 22–23)

These authors go on to remark, "Where images are at the center of the analytical framework, as they are for us, one must address the efforts of policy entrepreneurs in attempting to alter other people's understandings of the issues with which they deal" (Baumgartner and Jones 2009: 42).

Gary Goertz (2003: 172, italic in original) quotes Panama's former president Omar Torrijos' pithy remark: "To resolve a problem, the first thing you have to do is *make* it a problem." The struggle to define issues or give new meaning to old issues requires political entrepreneurship. Someone (such as Ralph Nader on automobile safety) or some group (such as the Sierra Club and Nature Conservancy on protecting the environment) will have to raise public awareness of a problem.

A good example comes from the efforts of anti-smoking groups to reframe tobacco's harm in terms of people's right to workplace safety due to second-hand smoking and in terms of the right of state governments to claim reimbursement for medical expenditures to treat their citizens' health issues arising from smoking. An important part of political entrepreneurship in changing the institutional landscape involves "shopping" for alternative policy venues that are more sympathetic to those agitating for change, or in some cases encouraging and assisting ambitious politicians to establish an entirely new venue to address a redefined problem.

The campaign to challenge and upend the policy monopoly once held by the nuclear power industry reflects "the ability of policymakers to appeal to different institutional venues for decision making by raising new understandings of old issues" (Baumgartner and Jones 2009: 59). The process leading to the breakup of this monopoly succeeded in part because its opponents were able to exploit the divided opinions among the relevant experts, to propagate a new understanding of the problem by mass media, and to engage the attention of various political actors, such as the energy administrators, the Congress, the judiciary, and finally the state regulators – leading eventually to responses from the financial market on energy provision (Baumgartner and Jones 2009: 79).

As just mentioned, political entrepreneurship also involves the engagement of mass media to influence and mobilize public opinion. Media coverage often precipitates political attention by placing an item on the public policy agenda, such as in motivating congressional hearings in the United States.

Public, media, and governmental concern for the long-standing social problems of drug addiction, alcoholism, and child abuse has varied much more than the underlying social realities have changed. In all three cases, we have observed what seems to be a recurring characteristic of the agenda-setting process – attention lurches ... These new institutions and the people who work for them do not disappear, even if public or media concern with the issue fades away. (Baumgartner and Jones 2009: 169)

Mass, elite, and media attention rises and wanes; it cannot be maintained forever. Thus, "the entire system must be subject to lurches and lulls" (Baumgartner and Jones 2009: 250) with each round leaving behind it institutional legacies and vested interests until the next time for change. "The most important influence on stability is scarcity of attention" (Baumgartner and Jones 2009: 256).

New policies often come about from a combination of a new issue image and a new policy venue. Baumgartner and Jones (2009: 31, italics in original) explain the concept of policy venue in these words, "some institutions or groups in society must have the authority to make decisions concerning the issue. We term this the *policy venue*." The interaction between policy image and policy venue is crucial. "[T]he searches for favorable venues and reinforcing images are related," and "changes in image are used purposefully, in an effort to attract the attention of the members of a particular new venue" (Baumgartner and Jones 2009: 35, 36). "The interactions of image and venue may produce a self-reinforcing system characterized by positive feedback. Such systems can produce long periods of no change or dramatic reversals in outcomes in relatively short periods of time…" (Baumgartner and Jones 2009: 37).

To interject an example from Sino-American relations, public discourse on and depiction of China being "unfair" in its trade with the United States have been on the rise recently, evidently reflecting American politicians' pursuit of voter support. This rhetoric is of course designed to mobilize the support of those American companies hurt by Chinese commercial competition and those American workers who feel that their jobs have been "outsourced" to the Chinese. Alleged unfair Chinese practices also mobilize those US companies doing business in China, who feel aggrieved by their mistreatment by the Chinese authorities, and at the same time, hamstring pro-China lobby groups such as those US companies that have profited from trading with China given the obvious pressure coming from slogans such as "Buy American." Once having made their presence felt, such rhetoric and its political consequences can be self-perpetuating and produce a series of cascading effects. There has clearly been a reversal in the popular narratives and images prevailing in the USA and other Western countries showing a major transformation in elite and public views on "free trade," "open borders," and "globalization."

Although they are rare, when policy changes occur, they can spread quickly. They can have a cascading or contagion effect. An example comes from the anti-smoking campaign in the United States. The lawsuit filed by Mississippi's Attorney General Michael Moore against tobacco companies was joined subsequently by other states. This lawsuit sought to recover on behalf of taxpayers the costs of treating sick smokers enrolled in Medicare (Baumgartner and Jones 2009: 278). This lawsuit represented a new "solution" to an existing problem. Other political entrepreneurs introduced yet another new conception or image of the problem by framing it in terms of the harm caused by second-hand smoking and thus redefining the problem of smoking as a matter of workplace safety. These new definitions of an old problem caught on as more and more states joined the anti-smoking bandwagon. They dislodged the tobacco companies' argument that sought to defend smoking as a matter of personal choice and informed consent. The transformation of national discourse and policymaking on tobacco smoking is illustrative of another important point. "One remarkable aspect about the outbreak of bursts of creative destruction in politics is how seemingly small events and trends, that seem routine at the time, can cascade into large disruptions" (Baumgartner and Jones 2009: 288).

Another important conclusion to be drawn from this example on tobacco smoking is that the issue images and problem definitions being promoted by the contesting camps rarely intersect. That is, these debates are not usually carried out on the basis of an agreed agenda, one that allows the audience or the relevant officials or public to adjudicate the pros and cons presented by the opposing sides on the same set of issues. The real battle is waged not on the relative merits of particular issues being articulated by the parties but is rather typically settled on the basis of which policy image or problem definition wins the day. The partisans in such disputes diverge fundamentally over their understanding and presentation of the problem, and their discourse can thus be characterized reasonably as "talking past each other." Once one side's view of the problem prevails; its favored solution tends to follow readily. Thus, another point underscored by this discussion is that (ostensible) problem and (supposed) solution are "coupled" tightly. Win the struggle to define a problem, you have practically won the acceptance of your favored solution.

Policymaking pertaining to tobacco smoking also suggests the difficulty involved in pinpointing a specific precipitant for change.

Isolating *the* punctuation that upended the tobacco industry turns out to be harder than pointing to the self-reinforcing processes that caused an explosive process to get underway. There may be many events adding up to more than any single one of them alone ... So a positive feedback process has unfolded over many years, not only in a single punctuation. (Baumgartner and Jones 2009: 280, italic in original)

Continuing this line of argument, Baumgartner and Jones (2009: 281) remark:

Tobacco policy dynamics might be characterized as disjoint, episodic, and disruptive. There was no single punctuation nor was there a lasting equilibrium after any punctuation. The rolling disruptive dynamics is due to the complex interactions of positive and negative feedback processes ... Perhaps the proper conception is to think of punctuated equilibrium as one manifestation of complex evolutionary policy dynamics, one that yields occasional punctuation in at least some policy areas, but which may not settle down to an equilibrium for a very long time.

Seen in this light, we may be witnessing today a gradual erosion of the dollar's dominance in international trade and finance. Many factors and developments combine to cause this decline which may, however, accelerate quickly, causing suddenly its demise as the world's premier currency. As in so many things in life, this development can be traced back to multiple sources with a cumulative effect. Should the dollar's dominance come under assault and become destabilized, it would provide another example of the disruptive dynamics discussed by Baumgartner and Jones.

As suggested earlier, resistance from vested interests and rigged rules of engagement tend to hold back necessary policy change. When this change comes, it can be long overdue, thus explaining the appearance of occasional sharp and discontinuous break with the status quo ante. This latter phenomenon in turn leads Baumgartner and Jones (2009: 9) to remark, "The destruction and creation of policy monopolies may be much faster than people realize, so the cumulative impact of the continual, but sporadic, creation and destruction of policies monopolies may be that a competitive and pluralistic political system is much less conservative than it sometimes appears." These authors were referring to the political system of the United States.

The conservative nature of the US political system – with its checks and balances at the federal level, the division of power between the federal and state governments, and multiple local and state jurisdictions – may not be as great as might have been imagined previously. Although some people have thought that a federal form of government works to dampen the operation of positive-feedback processes, "[t]he numerous venues provided by federalism make change far more unpredictable than in a unitary system," even though this form of government "ought to act as a brake on positive-feedback processes in policy dynamics" (Baumgartner and Jones 2009: 217, 227). Decentralization of policymaking authority and the availability of multiple points of access to policymaking should reduce the systemic effects of policy conservatism. The opposing influences just described led Baumgartner and Jones (2009: 236) to conclude:

Our primary thesis is that the American political system. built as it is on a conservative constitutional base designed to limit radical action, is nevertheless continually swept by policy change, change that alternates between incremental drift and rapid alterations of existing arrangements. During quiet periods of policymaking, negative feedback dominates; policy innovations seldom capture the imagination of many individuals, so change is slow or rare. During periods of rapid change, positive feedback dominates; each action generates disproportionately large responses, so change accelerates. Critical points occur before the initiation of a positive-feedback process; such periods are referred to as windows of opportunity. Punctuated equilibrium, rather than stability and immobilism, characterizes the American political system.

Punctuated Equilibrium and US Federal Policies

Baumgartner and Jones' ([1993] 2009) major contribution lies in showing that in addition to the prevailing view that policymaking tends to reflect a strong bias in favor of maintaining the status quo, it can also sometimes undergo sudden and major transformation. Even more importantly, their work introduces a perspective that can accommodate both stasis and change, explaining why these phenomena can coexist and are indeed mutually constitutive. As I have already indicated earlier in this chapter, since their initial book this perspective of punctuated equilibrium has "caught fire," inspiring and motivating a large and continuously expanding and seemingly ubiquitous literature. Any literature review is likely to be incomplete because of the rapid proliferation of studies sharing this perspective.

Baumgartner and Jones' seminal work, *Agendas and Instability in American Politics*, was originally published in 1993. This book was preceded and followed by other research that these authors, their students, and their collaborators have published (e.g., Baumgartner and Jones 1991, 2002a; Baumgartner et al. 2000; Jones and Breunig 2007;

Jones et al. 1993, 1998, 2003; Talbert et al. 1995). As already remarked, the initial thrust of empirical evidence supporting the perspective of punctuated equilibrium came from budgetary decisions, an area where the traditional view of incremental adjustment and even stasis has dominated. Principles such as "base" and "fair share" suggest next year's budget should be a close approximation of this year's.

A major quantitative study (Jones et al. 1998) examining all areas of federal spending since 1946 provided strong support for the conclusion that this traditional view of incremental adjustment and limited change has been exaggerated. There were two major punctuations in US government spending since World War II, presenting three epochs: postwar adjustment (1947–1956), robust growth (1956–1974), and restrained growth (1976–1995). While budgets in most years appear to show great stability or "drift," sharp breaks do occur to shift spending to a new level – and not just for specific funding categories but throughout the government. The epochal hypothesis was tested against competing explanations referring respectively to macroeconomic conditions, partisan divisions, and public opinion, and it survived all these challenges. This study's conclusion is important because the epochal proposition reflects a general understanding of a government, and this understanding is more influential in allocating public spending than those other factors suggested by the competing explanations.

In addition to showing major though rare discontinuities in federal spending programs and the importance of epochal influence, Jones et al. (1998) make another important point. Although we may understand well individual factors affecting budgetary decisions, these forces can interact in complex and unexpected ways, thus defying efforts to make specific predictions – a point that I have stressed in Chapter 1. "In policymaking, new ways of thinking about public problems, rapid mobilizations of new constituencies, changes in institutional structures, and the self-reinforcing effects of these trends occasionally combine to create dramatic and unpredictable policy changes in an issue-area" (Jones et al. 1998: 2). The authors acknowledge forthrightly:

The theory of policy punctuations does not lead simply to point predictions of when and in what area the next punctuation will occur. Punctuations are not easily associated with the ebb and flow of political and economic forces. If episodes of disjoint change were simply and directly associated with such forces, then an independent theory of policy change based on notions of punctuated equilibrium would not be necessary. (Jones et al. 1998: 4)

This is an important point, echoing my view stated earlier in Chapter 1 and also encapsulated in my conclusion to be presented in Chapter 7.

As already mentioned, the surge of studies on punctuated equilibrium after Baumgartner and Jones ([1993] 2009) has examined additional policy areas beyond those addressed by these authors (e.g., environmental protection, forestry management, civil defense, and election results) as well as some further studies of the same policy areas that they have investigated (e.g., tobacco smoking, budgetary decisions). There were also efforts made to extend the study of policymaking beyond the federal level in the United States to its state and local governments. These studies were followed subsequently by other publications reporting on policymaking in countries and places other than the United States.

Many of these follow-up studies showed supportive evidence for punctuated equilibrium as a description of policymaking dynamics, specifically, that this process tends to be characterized by long stretches of stability that is sometimes disrupted by sudden lurches. There are also studies that fail to turn up strong supportive evidence for punctuated equilibrium, such as policy evolution in forestry management in the Pacific Northwest (Cashore and Howlett 2007) and regulation on tobacco smoking at the state level in the United States (Givel 2008). Michael Givel (2010) has criticized Baumgartner and Jones for supposedly adhering to an old formulation of punctuated equilibrium which Gould and Eldredge have since abandoned and revised. According to him, Gould and Eldredge have refined their argument that punctuated equilibrium is the norm but that it is not the only possibility in evolutionary history.

On the latter point, Gould and Eldredge (1977) and Gould (1989) clarified that they have never denied that gradualism can happen in theory or in fact. In their view, nature is too complicated for researchers to be dogmatic. It is a matter of relative frequency of occurrence rather than dichotomous absolutes. Gradualism and punctuated equilibrium have both occurred, thus leading Gould and Eldredge to accept evolutionary pluralism. Similarly, Baumgartner and Jones ([1993] 2009) explain that they have never claimed that punctuated equilibrium is everywhere. They have only argued that public policies tend to alternate between stability and punctuation. Thus, the failure to uncover evidence of policy punctuation in some cases is not viewed as a fatal flaw of the punctuated equilibrium perspective. It is offset by supportive evidence from a larger number of other studies of policy-making both in the United States and elsewhere.

Although much of the existing research has focused on budgetary allocation by the US federal government, there are also interesting studies that take us to other subject areas. For example, Michelle Wolfe (2012) took up the phenomenon of negative feedback in media attention. Her event history showed that media attention could counterintuitively lengthen the time required for US Congress to pass pertinent legislations. Heather Larsen-Price (2012) reported that the allocation of US presidential attention to five different issue areas corresponds to patterns of stability and surges described by punctuated equilibrium. Finally, Jeff Worsham and Chaun Stores (2012) presented a case study of resistance to change. Crowded agenda and indifferent and even hostile congressional committees and the Farm Bureau continued for a long time to discriminate against African American farmers until a landmark court ruling in 1999. These articles demonstrate that punctuated equilibrium has been applied to a wide array of interesting questions.

Extensions to US State and Local Governments

As already mentioned, the perspective of punctuated equilibrium was initially applied to policymaking by the US federal government. Subsequently, researchers turned their attention to the analysis of policymaking at the state and local levels, which was in turn followed by the extension of this research agenda to comparative politics and international relations. A large portion of these studies following the first wave addressed budgetary decisions. They often involved quantitative research utilizing large cross-sectional and longitudinal datasets on government expenditures.

Thus, for example, Christian Breunig and Chris Koski (2006) analyzed budgetary figures for the fifty US states, across ten spending categories during 1982–2022. Their principal finding is that all state budgets deviate from a normal distribution. This deviation would be expected if punctuated equilibrium was present. Their analysis shows that states' budget allocations tend to have a "tall head" and "fat tails." That is, there were many more cases of small changes than would be expected from a normal distribution of the data – hence a taller but narrower peak when researchers plot the distribution of the relevant budget data. There were also more cases in the outlying regions of the distribution, suggesting a larger number of budgetary swings (that is, more cases of major increases and decreases in spending) than one would have expected statistically if the data were distributed normally. Finally, the graphs plotting the states' spending patterns showed "slender shoulders" – that is, fewer cases of moderate changes than one would expect from a normal distribution. These characteristics show departures from a normal distribution, which would be expected if policymaking reflected incrementalism.

Breunig and Koski (2006: 372–373) conclude, "the budget distributions are marked by a large amount of small changes and a considerable number of extreme changes." Although the budgets of all states showed signs of punctuation, this tendency was more pronounced for some states (e.g., New York, Alabama, Texas) than for others (e.g., Massachusetts, New Jersey, Kentucky). A descriptive statistic – leptokurtosis – tells analysts the extent to which an observed distribution deviates from normal distribution, something one would expect to see when punctuated equilibrium is absent. A normal distribution is characterized by the familiar bell curve, with random and diverse events producing mostly small adjustments and rarely large, disjoint decisions. In contrast, a leptokurtic distribution is distinguished by the prevalence of small changes, few cases of intermediate change, and more cases of large changes than one would expect from a normal distribution.

Another study of expenditures by local governments in the USA reported similar findings indicating the presence of punctuated equilibrium (Jordan 2003). Still another study by Robinson et al. (2007) analyzed data from over 1,000 school districts in Texas during 1989–2001. They found that the distribution of these districts' budgets followed the characteristics of punctuated equilibrium. Their study also reported that more centralized organizations tended to show larger budgetary changes. The same leptokurtic pattern has characterized budget decisions at the federal level of the United States (Jones 1994; Jones et al. 2003). Another example from Graeme Boushey (2012) focused on the dynamics of policy diffusion, which can spread and cascade due to imitation and mimicking by state governments to adopt innovations started by one of their counterparts.

Whereas some researchers have undertaken a quantitative approach to analyze large datasets, others have adopted a qualitative approach using case studies to search for evidence of punctuated equilibrium. Researchers pursuing different questions at the state/local level of policymaking in the United States, and others pursuing similar inquiries in non-US settings have undertaken both quantitative analyses employing large datasets and detailed, qualitative studies of single cases. As mentioned already, Givel (2006) and Givel and Glantz (2001) used the latter approach to study policymaking on tobacco smoking at the state level. Deserai Crow (2010) has also taken this approach to study the management of water rights in Colorado. She found that evidence of punctuated equilibrium was more evident at the level of state policymaking than at the level of local communities.

Baumgartner and Jones (2015) and Jones (1994, 2001) have recast their theory to emphasize people's limited capacity to process information and therefore their resulting tendency to pay sequential attention to emerging problems. This consideration as well as cognitive rigidity – not to mention institutional ossification and friction (more on this topic later) – tend to hold back timely adjustment reflecting information on changing circumstances. This resulting resistance to change, however, can only maintain the status quo for so long until rising pressure for change overcomes the forces of conservatism to cause a sudden and dramatic transformation.

In a review of their research program to date (as of 2012), Jones and Baumgartner (2012: 8) use the stick-slip dynamic of earthquakes to illustrate this process:

The general punctuation thesis specifies an interaction between the flow of information into a policymaking system and the resistance, or friction, to adjustment that is built into the system. In the natural world, there are various specifications for friction, but all of them involve the interaction of two forces: a retarding force and a force directed at overcoming the retarding force. Earthquakes are a primary example of one type [of] friction. The general process that generates earthquakes is known as stick-slip dynamics. The earth's tectonic plates are held in place by a retarding force, the "friction" of the plates, while the dynamic processes generated by activities in the earth's core push on these plates. When the forces acting on the plates are strong enough, the plates release, and, rather than slide incrementally in adjustment, slip violently, resulting in the earthquake.

In this view, policy systems respond to signals from their environment disproportionately, by either not making enough adjustment or overreacting. This phenomenon explains that in most cases for most of the time, incrementalism prevails. It also explains why change can happen suddenly and abruptly, giving the impression of policy surges or lurches. Whether and how well a policy or political system responds to incoming information depends on the extent of its institutional friction. An institution's decision protocols, the size of its membership, and the convergence or divergence of its members' preferences affect the degree of its institutional friction. Those that require a supermajority and even unanimity to reach a decision, and those that have a large membership with heterogeneous preferences are less able to make timely adjustments, and they are therefore more susceptible to punctuated dynamics. I will return to this important point again when discussing cross-national differences in policymaking.

A special issue of *Policy Studies Journal* in 2012 brought together a collection of essays on punctuated equilibrium. Christopher Breunig and Chris Koski (2012: 50) argue that "punctuated equilibrium positions itself as a broader theory of policy change in which incrementalism is but a special case." They state succinctly:

The core argument of punctuated equilibrium theory is that institutional stickiness creates policy stability which, over time, creates a gap in the institutionalized preferences of the status quo and the observed policy outcomes ... Eventually, exogenous shocks – typically in the form of new information – rupture a policy subsystem leading to a positive feedback cycle in which the public agenda undergoes dramatic, radical policy change to settle back into a new equilibrium. The new equilibrium, for the time being, then reflects the agenda of the status quo. The argument rests on a mechanism of how people and institutions process information. Given cognitive and institutional carrying capacities, attention to new ideas is difficult and radical at the same time. Thus, in such systems, moderate changes are actually quite difficult to achieve as strong institutions want to maintain their existing foci long after the general policy environment has changed. (Breunig and Koski 2012: 50)

Extending their earlier research on budget allocations at the state level in the United States, these researchers report two important insights. First, states with a history of punctuated equilibrium turn out to grow their budgets less than others that show, relatively speaking, more incrementalism. Second, it is important to attend to budgetary categories in addition to the level of aggregate spending. State legislators give a higher priority to funding education, welfare, and health because they are mandated by existing laws or because these issues are more salient to voters. Secondary budget items, such as funding for parks and police are more susceptible to spending surges or drops. These are also items over which the legislators have more discretion.

Looking beyond the United States

It should be evident from the discussion thus far that the perspective of punctuated equilibrium as applied to the study of politics and policy-making owes its theoretical inspiration and empirical foundation to the research on the United States. As this research program becomes more mature, more works that study non-US cases emerge to enhance our understanding of politics and policymaking in other democratic and welfare states in Europe. The overall conclusion of these studies indicates that punctuated equilibrium is a broad phenomenon that also characterizes the European countries. But as I will discuss in more detail later, there are meaningful variations in the extent of this phenomenon. For example, policymaking in a unitary system like Britain is less likely to experience punctuated equilibrium than a federal system, such as the United States with its more decentralized structure for policymaking, multiple venues of making policies, and checks and balances in the policymaking process.

In 2011, the journal *Comparative Political Studies* featured a special issue on agenda setting in a broad comparative context (Baumgartner et al. 2011a). This collection of essays, with a lead article providing introduction by Baumgartner et al. (2011b), shows that research on agenda setting has itself become a research agenda with increasing involvement and participation by analysts interested in comparing attention to issues by building large longitudinal datasets. It demonstrated that the study of policymaking dynamics had indeed taken off. This research program has shown vibrancy and progress.

As in the US context, the bulk of evidence on punctuated equilibrium has come from budgetary studies of Western European countries. When researchers studied budgetary data from these countries, they observed patterns reminiscent of those found in the United States. Leptokurtic distributions characterized the national budgets of countries such as Belgium, Britain, Canada, Denmark, France, and Germany (Baumgartner et al. 2009; Jones et al. 2009; John and Margetts 2003). Christian Breunig (2006) has presented similar results in studies of

Britain, Denmark, Germany, and the United States. The same phenomenon is evident at the subnational level and not just for state and local governments in the USA as reported earlier. For example, local spending in Denmark also offered evidence supporting punctuated equilibrium (Mortensen 2005). Naturally, that the same phenomenon shows up in different political systems and at different times gives greater credence to the perspective's empirical validity and significance.

In their study of three democracies (Belgium, Denmark, and the United States) in different policy areas and over an extended period, Baumgartner et al. (2009) found abundant evidence of punctuated equilibrium as evidenced by changes that depart significantly from a normal distribution. Moreover, there is a common pattern that as an issue moves through the various stages of policy process, this departure becomes more pronounced, suggesting that institutional frictions tend to increase as an issue makes its way from the initial stage of articulation to the final stage of decision. The influence from different stages of policy process turned out to be substantially stronger than that of the differences between countries in shaping policy distributions. Examination of extended series of government spending in France also shows significantly higher kurtosis values than one would have expected from a normal distribution if this spending were proportionate to changes in social inputs (Baumgartner et al. 2006).

The budgetary patterns of all countries studied thus far show evidence of leptokurtosis. As noted in the last paragraph, they also show meaningful variations according to different stages of policymaking. Moreover, such variations extend to differences among political systems. Those countries with a unitary form of government concentrating policymaking power at the national level such as Britain have less institutional frictions than others with decentralized, dispersed policy processes such as in US federalism with its many veto points. We should therefore expect to see stronger evidence of punctuated equilibrium in the latter case than the former case. Moreover, countries that occupy intermediate positions between Britain and the United States should manifest a middle range of punctuated equilibrium, depending on the stickiness of their institutional designs. As David Prindle (2012: 34) has noted, the cross-country data patterns are in fact supportive of this proposition, with their degree of experiencing punctuated equilibrium rising as their institutional frictions rise to impose greater transaction costs.

As with those studies on the United States, research on other countries has moved beyond an exclusive focus on budgetary decisions. The special issue of *Policy Studies Journal* in 2012, mentioned briefly earlier, featured articles addressing punctuated equilibrium beyond national or local budgets. Petya Alexandrova et al. (2012: 69) wrote about agenda setting by the European Council (1975–2010), concluding that its distribution of attention to agenda items followed a leptokurtic pattern. Peter John and Shaun Bevan (2012) studied British government's legislative agenda, which showed a similar leptokurtic distribution of items taken up for consideration. In their words, "Institutional stickiness and cognitive rigidity hold back change, but after pressure builds up over time and reaches a certain threshold, policymaking and policy agenda exhibit disproportionate changes that are manifested by positive feedback and cascades" (John and Bevan 2012: 90).

There are other more recent studies applying punctuated equilibrium to novel topics and contexts. For example, Andrew Gibbons and Rhonda Evans (2023) studied Australia's executive lawmaking agenda, reporting that changes in individual prime minister have had a greater influence on this agenda than changes in the governing party. Daniel Casey (2023) compared letters to Australia's prime minister and US president to study punctuations in public opinion and political participation. In another interesting study, Nick Hin-Kin Or (2019a, 2019b) applied punctuated equilibrium to agenda setting in Hong Kong's Legislative Council. He examined the crosscutting effects imposed by the costs of information exchange and those of bargaining transactions. He showed that the benefits from information exchange tended to be stronger than the transaction costs of bargaining initially in Hong Kong's liberalization process. But the costs of transaction bargaining tended to override the former's benefits in the later stages of liberalization. In other words, bargaining costs started to subsequently shrink policy space, forcing officials to focus their attention on fewer issues.

Comparing Democratic and Authoritarian Systems

The study by Or (2019a, 2019b) points to a new exciting research direction. Researchers have turned increasingly to comparative research, not being content just to demonstrate that punctuated equilibrium provides a good description of the policymaking process. They have started to ask probing questions such as whether authoritarian systems are more prone to suffer from punctuated equilibrium than democracies, and if so, why (Jones et al. 2019).

This research reveals that several variables are likely to be at play. First, they pertain to the forces maintaining the status quo versus the forces agitating for change. Conservative forces in favor of maintaining the status quo usually have the upper hand whether a country is a democracy or an autocracy. The default is always to continue with the existing policy, for change requires resources – including attention, energy, and political capital which are always in short supply. The next question is which kind of political system is more likely to suffer from policy gridlock or stalemate, postponing important decisions even though a situation calls for decisive action. Decentralized power and multiple veto players suggest greater difficulty in mounting major policy overhauls in democracies. An example is the looming disasters facing the social security program and national debt in the United States. Gradualism, or kicking the proverbial can down the road, appears to be a more prevalent situation in a democracy like the USA. However, this remark is not as much about the nature of democracy per se as it is about its decision structure in the USA compared to a more centralized format such as in a unitary system like Britain. Nevertheless, everything else being equal, it is more difficult for democracies to reach a consensus for decisive action and the solutions to perceived problems tend to be watered-down compromises, because compared to authoritarian systems, they have a larger selectorate (Bueno de Mesquita et al. 2003, Bueno de Mesquita and Smith 2012). A selectorate consists of those groups or individuals who "select" or are responsible for putting a leader in a position of power, and whose support this leader needs to stay in power. Moreover, according to Mancur Olson (1982), those democracies that have enjoyed long, uninterrupted peace and stability tend to accumulate entrenched distribution coalitions, powerful groups that resist change in order to protect their particularistic interests.

The preceding observation refers more to how easily can a policy change be made rather than the quality of decisions. Naturally, "problems must be detected and defined before they are addressed" (Jones et al. 2019: 12), which in turn requires information. Specifically, democracies have better information and more access to information for making policies. In authoritarian systems such as China, there are fewer channels for leaders to stay in touch with society and the information available to officials is less reliable because of distortions in the political system – including the tendency for this information to please or support rather than challenge the leaders' predispositions. Therefore, whereas a country like China is more capable of launching major policy initiatives like the Great Leap Forward, the Cultural Revolution, and most recently the Covid-19 Lockdowns, there are fewer safeguards to check against bad decisions and fewer dissenting voices to call for course correction. A bad policy can have system-wide ramifications in contrast to a more decentralized system where separate local jurisdictions present barriers to contain its deleterious effects. As suggested by van den Dool and Li (2023), this discussion hypothesizes that authoritarian regimes tend to experience less institutional friction, but they suffer more from restrictions on information flow that compromise the quality of their decisions and cause larger policy punctuations.

Commenting on the contrast in the history of China and Europe's economic development, David Landes (1999: 38) remarks that unlike China's political unification and centralization, Europe's decentralization and "fragmentation was the strongest brake on wilful [*sic*], oppressive, behavior. Political rivalry and the right of exit made all the difference." Similarly, Joel Mokyr 1990: 208) emphasizes, unlike China, Europe's "political fragmentation guaranteed that no single decision maker could turn off the lights, that the capriciousness or piety of no single ruler could prevent technological advances and the economic growth they brought." Although in a more autocratic and centralized system there may be fewer institutional frictions and veto players to stall and prevent decisive action, these top-down systems are more prone to issuing orders that are detached from reality on the ground, and they are more likely to be carried out without critical examination. When they fail, they fail spectacularly with system-wide, lasting effects. "Europe, in contrast [to imperial China], did not have all its eggs in one basket" (Landes 1999: 39). Authoritarian systems are more susceptible to ideological or political correctness that distorts information, creates false optimism, and thus amplifies positive-feedback loops over an extended period, causing "policy bubbles" or overreaction (Jones et al. 2014; Maor 2014).

E. J. Fagan (2023: 243) has studied policy disasters defined as "avoidable, unintended extreme negative policy outcomes." Using predictions from punctuated equilibrium, he hypothesizes that "Systems with more veto players and weaker information flows will experience more policy disasters, but information flows will have a stronger impact than veto players." Coming from a different angle, his study concurs with the thrust of the argument presented in the last paragraph. It also suggests that systems with both weaker information flows and more veto players have the greatest exposure to policy disasters. Information flows and veto players are of course important in affecting a government's policymaking capacity, specifically in the timely detection of problems and in their effective resolution. Low-friction governments with these capabilities are better equipped to avoid policy disasters (Fagan et al. 2017; Jones et al. 2009).

Jones et al. (2019) and Fagan (2023) postulate that policy disasters can occur due to two reasons: Poor information flows cause errors to accumulate and delay the necessary action to address them, and when such actions are taken, they tend to be overreactions. Democracies should have fewer disasters than authoritarian systems because of their stronger information flows, even when they have more veto players. Authoritarian systems with weak information flows and strong veto players are most likely to experience policy disasters. Fagan (2023: 247–248) concludes, "An emerging consensus in the punctuated equilibrium theory literature finds that authoritarian regimes tend to have a more punctuated pattern of policy changes ... While all governments produce patterns of policy change significantly more leptokurtic than normal, authoritarian countries produce considerably more leptokurtic distributions than democracies." He cites various studies on Brazil (Baumgartner et al. 2017), China (Chan and Fan 2021; Chan and Zhao 2016), Hong Kong (Lam and Chan 2015; Or 2019a, 2019b), Hungary (Sebők and Berki, 2018), Malta (Baumgartner et al. 2017), Russia (Baumgartner et al. 2017), and Turkey (Baumgartner et al. 2017; Bulut and Yildirim 2019).

Jones et al. (2019: 1) use extreme policy punctuations as an indication of maladaptive policymaking, and they suggest that four related factors contribute to more punctuated policymaking: "friction imposed by formal rules and informal norms on the policymaking process, the absence of incentives to address problems, centralization in policymaking, and lack of diversity in channels of information." These factors address both the incentives to engage in policy change and the availability and quality of information to guide this endeavor.

There are gradations for these variables among political systems, including democracies, autocracies, and hybrid types. Democracies generally tend to have less severe punctuations than their authoritarian counterparts primarily because information availability and quality appear to play a larger role than the presence and strength of veto groups. In comparing countries undergoing political transition such as Brazil, Malta, Russia, and Turkey, Baumgartner et al. (2017) found that budgetary punctuations became less pronounced when these countries became more democratic. As expected, Miklós Sebők and Tamás Berki (2018) found the opposite trend for Hungary as it became less democratic. In an earlier study, Jones et al. (2009) hypothesized that among democracies, presidential systems should have more institutional frictions than parliamentary systems. Similarly, federal governments should have more frictions than unitary governments, and likewise, minority or coalition governments compared to governments dominated by a single party. The same logic argues that bicameralism should have more frictions and hence experience more punctuations compared to governments with only one legislative body.

Applying Punctuated Equilibrium to International Relations

In the realm of international relations, scholars have applied punctuated equilibrium to the study of international law, interstate rivalries, and international regimes. For example, Paul Diehl and Charlotte Ku (2010) seek to develop a general theory of legal change. They provide a framework to study the evolution of international law, a framework consisting of an operating component and a normative component which are mutually causative in bringing about change. This change is infrequent but when it occurs, its influence can be substantial. As with the development of international law, Paul Diehl and Gary Goertz (2000) show that long-standing feuds between pairs of countries, which they call enduring rivalries, appear to follow the dynamics of punctuated equilibrium. These hostile and competitive relationships can last for a long time but come abruptly to an end due to some type of shock. Thus, there can be a sudden and dramatic breakthrough terminating a protracted impasse or deadlock. The Camp David Accord between Egypt and Israel comes to mind as an example. This accord was of course itself the culmination of a process started by Egypt's President Anwar Sadat when he announced his decision to visit Israel – a radical decision that broke the "logjam" and turned a new page for relations between Egypt and Israel.

Still other international relations scholars have applied the perspective of punctuated equilibrium to the development and evolution of international regimes. For instance, the study by James Colgan et al. (2012) mentioned in the previous chapter applied it to the study of the international energy regime complex. They showed that innovation can take two forms, being either path-dependent (thus incremental) or de novo (thus representing sharp departures from the status quo, including the introduction of new institutional fora). Whether change takes one or the other form depends on the degree of the relevant states' dissatisfaction, especially those that are strong and are therefore capable of organizing and leading a powerful coalition to introduce and implement change. Environmental shocks also play a role in presenting choice opportunities, thus serving as a trigger to produce change. Path dependency prevails when major actors have homogeneous interests. Conversely, when these interests are heterogeneous and powerful actors are very dissatisfied, the creation of new or de novo institutions becomes likely because reform of the existing institutions is perceived to be difficult or impossible (thus causing this option to be eschewed by powerful actors that are dissatisfied). In this formulation, dissatisfaction is a necessary but insufficient condition for change. The dissatisfied actors must also have the wherewithal to initiate and force change.

Although he did not study the process of punctuated equilibrium specifically, Oran Young (2010) introduced this characterization as one of the five historical patterns in his comparative analysis of five international environmental regimes. He described the evolution of the Antarctic Treaty System as a process of punctuated equilibrium. The other international environmental regimes studied by him dealt with ozone depletion (which was labeled by Young as progressive development), climate change (an example of arrested development), whales and whaling (an example of "diversion"), and the harvesting of northern fur seals (an example of "regime collapse"). Young focused on the alignment of endogenous and exogenous factors, arguing that too much institutional rigidity means an inability to adapt to changing environment, but too much suppleness can have the opposite adverse effect of causing a regime to be overwhelmed by its environment. The key is thus to strike an appropriate balance whereby institutional robustness enables a regime to withstand environmental pressure and resilience enables it to adapt and adjust to a changing environment. As with other authors such as John Kingdon (1984) and Baumgartner and Jones ([1993] 2009), Young stressed the conjunctive logic, that is, the importance of interactive effects among the trinity of interests, power, and ideas (knowledge) in shaping institutional dynamics.

As with Young's (2010) study, Magnus Lundgren et al. (2017) focused on policymaking in international organizations. They compared agenda setting in five international organizations during 1985–2015: the United Nations, the European Union (EU), the African Union, the Organization of American States, and the Organization of Islamic Cooperation (OIC). Their research focused on the effects of institutional friction on policy punctuation, with institutional friction operationalized in terms of each organization's decision rules, membership size, and preference heterogeneity. This research led them to three main conclusions. First, policymaking in all these international organizations displays signs of punctuated equilibrium, thus "Long periods of inattention will be supplanted by short periods of attentiveness in a pattern of infrequent and disproportionate response" (Lundgren et al. 2017: 550). Second, institutional friction tends to produce punctuated equilibrium. Those international organizations such as the OIC characterized by a large and heterogeneous membership are more likely to experience institutional frictions and consequently punctuated equilibrium. In contrast, when institutional friction is lower – such as when decision-making rules are laxer, membership consists of a small number of states, and/or the members share homogeneous views and similar preferences, international organizations can respond more efficiently to societal pressure such as in the case of the EU. The results of this research correspond to and reinforce the evidence found at the national level regarding budget allocations (Baumgartner et al. 2009; Jones et al. 2009), namely the proposition that policy or political systems with higher institutional frictions are more likely to experience punctuated equilibrium.

Another example from the field of international relations is provided by Bahar Leventoglu and Branislav Slantchev (2007), who applied punctuated equilibrium to study how belligerents reach an agreement to terminate combat. After a war has started, how does it come to an end? These authors showed that windows for peace often appear following protracted fighting. These opportunities for a negotiated settlement vary in their duration but show up typically after a series of battles. They can disappear thereafter, only to reappear again later after another round of fighting. A negotiated settlement becomes more possible after one side's threat to punish the other side for exploiting peace negotiation has been made more credible. In this sense, fighting prepares a conflict to become "riper" or more ready for resolution. "It is this pattern of windows of opportunities for peace, which cluster toward the military end of war that leads us to view war as a punctuated equilibrium" (Leventoglu and Slantchev 2007: 769). Protracted fighting in this case is the normal situation, whereas punctuation is provided by the breakthrough of peace.

As already mentioned, the literature on punctuated equilibrium is vast as this idea has caught the attention of scholars in many diverse fields. It is difficult to do justice to this rapidly expanding literature. Just to mention a few final examples, Surinder Mohan (2022) used this perspective to study the life cycle of Indian–Pakistani rivalry. Jeroen Joly and Friederike Richter (2023: 42) showed that in foreign policymaking as in domestic policymaking, the politics of gridlock can prevent "large policy changes, leading to mostly small, incremental, changes instead of policies that are proportionate to solving the problem. Yet, disproportionately large policy changes can occur when the way an issue is understood changes (issue definition) and/or previously uninterested people get involved (agenda setting)." On these relatively rare occasions foreign policy can alter its established course. The terrorist attack on September 11, 2001, served as a shock and a focusing event that mobilized attention and resources for Washington to abandon business as usual. Such dramatic events calling for decisive action can present a "window of opportunity" (Birkland 2004; Mazarr 2007) to implement an ostensible solution (such as attacking Saddam Hussein) that has already been conceived and one that has just been waiting to be applied to a supposed problem (his perceived threat to US interests in the Middle East) when a choice opportunity presents itself.

My final example comes from a case study of US policymaking on its hydrogen-bomb program. Warner Schilling (1973) wrote about this policymaking – or rather, non-policymaking – long before punctuated equilibrium became a popular research topic. He did not use the terminology of punctuated equilibrium, but his study showed all the hallmarks of the politics of policymaking described by Baumgartner and Jones. Various US agencies competed to define the issue(s) at hand,

to set the agenda for presidential decision, and to include or exclude
participants who might be allies or alternately, adversaries on the
question of whether to expand the H-bomb program. Bureaucratic
stalemate, or letting the status quo continue to drift, was one of the
outcomes – a situation described by Warner as "deciding without
choosing." Significantly, the preferences of the State and Defense
Departments eventually prevailed over that of the other bureaucratic
actors (such as the Atomic Energy Commission) involved in this inter-
agency struggle – even though they preferred the same outcome for
different reasons.

Useful Imports and Tantalizing Metaphors

I conclude this chapter with a few remarks about arguments in favor of
and against importing concepts from other disciplines. Michael Givel
(2010: 187) cautions us that borrowing from the natural sciences
requires "a clear and viable syllogism linked to appropriate methodology." He points out that important differences exist between biological research and studies of public policy, "including time frames for
change, what constitutes outside disturbances of equilibrium, venues of
punctuated equilibrium, levels of analysis for change, and patterns of
change" (Givel 2010: 187). All of this is true, but does it mean that we
should not accept insights from other disciplines? David Prindle (2012)
also warns about the pitfalls of borrowing a concept from a different
field but at the same time acknowledges that this import can be a
source of inspiration, when remarking about "broader metaphors that
can surely nudge the mind into productive channels, but that make no
explicit claim for causal continuity or unification" (Gould quoted in
Prindle 2012: 26).

Prindle (2012: 26) observes that Gould (1995, 2002) does not
dismiss the usefulness of metaphors. He quotes Gould saying, "...we
need carriers, or metaphors, to make ... imaginative jumps. Moreover,
a scholar's choice of metaphor usually provides our best insight into
the preferred modes of thought and surrounding social circumstances
that so influence all of human reasoning, even the scientific modes
often viewed as fully objective in our mythology" (Gould 1995: 444).
Prindle (2012: 27) also quotes other scholars on the usefulness of
metaphors. "The very nature of science ... is such that scientists need
the metaphor as a bridge between old and new theories" (MacCormac

1976: 36), and "... many theorists have been arguing for the constitutive nature of metaphor in virtually every natural and social science
discipline" (Gibbs 1994: 171–172). Prindle (2012: 27) goes on to
provide the following long list, showing the common phenomenon of
political scientists employing metaphors in their language:

As a matter of common observation, the profession of political science is rife
with metaphors. Those who study elections lament that too much attention is
given to the horse race and wish to avoid media feeding frenzies, unless that
would lead to a landslide for the right side but only if the wrong side can be
prevented from bringing up wedge issues. Whatever the other possibilities,
they hope that no one will play the race card. Budgeting scholars wish that
Social Security could be put in a lock box, an action that might prevent
another economic meltdown. Or it might be headed off if the Fed makes sure
that the economy does not overheat or cool down too much. Judiciary
scholars fear that blind justice will be compromised if the scales are tipped
the wrong way, an especially likely occurrence if the courts start down a
slippery slope. Specialists in international relations worry about the balance
of power, while specialists in domestic politics worry about the nanny state.
Everyone knows that elected officials will not survive if they touch one of the
third rails, an action that they can avoid if they connect the dots while they
are competing for political space.

Prindle points out that political scientists often do not operationalize
the relevant concepts introduced by metaphors which therefore remain
mainly "pedagogical" to insinuate, evoke, or tantalize. In his view, in
the social sciences punctuated equilibrium has remained as a metaphor
lacking any empirical explanatory power, not a scientific concept –
unlike in biology, where it is part of a "theory [that] is based on
measurable trends in the fossil record and backed by an explicit model
of historical process" (Prindle 2012: 29). Baumgartner and Jones
(2009: 18) give their rationale for adopting the idea of punctuated
equilibrium in their research in these words: "We have adopted the
terminology of punctuated equilibrium because it evokes the images of
stability interrupted by major alterations to a system." "Punctuated
equilibrium, rather than stability and immobilism, characterizes the
American political system" (Baumgartner and Jones 2009: 236).

Some time ago, Davis Bobrow (1972) used "metatheory" to describe
the adoption of a particular perspective to illuminate our understanding
of some empirical phenomena. Metatheories do not predict specific
outcomes or indicate the necessary or sufficient conditions for their

occurrence. They are basically an invitation to researchers to put on a particular analytic lens to interpret events, but they in no way exclude possible alternative interpretations. In reference to Graham Allison's (1971) well-known models for explaining the Cuban Missile Crisis, they in effect say to us, think about a country's foreign policy as if it were the outcome of rational deliberations by unitary actors, the output of large inertial organizations, or the result of bureaucratic pulling and hauling. The value and relevance of these models "come in the form of metaphor rather than prediction" (Bobrow 1972: 206).

As a metaphor, the unitary actor model formulated by Allison, for example, presents one way of thinking about how foreign policy decisions are made – but by no means the only way. It suggests how analysts or for that matter, amateur observers of foreign policy can go about imagining how government officials might have tried to understand the foreign policies of other states. The way these officials do so, according to the rational actor model, is to treat the government in question as if it is a unitary and purposeful actor, even though this assumption can be challenged seriously as a depiction of reality. The analyst or pundit adopting this model goes about *reconstructing* history, asking what objectives and calculations *could* have disposed the relevant officials to reach the choice that they did. This reconstruction, however, only provides one *plausible* manner in which this choice could have been reached. In other words, it by no means rules out many other plausible, or conceivable, ways by which the same choice could have been made. All these remarks, however, do not in any way diminish the accolades that Allison's book has received and the influence that it has had on the analysis of foreign policy.

Prindle (2012: 32) concludes, "Our criteria for adopting an outside concept must be, 'Can it be made useful to us?' In the case of punctuated equilibrium, Baumgartner and Jones' answer was a resounding 'Yes.'" Obviously, I agree with Baumgartner and Jones on this point. Moreover, as researchers continue to develop and refine their understanding of punctuated equilibrium, it is not quite true to say that studies associated with this concept are completely devoid of causal content. This point should have come across clearly from the preceding literature review. Insights about the nature and sources of institutional frictions and about people's information-processing tendencies have advanced this collective research agenda considerably even if we do not yet have a full-blown theory. But then, such theories are elusive even in the natural sciences. Thus, as already mentioned, scientists cannot yet predict the timing and location of specific earthquakes or fully explain evolutionary outcomes even though they have a reasonably good grasp of the relevant dynamics.

As mentioned earlier, Baumgartner and Jones do not deny that incrementalism exists, and Gould has also not excluded the occurrence of evolutionary gradualism. The available possibilities ought not present to us binary choices. Prindle (2012: 36) makes a good point suggesting that we should consider replacing "punctuated equilibrium" with "punctuated incrementalism." As Michael Howlett and Andrea Migone (2011) have pointed out, Baumgartner and Jones do not try to apply a biological theory to political science, but rather seek to improve traditional views of incrementalism in policymaking with new insights inspired by biology. As a descriptive term, "punctuated incrementalism" is more accurate than "punctuated equilibrium" at least in political science. Having said this, I have not followed my own judgment on this issue, and I have instead continued to use "punctuated equilibrium" rather than "punctuated incrementalism" for fear of muddying the water by adopting a different terminology than the prevalent one in this area of study.

3 | *Epochal Breaks in Sino-American Relations, and Lulls and Lurches*

Americans have a love–hate relationship with China. There were moments of outpouring of support and sympathy for the Chinese people such as when they were fighting Japan's aggression during World War II, and perhaps even euphoria such as when Americans were caught up in the "panda maniac" after Richard Nixon's visit to Beijing in 1972. There were also times of open hostility and loathsomeness such as when concerns about cheap Chinese "coolies" motivated Washington to pass the Chinese-Exclusion Act with widespread popular support, and mass hysteria concerning the "red menace" during the height of McCarthyism. Americans sometimes romanticized about China, and they were often attracted by the prospect of selling to its huge market. Many missionaries were drawn to that country to proselytize and convert its people to Christianity. Nebraska's Senator Kenneth Wherry's words in 1940, professing that "With God's help, we will lift Shanghai up and up, ever up, until it is just like Kansas City" (quoted in Carillet 2008), reflected this evangelical impulse, missionary zeal, and patronizing attitude. There were also Americans who dreaded the prospect of hordes of "yellow peril" that threatened to spill over China's borders. Nowadays, it is quite common to hear US politicians to rail against the "Chinese Communist Party" to demonstrate their patriotic credential, although in reality the policies being pursued by this political party often has little communist ideological content as understood by orthodox Marxists – just as perhaps, Republican establishment types from a few decades ago would have difficulty recognizing their party under the influence of Trumpism. For the US mass public, knowledge about China has always been scant and shallow. Most from my generation may remember caricatures depicted in popular media, such as Fu Man Chu, Charlie Chan, and Jackie Chan. I doubt many Americans can name any Chinese celebrity today beyond Mao Zedong and Xi Jinping. The Chinese public also has many seriously distorted views about the United States, but there are many more people in China who study the English language or visit or study in the United States than vice versa.

How does the above paragraph relate to punctuated equilibrium? This chapter is intended to show important mood swings and abrupt and sharp changes in the US public and even elite's images of and official policy toward China. As such, we can speak of different epochs in Sino-American relations. A recent book on China (Doshi 2021) tries to discern Beijing's grand strategy based on its perception of US strength and intention. This book, entitled the *The Long Game*, demarcates Beijing's statecraft to displace the US as the world's premier power in recent decades in three periods. In the first period or phase (1989–2008), Beijing is said to be aiming to blunt US power over China, particularly in Asia. This strategy followed the traumatic trifecta (from Beijing's perspective) of the Tiananmen Square demonstrations, the Gulf War, and the Soviet Union's collapse, which led it to sharply increase its perception of US threat. In the ensuing second period (2008–2016), China pursued its second strategy seeking to build the foundation for regional hegemony in Asia. According to Doshi, it was launched after the global financial crisis precipitated by the US housing bubble, which led Beijing to see the USA as a declining power and emboldened it to take a more confident and assertive approach in foreign policy. With Beijing's invocation of "great changes unseen in a century" following Brexit, President Trump's election, and the coronavirus pandemic, China has, according to Doshi, initiated a third strategy, one that expands its blunting Washington's strategic initiatives and building efforts worldwide to displace the United States as the global leader. I introduce Doshi's book to show that periodization is not unusual in analyzing Sino-American relations. This chapter ties this idea of periodization to punctuated equilibrium's central idea – namely, policies tend to follow phases of lulls and lurches. That is, there are brief and sharp punctuations in these policies indicating the start of a new era or epoch to be followed by a protracted period of "business as usual" during which stasis or small changes tend to be characteristic. Eventually, pressures build to cause a rupture or punctuation which ushers in a new equilibrium.

The official governmental relationship between China and the United States has experienced change and continuity. Words like up and down, fits and starts, turns and twists, and peaks and valleys come to mind. In the context of the discussion on punctuated equilibrium in

the previous chapters, I prefer lulls and lurches to describe the vicissitudes of this relationship. Sharp punctuations have been followed by
periods during which this relationship has "normalized" – until the
next round of upheaval and subsequent return to yet another era of
"normalcy." As should be clear from the following discussion, this
"normalcy" refers to bilateral relationship settling around a new level
of comity or enmity, periods during which policies "drift" more or less
around a new equilibrium. This pattern of alternations between relative continuity and sharp breaks has been reasonably evident so that
any reasonably careful and astute observer can discern it. Incidentally,
China's entry into the Korean War also highlights the role of a focusing
event galvanizing policy attention and action that is required to upend
a status quo, a topic that I will return to later.

This chapter has a second purpose. It seeks to show how gathering
momentum as suggested by the idea of positive feedback loops can
eventually carry the day. As suggested by previous studies of major
policy transformation, politicians, bureaucrats, and ordinary folks
want to "go with the winner." No one wants to waste his/her time,
effort, and other resources on a losing or lost cause. This phenomenon
suggests that it is initially difficult to mobilize support to replace an
existing policy or overturn an existing consensus, which explains in
part the persistence of status quo. However, sometimes political entrepreneurs and perceptions of historical "inevitability" may galvanize a
movement such as mass mobilization against nuclear energy or in favor
of protecting the earth's ecology. Once an idea "catches fire" and as it
gathers momentum, more people join the movement and the more
likely a cause appears to be winnable. Sometimes this phenomenon is
described negatively as a "feeding frenzy" such as in reference to media
coverage. In any case, such positive feedback loops can produce transformative change. In this chapter, I also introduce the example of
China's admission to the United Nations to illustrate this process to
bring about a punctuation to a previous situation of gridlock.

Yet a third important idea from punctuated equilibrium is introduced and discussed in this chapter. It is the conjunctive logic arguing
that policy results usually stem from a convergence of problems,
solutions, participants, and opportunities. The timing of this confluence of factors tends to be random or accidental, thus accounting for
the fact that it is difficult to predict when a policy rupture will occur.
This emphasis of multiple factors coming together to produce a policy

output or choice is very different from prevailing narratives on Sino-American relations, such as the monocausal explanation being advanced by Thucydides' Trap (Allison 2017) emphasizing ongoing or pending power shifts to presage war. Quantitative studies on power-transition theory (Organski and Kugler 1980) also tend to lean on a single variable to explain war – namely, interstate power shifts, even though theoretically they are supposed to also take into account a rising state's revisionist agenda.

As the readers will see, this chapter introduces and discusses two more elements tied to the perspective of punctuated equilibrium in policymaking. One of them refers to the contingent nature of policy outputs. Much of the existing international relations scholarship appears to be deterministic – such as the proposition that power shifts are a recurrent cause of interstate war. The perspective stressed in this chapter instead argues that policies tend to be due to fortuitous timing and circumstances. Thus, historical events are contingent and not inevitable. The other element points to the role of political entrepreneurs to bring about change. In the case of China's counter-intervention in the Korean War and Nixon's visit to Beijing, dominant, decisive leaders played a critical role in these decisions.

Two Punctuations and Four Watersheds

The United States had interjected itself in the Chinese Civil War between the Nationalists (represented by the Kuomintang) and the Communists. By 1948 if not earlier, it became clear that the side backed by Washington would lose this contest. Washington appeared to have decided to wash its hands and abandon the Chiang Kai-shek regime in its last island bastion, Taiwan. The outbreak of the Korean War in June 1950 changed everything. Although Dean Acheson, the US Secretary of State, had previously left the Korean peninsula outside the US defense perimeter in a public speech given at the National Press Club, there was a change of mind after war broke out. Motivated by fears of the expansion of a monolithic communist bloc headed by the USSR with Beijing playing the role of its chief surrogate in Asia, the Truman administration decided to intervene in that conflict under United Nations auspice. One immediate consequence of this fateful decision was Washington's reappearance as a key participant in the Chinese Civil War, when Harry Truman ordered the Seventh Fleet to interpose itself in the Taiwan Strait. This decision to "neutralize" the Taiwan Strait had the effect of deterring a prospective Chinese invasion of Taiwan and protecting the Kuomintang regime installed on that island to this date (the Kuomintang had fled to Taiwan after losing the civil war on the mainland). The legacy of this decision continues to reverberate as Taiwan's status has still not been resolved. Beijing perceives the USA to be the chief stumbling block to accomplishing its sacred mission to reunify the country.

Washington's intervention in the Korean War led to Beijing's counter-intervention to defend its North Korean ally and to deny the USA a presence right up to its border. Beijing's decision also had a lasting effect, perpetuating the status quo on the Korean peninsula that has thus far divided the two sides of the Korean Civil War. More directly pertinent to the evolution of Sino-American relationship, Beijing's counter-intervention caused a fundamental change in these two countries' relationship, bringing them into a direct armed conflict. This action froze for all practical purposes this relationship for the next two decades, entrenching the intense hostility and deep suspicion that characterized it. It has had a profound influence on Washington's policy to develop bases and recruit allies in its effort to contain China, including fighting in Vietnam to forestall the so-called domino effect, a belief that was widely shared at the time suggesting that a communist victory anywhere would presage a chain reaction leading to setbacks elsewhere. In the United Nations, the United States claimed that the Kuomintang regime installed in Taiwan was the legitimate government of China – all of China on both sides of the Taiwan Strait. This claim of course sounds ironic today because Washington has now reversed its position to recognize the Beijing government's authority over just the mainland but not its claim of sovereignty over Taiwan. In the 1950s and 1960s, US leaders professed publicly their conviction that the government in Beijing would be a "passing phenomenon." They also characterized the government in Beijing as Moscow's stooge in Asia.

The Sino-American relationship remained frozen until February 1972 when Richard Nixon visited Beijing. The announcement of this visit was a shock as much as the Chinese entry into the Korean War. It was a shock in the dual sense that it came as a huge surprise to nearly all people, and that it signified a fundamental transformation of the relationship between China and the United States. It was "punctuational" – a breakthrough – in that it ruptured the previous state of affairs and inaugurated a new era in these countries' bilateral relations. After Nixon's visit to Beijing, their normalization of diplomatic relations in January 1979 became widely expected as almost the logical and inevitable outcome of this visit. For nearly two decades after this visit, Sino-American relations reached a new plateau of cooperation during the administrations of Gerald Ford, Jimmy Carter, and George H. W. Bush. China and the United States were practically strategic allies in their joint opposition to the USSR.

Policy punctuations are relatively rare but when they do happen, they are big and fast (Goertz 2003: 135). China's entry into the Korean War and Nixon's visit to Beijing were watershed events that established a new level, or equilibrium, in these countries' relationship. In this sense, they can be characterized as "epochal," separating one era of bilateral relations from another. Significantly, as in the research by Jones et al. (1998) on US budgeting, the "epochal" effects appear to be stronger than the effects introduced by changes of individual top leaders in both countries, the conditions in their domestic and international environment, and their popular and elite attitudes. That is, these breakthrough events set the general tone of bilateral relations for the subsequent years that overrides the effects of other sources such as those just mentioned. The two watershed events appear to capture, embody, and augur a fundamental alteration in the two governments' gestalt outlook that sets the broad parameters defining the nature of their overall relationship in the ensuing years. Although it would be an exaggeration to say that the management of this relationship was put on "auto pilot" or "cruise control," "business as usual" would not be an unreasonable description suggesting that Beijing and Washington's policies toward each other mostly drifted within a narrow band around a new consensus emerging from and following the two transformative events, whether reflecting comity or enmity, a consensus shared broadly by the elites and masses of both sides. Even though there might be individuals or groups who were dissatisfied with the new policy course, it is difficult for them to challenge and overturn it for the usual reasons that favor the persistence of the status quo, not the least of which is the very perception that such a struggle is unlikely to be winnable (I will expand on this point later in this chapter). As explained previously, it takes effort to upend an existing policy, and time and attention are among the scarcest commodities in policymaking, especially when an issue needs to reach the very top of the government echelon to be addressed.

One can imagine other plausible punctuations in Sino-American relations, but I tend to think that none are as significant and meaningful as the two just mentioned. Arguably, the Tiananmen Square crackdown in June 1989 can be a possible candidate as Doshi (2021) thinks along with the Gulf War and the USSR's demise although the latter events did not pertain directly to Sino-American relations. However, after the initial round of criticisms and sanctions by the West for the Tiananmen Square crackdown, George H. W. Bush led the way to restore bilateral relations to normalcy. This event therefore did not actually mark a sharp break in Sino-American relations, rupturing the state of affairs existing prior to the crackdown. It could have if the USA and its Western allies had wanted to use it to transform their relations with China, but they chose not to. Beijing's joining the World Trade Organization in December 2001 could be considered as another turning point. It increased the tempo of China's integration into the world economy and ended the annual debate in Washington on whether to accord China the most-favored-nation status in trade, a contentious issue that was an irritant in Sino-American relations. Although an important milestone in China's economic development, this event pertained to not just China's relationship with the USA but rather its economic ties with the world in general. Moreover, to the extent that "politics takes command," economics takes second place. The Beijing Summer Olympics in August 2008 could also be presented as a watershed event, signifying China's "coming out party." Yet, although this event did offer Beijing an opportunity to feature its accomplishments, it did not somehow transform its basic relationship with the United States or, for that matter, with other countries.

One can argue that the 2008–2009 economic recession brought about by the housing bubble in the United States was another watershed event, one that could have led Chinese leaders to conclude that the USA was getting weaker, therefore inclining them to adopt more assertive policies (Deng 2022; Doshi 2021). Although this proposition may be true, it did not appear to have had a direct and immediate impact in transforming Sino-American relations, one that is comparable to Mao Zedong's decision to intervene in the Korean War and Richard Nixon's decision to visit Beijing. Nevertheless, it was a salient event setting off a series of cascading effects that caused a downturn in

Sino-American relations in recent years. It highlighted relative US weakness in Chinese eyes and concomitantly, China's own rise as a formidable competitor in American eyes. Seen in this light, even though it did not represent a policy punctuation (that is, a policy initiative undertaken by either Beijing or Washington), the 2008–2009 economic recession in the USA can be considered to represent another turning point marking the onset of another epoch in Sino-American relations. Perceptions of an ongoing power shift on both sides of the Pacific Ocean as much as the reality of changing balance of power would be the primary leitmotif for increasing tension and competition in this most recent and current epoch in Sino-American relations.

In retrospect, there were signs of turbulence in this relationship long before 2008–2009. Even though it did not represent a deliberate policy punctuation such as China's entry into the Korean War and Nixon's visit to Beijing, the collapse of the Soviet Union and the end of the Cold War had serious reverberations impacting on Sino-American relations. As such, these monumental events (1989–1991) can be considered another turning point in these countries' relationship. They signified the ascendance of the USA as the world's indisputable and unassailable unipolar power. They also signified the end of China's value from Washington's perspective as a strategic partner to check the USSR. If anything, they could have elevated China's status as a substitute enemy for the United States if it were not for the events of 9/11 whereby Al Qaeda and global terrorism preempted this role. In any case, the USSR's collapse meant that China had lost much of its strategic usefulness and thus any substantial leverage vis-à-vis Washington (Zhang 2024: 148–149). At the same time, Wahington's resort to "muscular" policies during its "unipolar moment" became a concern for Beijing and Moscow (Brooks and Wohlforth 2008; Daalder and Lindsay 2005; Walt 2005). These policies included its attacks on Serbia in support of Kosovo's secession from former Yugoslavia (1999), its unilateral decision to invade Iraq without United Nations authorization (2003), and its attacks on Libya ending in the gruesome death of Mohammad Gaddafi (2011). Washington's promotion of color revolutions and regime change abroad, its justification of the novel doctrine of preventive war, and NATO's (the North Atlantic Treaty Organization) expansion (it invited Bulgaria, Estonia, Latvia, Lithuania, Romania, Slovakia and Slovenia to join in 2002) caused further alarm in Moscow and Beijing. As I will discuss shortly, starting from the early 1990s a series of incidents began to cause a deterioration in Sino-American relations.

The discussion thus far has proposed two punctuations that had fundamentally redefined and reframed Sino-American relations for the ensuing decades. These are China's entry into the Korean War in 1950 and Nixon's visit to Beijing in 1972. In addition to these two monumental decisions pointing to an immediate and direct change in Sino-American relations, the USSR's disintegration in 1989–1991 and the economic recession of 2008–2009 can also be considered watershed events that augured a transformation in Sino-American relations albeit in a more indirect and gradual way. This chronology therefore presents four epochs in Sino-American relations, each reflecting a new gestalt outlook on the part of their leaders and setting a new tone for these relations. They are China's entry into the Korean War putting bilateral relations in a deep freeze; Nixon's visit transforming their relations to a strategic partnership; the end of the Cold War and the US rise to unipolar status presaging a series of disruptive events highlighting assertive US unilateralism undermining Chinese trust (Chan 2017a); and most recently, the 2008–2009 economic recession signaling the onset of a new era of intense strategic competition motivated by perceptions as well as the reality of shifting power balance between the two countries.

These events are "shocking" in the sense of causing a fundamental reorientation in foreign policy. They illustrate nicely Paul Diehl and Gary Goertz's (2000) proposition that shocks play an important role in the life histories of enduring rivalries. They can initiate a feud that lasts many years, but they can also bring an end to it abruptly and unexpectedly. Between initiation and termination, there can be a protracted struggle between the rivals with recurrent rounds of confrontation and fighting. Thus, these authors have argued that the evolution of longstanding interstate rivalries is captured by the dynamics of punctuated equilibrium. Note, however, that the shocks relevant to Diehl and Goertz's discussion can have an exogenous source outside the actors' control. For instance, the Bolshevik revolution caused Russia to pull out of World War I, and the dissolution of the USSR "sucked the oxygen" out of contestation between Somalia and Ethiopia. In the two examples I have given for Sino-American relations – China's entry into the Korean War and Nixon's visit to Beijing – these shocks were administered deliberately by the relevant leaders themselves with their "eyes wide open." In other words, these are not blunders or accidents that could conceivably describe other monumental upheavals such as the assassination of Archduke Ferdinand, setting in motion a chain reaction leading to the outbreak of World War I. Rather, Mao's decision to intervene in Korea and Nixon's decision to visit Beijing are more similar to Anwar Sadat's 1977 decision to visit Jerusalem, a decision that broke the "logjam" and led eventually to the Camp David Accord. These shocks did not so much create a "choice opportunity" for other officials to act on; rather, they were themselves monumental choices that reoriented foreign policy, setting it on a new path in the years to follow.

By definition, a shock happens suddenly and unexpectedly (Chan 2023b). On both occasions of policy punctuation in Sino-American relations, the surprise was deliberate. Regarding China's decision to enter into the Korean War, there was clearly a trade-off (Slantchev 2010). Deterrence would require Beijing to tip its hand, demonstrating its intention or resolve (to intervene) by disclosing its troop deployment and perhaps by initiating skirmishes with the South Koreans and even Americans as a warning to show that Beijing meant business, that there would be war unless Washington reversed its policy course (by halting its military advances to the north). Such disclosure, however, would forfeit the military advantage of being able to surprise an enemy and catch it unprepared for a surprise assault. Similarly, Nixon's visit to Beijing was negotiated and arranged in utter secrecy. This secrecy enabled the leaders of the two countries to present the world with a fait accompli, and thus to prevent possible countermobilization domestically and internationally to thwart their initiative. Naturally, the impact of a shock is greatly enhanced if it happens abruptly, catching people off guard. The magnitude of the policy reversal, such as rapprochement by China and the USA that were practically sworn enemies before the announcement of Nixon's visit, of course also contributes to the shock's impact. Moreover, as presented in Chapter 2, the perspective of punctuated equilibrium argues that the very protracted stasis that has held change at bay is the source of accumulating pressure producing a subsequent change. Thus, when change happens, it does so with greater force and abruptness (the metaphor of a coiled spring comes to mind), causing policymakers possibly to overreact and their policies to overshoot.

In view of the literature review in Chapter 2, several features of the two aforementioned policy punctuations in Sino-American relations deserve commenting. First, the role of focusing events in bringing about policy change. These are dramatic occurrences calling elite and public's attention to a problem. Tragedies such as the Triangle Shirtwaist Factory fire in New York in 1911 and the Mississippi River flood of 1927 had also jolted officials to undertake regulations and legislations aimed at fire prevention and flood control, although the Monongah Mine Explosion of 1907 did not have a similar impact on mine safety (Niles 2011). The discovery of a hole in the earth's ozone, and nuclear accidents at power plants at Three Mile Island and Chernobyl had similarly raised the public's awareness of the consequences of greenhouse emission and the hazards of nuclear energy, thus spurring the environmental and anti-nuclear movements respectively. Similarly, the US Supreme Court's ruling on abortion rights (Roe v. Wade) and its more recent decision to curtail these rights also galvanized opposing groups on this issue. When US troops crossed the 38th parallel in Korea in pursuit of the retreating North Korean forces in disarray, this development was also a focusing event forcing leaders in Beijing to decide. They were compelled to act before the window for this choice opportunity closed should the approaching US forces reach the Yalu River separating China and Korea when it would be too late for Beijing to act. Its effect would be comparable to a situation that US leaders would confront if a hostile foreign army was marching rapidly toward Rio Grande and threatening to establish a pro-Beijing government in Mexico. In contrast to China's entry into the Korean War, it is difficult to point to a single shock or catalyst that motivated Nixon's decision to visit Beijing. Naturally, opposition to the USSR and assistance from Beijing to ease the US exit from the then ongoing war in Vietnam War were on US leaders' minds.

Second and as suggested by the various case studies on US policymaking such as on the regulation of nuclear energy, automobile safety, tobacco smoking, and pesticides, intense media coverage often preceded government action. The mass media was important for elevating public and elite awareness and calling attention to the existence of a problem and mobilizing support for change. In the case of the two policy punctuations in Sino-American relations, mass media did not play this role. As already mentioned, both punctuations were initiated by top leaders in complete secrecy. The media, however, did play a subsequent role in the "mobilization of enthusiasm" discussed earlier. After China's entry into the Korean War, there was a massive media

campaign organized by Beijing to generate support for this decision –
the "Resist America, Assist Korea" campaign. The US media also
played a post hoc role after the announcement of Nixon's visit to
Beijing. There was a large uptick in favorable publicity about China,
sometimes dubbed "panda maniac." Therefore, in these cases the
mobilization of media followed rather than led policy punctuation.

Third, the impetus and pressure for a new policy can come from
different sources. One possibility is the mobilization of public opinion and mass sentiments from below. Gary Goertz (2003: 173) points
to the anti-slavery, anti-apartheid, and anti-colonial campaigns
undertaken by societies located in the Global North or the Global
South, sometimes both. Another source or path for policy change
stems from or is related to the diffusion of ideas across national
boundaries or as reviewed in the last chapter, across subnational
political units such as among state governments in the USA on
tobacco smoking or legalized gambling. Interesting examples come
from the extent to which California sets the national standard for
automobile fuel efficiency, and Texas playing the same role in the
publication of textbooks for college and high school. This second
process suggests policy contagion operating horizontally. Naturally,
a third possibility is a vertical or top-down process, with major and
dramatic policy turns being initiated by top government leaders.
Of course, the two policy punctuations in Sino-American relations
came from this third source, with popular support and political
endorsement occurring only subsequently. I will return later to discuss the idea of domestic ratification of foreign policy deals. Finally,
policy transformation can come from pulling and pushing reflecting a
combination of dynamics just described.

Fourth and as already mentioned several times, the two policy
punctuations in Sino-American relations were the result of deliberate
decisions undertaken at the pinnacle of the Chinese and US governments. These decisions involved a small circle of top officials, thus
bypassing the regular bureaucracies. Henry Kissinger, Nixon's foreign
policy advisor, arranged his visit to Beijing in complete secrecy. It has
been rumored that even the US Secretary of State William Rogers was
kept in the dark as he was excluded from the small and tight decision
circle. This being the case, we lack any information reporting on the
activities of political entrepreneurs in these cases engaging in "forum
shopping" and lobbying efforts to promote their ideas. Mao Zedong

and Richard Nixon *were* the venues. In sharp contrast, various episodes of punctuating public policy in the domestic setting told by Baumgartner and Jones ([1993] 2009) and others often show the presence of advocacy groups seeking access to the policymaking process, seeking sympathetic venues whether in the executive or the legislative branch to advance their agenda.

Sino-American relations have deteriorated in recent years, entering yet another epoch characterized by acrimony and tension. Washington has publicly identified China as a revisionist power and a strategic rival. Although Beijing has not officially designated the USA as its main adversary, Chinese leaders have pushed back. They claimed that it is not just up to the USA to judge the superiority of its democratic institutions and declare unilaterally the rules of international relations. They insist that China will only abide by the international order based on the United Nations Charter. Xi Jinping stated pointedly that "China welcomes helpful suggestions, but will not accept sanctimonious preaching" (quoted by Xinhua 2021: no page number). Chinese officials and academics have hinted that a majority of Americans have deep doubts about the legitimacy or competency of their leaders and harbor great distrust and skepticism about their political institutions – even while US officials routinely proclaim that their form of government is the best model for the rest of the world. About a third (30 percent) of Americans believe Biden won the presidency due to electoral fraud (Kamisar 2024), and a majority feels that their country has been heading in the wrong direction.

A careful reader would have noticed that I have so far argued that China's entry into the Korean War and Nixon's visit to Beijing represented two policy punctations that set the stage for subsequent decades of hostile and amicable Sino-American relations respectively. Until now I have not said much about the current state of the relationship between China and the United States that has clearly experienced a sharp downturn since the second decade of this century. The administration of George W. Bush was of course preoccupied with the war against terrorism and the invasion of Iraq. Barack Obama started to reorient US policy toward China with his "pivot to Asia" which, however, communicated more a symbolic than substantive change while he was in the White House. It was Donald Trump who started to ratchet up the heat with his imposition of US tariffs on imports from China, his charge that China had committed "rape" against the US economy, and his initiation of a technological embargo against Chinese companies such as Huawei. Despite Joe Biden's criticism during his 2020 presidential campaign that Trump's policies toward China had hurt the US economy, his administration had basically adopted the same approach and even increased the tempo of "economic decoupling" from China. In short, then, it is difficult to trace the recent deterioration in Sino-American relations to a single punctuation in policy. It rather appears to reflect a cumulative process reflecting a series of reinforcing positive feedback to bring about a reversal in this relationship. In the phraseology of Baumgartner and Jones, one may say that the process of deteriorating bilateral relations can be described as being driven by a series of "rolling disruptive dynamics" as in their study on restrictions placed on tobacco smoking in the United States (a series of regulations that cannot be traced to any one pivotal event or moment). It is difficult to say whether this relationship has settled down on a new equilibrium.

There was trouble brewing in Sino-American relations long before the recent spats. There were incidents such as the US bombing of China's embassy in Belgrade in 1991 (killing three Chinese citizens and injuring at least twenty – something that Washington claimed to be the result of an innocent mistake but Beijing suspects to be a deliberate act), George H. W. Bush's decision in 1992 to sell F-16 fighter jets to Taiwan (which, in Beijing's view, was a major betrayal of the US pledge to reduce its armament sales to Taiwan over time), the granting of a visa by Bill Clinton's administration in 1995 for Taiwan's President Lee Teng-hui to visit his alma mater Cornell University after it had reassured Chinese diplomats to the contrary (an incident that was followed by Chinese missile tests around Taiwan to signal Beijing's displeasure and the US response in turn to send two aircraft carrier battle groups to the Taiwan Strait – something that Chinese officials recalled bitterly and were determined to prevent from happening again right up to their coastline), and the collision of a US intelligence aircraft (EP-3E ARIES) and a Chinese fighter jet in 2001 off the coast of Hainan Island (causing the death of the Chinese pilot and the US aircraft's unauthorized emergency landing on the island with the historical backdrop of a huge number of previous US intelligence overflights violating China's airspace). Although Washington claimed that its bombing of the Chinese embassy was an honest mistake, even Western news media had reported that this attack was intentional (e.g., The Guardian 1999a, 1999b). Regardless, one can imagine Washington's reactions if one of its embassies abroad were attacked by China's air force, intentionally or otherwise. One just needs to recall the anger felt by Americans over the Iranians' seizure of the US embassy in Tehran.

Fast forward to the most recent event rocking Sino-American relations, Nancy Pelosi, the former Speaker of the US House of Representative and the third highest ranking official in the US government, visited Taiwan in August 2022. China lodged its strong protest, and it undertook another round of missile tests in Taiwan's vicinity to underscore its displeasure. There was therefore a series of events dating as far back as the early 1990s shortly after the USSR's demise that began to destabilize Sino-American relations. Although after each incident, the two sides managed to stabilize their relationship, it became increasingly clear that this relationship had deteriorated from its heydays of strategic partnership and cooperation. During those days of "honeymoon," the United States had, for example, stood aside when Chinese and South Vietnamese (a US ally) forces clashed over the Paracel Islands in 1975, and Washington gave its tacit blessing before China initiated its border war against Vietnam in 1979 to "teach" Hanoi a "lesson" for its invasion of Pol Pot's Cambodia (or Kampuchea, a Chinese ally) and alignment with the USSR (at that time, China's main adversary).

Thus, the transformation of Sino-American relationship after the second epoch cannot be traced to any single punctuation but has rather reflected a gradual but steady process of deterioration stemming from a series of reinforcing positive feedback loops. Nor, as already remarked, is it clear that this relationship has settled into a new equilibrium. There does not appear to be a "grand bargain" or even tacit mutual understanding after meetings between the presidents of the two countries, most recently at Woodside, California in November 2023.

This ongoing process is entirely compatible with the perspective of punctuated equilibrium. I have already quoted in Chapter 2 Baumgartner and Jones' comment and as mentioned briefly earlier in this chapter that in the case of US policymaking on tobacco smoking, it would be difficult to point to any single event that precipitated change; rather, the process involved a series of episodes unfolding over many years.

"Rolling disruptive dynamics" is an apt description of Sino-American relations since the end of the Cold War. It started gradually after the USSR's demise and the rise of the USA as the world's unipolar power.

On the one hand, China's value as a strategic ally evaporated for Washington. On the other hand, Beijing's suspicions about Washington's international agenda increased after a series of US unilateral assertive actions (e.g., attacks on Iraq, Libya, and Serbia based on what Moscow and Beijing perceived to be false pretenses, such as Saddam Hussein had weapons of mass destruction and connections with Al Qaeda). The subsequent US economic recession in 2008–2009 brought about a further perceptual shift on the balance of power on both sides of the Pacific Ocean. The deterioration in bilateral relationship began to gather momentum during the Trump administration, and it has remained at an elevated level of antipathy and acrimony during the Biden administration. This relationship has entered a new, more complex era with greater volatility and more animosity. It could be a while before it reaches a new equilibrium, and it can even undergo a sharp downturn in the coming days during Trump's second presidential term. The opposite possibility of an uptick is less likely given the current political climate in both countries.

Dynamics of a Second Cold War?

Why this pessimism? It reflects policy and political stickiness and politicians' incentive structure. As already mentioned earlier, the default option is always the continuation of the existing policy course. The reason is simply that change always requires the commitment of scarce resources: attention, time, and political capital and courage which are always in short supply. Moreover, people's limited capacity to process information and their consequent tendency to attend to only a few problems at a time means policy persistence most of the time. Policy agenda becomes increasingly crowded as issues rise higher up the bureaucratic and political echelon. As a global power, US leaders are always being distracted by events around the world – and not just those pertaining to Sino-American relations. The campaign against international terrorism, instability in the Middle East, and the ongoing Russo-Ukrainian War are just a few examples. Moreover, domestic politics compete for officials' time, attention, and political capital. They include such pressing concerns as electoral competition for the government's top offices, the passage of the federal government's budget and national debt ceiling, controversies surrounding divisive issues such as abortion rights, gun control, and the insurrection by Donald Trump's supporters on January 6, 2021, not to mention the threats of impeachment and litigation of personal or family legal problems. These competing concerns can divert the top leaders' attention, drain their energy, strain their patience, exhaust their goodwill, and deplete their resources (which, of course, include intangibles such as political capital which is naturally also subject to depletion or exhaustion). On top of all these factors, there is the consideration of the top leaders' physical stamina and mental acuity as demonstrated by the two candidates for US presidency (before Joe Biden decided to withdraw his candidacy after his senility was on full display in his televised debate with Donald Trump).

Information costs, transaction costs, cognitive costs, and decision costs mount to limit the amount of feasible change, not to mention resistance from established vested interests. Add to this combination the politicians' usual tendency to be risk-averse, and the popularity of scapegoating and demonizing foreigners (and immigrants as attested by the 2024 US presidential contest) as a campaign strategy to win votes and gain popularity (Colaresi 2005). Donald Trump took a page from this playbook when he mounted sharp attacks on China for a variety of alleged misconduct, from trade violations to Covid-19 malfeasance. Politicians therefore compete to demonstrate their patriotic credentials lest they be accused by their domestic opponents for failing to stand up to foreign adversaries. In US history, incumbent presidents have been known to postpone conciliatory gestures to foreign competitors or adversaries until they have won their second term in office, whether it is to conciliate with Castro's Cuba, to recognize the government in Beijing, or to end the Vietnam War.

My remark about taking risks is not just an abstract idea. A leader trying to reach compromise with a foreign adversary can cause serious domestic resistance and political fallout, including putting not only her political career in jeopardy but also quite literally her life at risk. Anwar Sadat paid this ultimate price for his audacity to reach détente and rapprochement with Israel. It is difficult to imagine that any Chinese leader can survive politically if she were to renounce the sacred mission of national reunification with Taiwan. During the Cuban Missile Crisis, John Kennedy's inner circle considered not only the likely setback for the Democratic Party in the then upcoming Congressional elections, but also quite seriously the prospect of the president being impeached should he fail to take decisive action against Soviet missiles installed on the island (Allison 1971: 184–185). One of

Kennedy's advisors reportedly remarked that although the Soviet missiles might not pose a mortal danger to the nation, they certainly represented a threat to the presidency.

That an adversarial relationship between two countries can persist for a long time can reflect these realities – or perceptions of such prospects – on the minds of leaders of both sides. Robert Putnam's (1988) well-known formulation of two-level games shows that top executive officials on both sides must be able to have any deal negotiated by them ratified domestically (ratification used here does not refer to just the limited, formal legal sense of receiving legislative approval but rather includes more generally the support, endorsement, or at least acquiescence by important domestic individuals and groups, ones whose support is critical for a politician to hold on to his power or office). Importantly, this requirement means that any conceivable deal must be acceptable to influential domestic constituents of both sides' leaders, or their respective political base and selectorate. Naturally, the "win sets" of both sides' top leaders must overlap for a deal to be reached which in turn means that the window for reaching a negotiated deal must be open concurrently for both of them. A "win set" is the range of politically feasible deals for each side's top leaders. Their political clocks must be in sync (Nincic 2011). This is a demanding standard, suggesting one of the reasons why policy punctuations are infrequent in international relations. As discussed further later, Nixon's visit to Beijing happens to be one of those rare occasions. Of course, when more than two sides are involved such as in the triangular relationship involving Taipei, Beijing, and Washington, it is even more difficult for the "stars to line up."

When politicians' grip on power is precarious and when they face challenges from multiple sources, they are constrained from launching bold new initiatives. One telltale sign comes from polls showing that most Americans did not support either Biden or Trump as their next president before Biden dropped out of the race. Both candidates were unpopular. Even though Kamala Harris had lost the 2024 election to Donald Trump by a decisive margin in the Electoral College and Republicans had gained control of both legislature chambers, Democratic opposition could still cause policy gridlock and discord in Washington. One can even push the argument further by pointing out that politically vulnerable officials try to leverage their nationalist credentials to win popularity. Demonizing foreigners can be a winning election strategy. In 1775, Samuel Johnson quipped, "Patriotism is the last refuge of the scoundrel."

Multiple reasons can cause windows for conciliation and compromise to be or to remain shut. When a politician needs to campaign for elected office, when her ruling coalition faces serious internal discord, when a strong opposition party is in control of the legislature, when the country is gripped by economic distress and hardship, when a politician's popularity is low or besieged by personal scandal, or any number of other possible situations distracting a leader's attention and constraining her policy space, it is unlikely for her to reach out to a foreign counterpart to seek détente or rapprochement. Although leaders in autocracies do not face some of these challenges or at least not to the same extent as democratic leaders, domestic political and/or economic disarray can have the same effect. Politically secure leaders are typically less vulnerable to domestic challenges when they seek to reach a negotiated settlement with a foreign adversary (Huth 1998; Huth and Allee 2002).

It is not often that one finds the window for compromise to be open simultaneously on both sides of an adversarial relationship. In the language used to describe punctuations in public policy, a choice opportunity must present itself to leaders of both countries. Nixon's visit to Beijing was one of those relatively rare circumstances when decisive leaders on both sides were ready and able to forge a new relationship. On this latter point, strong autocratic leaders can be more likely and easily "pushed around" to make concessions to reach a deal for the simple reason that this person is more politically secure and less beholden to domestic constituents whose support is necessary to ratify this deal and for this politician to stay in power. The obvious implication is that Xi Jinping, who is supposed to have consolidated much personal power, has more leeway to negotiate a deal with the United States than Kamala Harris or Donald Trump vis-à-vis China.

Limitations in human beings' cognitive capacity and their tendency to attend to only a few items at the same time tend to promote policy stability or persistence. Bounded rationality, satisficing, and muddling through are well-known hallmarks of policymaking, inclining officials to make small, incremental adjustments rather than radical shifts in policy (Lindblom 1959; Simon 1957, 1977; Wildavsky 1964). Gary Goertz (2003) calls such "normal" behavior "fiddling," that is, making marginal adjustments to existing policies, which characterizes policymaking most of the time, giving these processes and their output the appearance of stasis or slow change. Stasis and slow change are further enhanced by officials' general conservative tendency, or what James Thomson (1973) has called the bureaucrats' "curator mentality," as expressed by the adage "if it ain't broke, don't fix it." "Fiddling" is an appropriate word describing diplomatic interactions during the intervals between those landmark events in Sino-American relations described earlier.

Those tendencies just described are further reinforced by vested interests predisposed to protect their bureaucratic turf and perpetuate their organizational mission, thus providing another source for maintaining "business as usual," reflecting a predilection to follow accustomed ways of addressing problems. The standard operating procedures of large organizations contribute even further to institutional rigidity (Allison 1971). Finally, until displaced by a new paradigm, established orthodoxy preserves political or bureaucratic consensus on the nature of policy problems and their supposed solutions. As the saying goes, you cannot beat something with nothing. For both political, personal, and socio-psychological reasons, bureaucrats are leery of "rocking the boat" (Janis 1982). These impulses and inclinations again combine to cause strong resistance to change. In short, the combined effect of these factors suggests that the frigidity characterizing current Sino-American relations may persist for some time. Whether they are conciliatory or confrontational, policies usually get "stuck" in these circumstances.

These same forces suggest that policymaking and its output rarely depart from established patterns but when they occur, changes tend to be large and abrupt. Thus, we encounter the phenomenon described by punctuated equilibrium: Protracted periods of stability or stasis are followed occasionally by sudden, sharp breaks. As described by Baumgartner and Jones ([1993] 2009), policymaking and their outputs tend to "lurch" after protracted periods of stationarity. As discussed in Chapter 2, this formulation has been influential because it can account for both change and stability.

Contingency, Conjunction, and the "Garbage Can" Model

How do changes come about? Baumgartner and Jones ([1993] 2009) and before them, Kingdon (1984) adopt a conjunctive logic. In other words, they see changes in policymaking and policy output to be the joint product of several factors. Thus, as discussed in the last chapter, Baumgartner and Jones emphasize that a new "policy image" (that is, a new definition or understanding of a policy problem) and the successful shopping for a new policy venue interact to provide the impetus for policy change. The mobilization of new participants (those that were previously uninvolved or sidelined) is also often another necessary condition to bring about this change. Finally, a crisis and mounting socio-political pressure also play an important role, causing increasing media coverage which in turn focuses policymakers' attention and jolts them into action. Similarly, Kingdon (1984) discusses agenda setting as the fortuitous and joint product of a new awareness of a problem that needs to be solved, a perception of available solution(s) to address this problem, and the activities of capable political entrepreneurs to promote and propagate the new problem definition and solution. Changes in public policy come from the confluence or convergence of these factors. This perspective implies that major policy changes are rare and contingent.

As just indicated, Kingdon's (1984) research suggests that agenda setting is best conceptualized as the convergence of independent streams of problems, participants, and politics interacting to present periodic fleeting opportunities for making policy changes. As Gary Goertz (2003 136) points out, this perspective is largely based on the "garbage can" model of policymaking (Cohen et al. 1972). Significantly, this model suggests that policymaking and policy outputs are often serendipitous. According to it, four independent streams feed into the policymaking process, and policy output (or the failure of this output to materialize) is due to fortuitous timing, the matching or mismatching of these components of policymaking. These components or streams represent (1) problems, (2) solutions, (3) participants (with the wherewithal to act, that is, the power, incentives, and resources, including time and attention, to act), and (4) choice opportunities (or context, which is often precipitated by some focusing event such as crises or other kinds of shocks). "The four factors in addition to being individually necessary are *jointly sufficient* for institution creation" (Goertz 2003: 186, italics in original). That it takes all these factors coming together at the same time to produce change explains why it is difficult to transform policies. This is also the reason why it is difficult to predict the timing of transformative policies because the convergence of these factors tends to be highly irregular and idiosyncratic, and hence not within anyone's capacity to control.

When this confluence occurs, the [policy] item makes it onto the agenda of high leaders. For this to happen, policy windows occasioned by problem opportunities must open, viable solutions must be available and then be coupled to the problem by entrepreneurs operating within policy communities, and the political environment (e.g., the national mood or partisan predispositions in the U.S. Congress) must be amenable to policy change. In sum, Kingdon's overview of agenda setting portrays a decidedly nonincremental ebb and flow of items that appear and disappear with striking rapidity. (Goertz 2003: 136–137)

Two features of this conception are important to underscore. First, timing is critical as problems, solutions, participants, and choice opportunities come and go. Decisions reflect the fortuitous circumstances created by the combination of these streams. Major policy shifts require that these streams converge just at the right moment to enable change – which in turn explains why these shifts are rare because they require all the necessary conditions to be present. Misalignment in the sense that one or more of these necessary conditions are missing suggests the continuation of the status quo. In this "garbage can" model, solutions can be looking for problems to which they can be applied, just as problems may be searching for solutions. Similarly, participants can be seeking problems and solutions – and vice versa in the sense that problems and solutions are always on the lookout for sympathetic ears, that is, waiting for sponsors to promote them to a higher priority in the policy agenda. Policymaking is contingent on their matching (or mismatching) as well as the circumstances in which they encounter one another.

Second, this conception of the policymaking process suggests that it is inherently difficult to predict when a major policy change will occur. As discussed in the previous chapter, most studies of punctuated equilibrium tend to be descriptive. They show that the distribution of policy outputs tends to follow the statistical pattern that one can expect to see from the operation of punctuated equilibrium (that is, they approximate a leptokurtic rather than normal distribution). They also explain why large policy shifts happen when they do by pointing to the role of political entrepreneurs, the availability of a sympathetic venue, the emergence of an alternative understanding or definition of an existing problem, the mobilization of previously uninvolved participants, and the stimulus provided by a dramatic, focusing event (such as the accidents at Three Mile Island and Chernobyl plants to spur the antinuclear movement, and the discovery of a hole in the earth's ozone for the banning of harmful chemicals) in raising public as well as official attention, elevating an item to a higher priority in the policy agenda.

In the case of China's entry into the Korean War, the choice opportunity was created by US General Douglas MacArthur's march north of the 38th parallel in pursuit of North Korea's armed forces that were retreating in disarray. Beijing faced the prospect of its ally's collapse and the installation of a pro-Western regime on its border. This problem was clear, urgent, and compelling, and Beijing had to make a quick decision before these possibilities came to pass. US hawks, including MacArthur, were calling for "rolling back" communism in Asia – thus, suggesting the danger to Beijing that China might have to fight US forces on its own soil. Mao Zedong, China's paramount leader had the stature to make the bold decision to intervene militarily in the Korean conflict as his authority was unchallenged. Even though Mao and other Chinese leaders struggled with the implications of this monumental decision, there was evidently on their mind no other feasible alternative to this solution for the problem that they were facing as Washington was undeterred by Beijing's earlier threat to intervene in the war when MacArthur's troops crossed the 38th parallel, thus changing his mission from preventing North Korean forces from overrunning the peninsula to one of unifying it under a pro-Western regime. Support from Moscow made Beijing's decision more acceptable to its leaders but there was no doubt that it was a difficult decision (Chen 1994; Whiting 1960).

With respect to Nixon's visit to Beijing, this breakthrough seemed to have defied the high odds against it. The United States and China were sworn enemies. At the same time, in the early 1970s they both perceived an aggressive USSR as their chief problem in foreign policy. Moreover, Washington was looking for help from Beijing to ease its exit from its protracted involvement in the Vietnam War. The punctuation provided by Nixon's visit was more amazing because unlike China's unilateral decision to intervene in the Korean War, it was a bilateral decision negotiated by the two sides. The two countries basically agreed to set aside the thorny issue concerning Taiwan's eventual status, and to proceed with their higher priority to oppose Moscow jointly. There was not any clear precipitant such as a crisis that created a choice opportunity. It looked more like the existing situation was ripe for change given the worldviews shared by these countries' respective leaders, Ma Zedong on the Chinese side and Richard M. Nixon and Henry Kissinger on the US side. Their solution to the problem of an aggressive USSR was to create a strategic partnership – despite their political and ideological differences. In this case, decisive and powerful leaders with a compatible vision of world politics made all the difference.

Timing was propitious for this policy breakthrough. China's domestic chaos due to the Cultural Revolution was winding down to an end. In September 1971 Lin Biao, the heir apparent to Mao, had died mysteriously in a plane crash in Mongolia after the failure of his alleged plot for a coup d'état. On the US side, Richard Nixon appeared to be politically unassailable, well on his way to win a second term as he did subsequently in a landslide victory in November 1972 (winning 60.7 percent of the popular vote and carrying forty-nine states in a historic victory over his Democratic opponent, George McGovern). The Watergate break-in which caused him later to resign in disgrace had not yet happened (it occurred in July 1972). It thus appeared that the "stars were aligned" at least in the sense that there were not any serious political obstacles or insurmountable impediments to reconciliation. The Chinese and American leaders' convergent outlook on foreign policy, especially their shared perception of the threat being posed by an aggressive USSR, and their political stature and seeming political invulnerability domestically were important. Both sides had wanted something from their rapprochement besides their joint opposition to Moscow. Nixon wanted Chinese help to extricate the USA from the Vietnam War, and Mao wanted US help to isolate Taiwan. Problem, solution, and the "right" participants thus came together to produce this policy breakthrough. Henry Kissinger's personal skills also played a role in political entrepreneurship in "selling" this transformational reorientation of foreign policy first to Nixon and later to the US domestic audience.

As a *Gedanken* experiment (a thinking experiment, or an exercise of counterfactual reasoning), imagine that Lin Biao's alleged coup was delayed for two or three months, or the proceedings to impeach Nixon were to happen a year earlier, would the decision circumstances for Nixon's visit to Beijing be fundamentally different for the Chinese and

American sides respectively? Alternately, had George McGovern been elected as president for the United States, would he have the necessary political space or capital to travel to Beijing as Nixon did? McGovern would probably face a much more challenging decision due to the likely backlash from the political right whereas Nixon's credential as an anti-communist would protect his political flank and reduce resistance from this source. Similarly, had someone else other than Kissinger been Nixon's national security advisor, would that make a difference? Would this individual have the same entrepreneurial skill and access to Nixon's ears as Kissinger did?

Ned Lebow (2000/2001) has argued that if the assassination of Archduke Ferdinand were delayed for just three years, the combustible combination of factors igniting World War I would no longer have existed and therefore that this conflict would have been avoided. As another example of counterfactual reasoning, had the Germans committed just one more battalion to the siege of Stalingrad, they would probably have been able to seize that city (Mercacante 2012: 156). German soldiers had come within a few blocks of Stalingrad's city center, and even a relatively small reinforcement could very well have altered the outcome of Hitler's campaign against the USSR.

What is most terrifying is that Hitler and his military leadership held numerous and repeated opportunities to make decisions that had they chosen differently in *just a few of these circumstances*, even still allowing for all their other mistakes, they may very well have altered the course of history. (Mercacante 2012: 166, italics in original)

As a final example, Thomas Jones Barker had remarked that victory over Napoleon at Waterloo was "a damn close run thing" (Barker 2015) Lord Wellington said in the same vein the day after victory at Waterloo, describing the battle as "the nearest run thing you ever saw in your life" (Quora 1815). History is replete with anecdotes of near misses and close calls – thus again underscoring the serendipitous nature of policymaking and its unpredictability.

The policymaking process as just sketched provides an initial cut to investigate decision choices. It offers a combination of "closed" and "open" elements – or in Goertz's (2003: 185) words, both rigidity and flexibility in an incipient theoretical structure, "requiring that each determinant [that is, each of the policy streams or categories mentioned earlier] be present provides a rigid foundation; but allowing multiple ways of filling each structural prerequisite permits a wide range of institution creation possibilities." The possibility of assigning different content to each element introduces the idea of substitutability (Most and Starr 1989). For instance, a choice opportunity can be due to a crisis that shocks the policymakers into action, or it can stem from a window of opportunity with the appointment or election of a new leader with a different policy outlook or agenda.

The rudimentary theoretical structure as just described postulates that "the four factors [or causal categories presented by the policy streams] in addition to being individually necessary are *jointly sufficient* for institution creation" (Goertz 2003: 186, italics in original). This formulation in turn points to a path for preliminary testing and perhaps even tentative forecasts. According to this formulation, a major policy shift requires the presence of all four factors or conditions. The converse of this proposition claims that if any of these factors or conditions is missing, a major policy shift will not happen. As thus stated, this claim is perhaps too stringent or demanding. It is sometimes difficult to assert categorically whether a factor is present or absent. If so, the argument that just one disconfirming case should be enough to reject the assertion of necessary condition may be excessive. "... Theoretical controversy about concepts, gray zone cases, and measurement errors are three good reasons" that may incline us to accept a more lenient standard for rejecting this claim (Goertz 2003: 190). Goertz made this point in objecting to the more stringent view expressed by Oran Young and Gail Osherenko (1993: 346) that one instance of disconfirmation (that is, when something happens even without a necessary condition being present) would suffice to invalidate a proposition.

How to fill the four analytic categories with empirical content can be challenging and problematic. The formulation presented thus far is underspecified. For example, who deserve to be included in the category of "participants?" Presumably, not any participant will do. It matters who are the gatekeepers, the veto players, and the power brokers. At a minimum, for a major policy shift to occur, the relevant players agitating for change must be both dissatisfied and powerful as Colgan et al. (2012) have shown. They must also have different interests and preferences from those of the existing stakeholders. Similarly, external shocks can jolt policymakers to reexamine their understanding of a problem and motivate them to look for new solutions to address it. But it is also imaginable that large shocks can create policy disarray and produce stupor that immobilizes officials. Thus, although formulations based on the "garbage can" conception of policymaking can be quite evocative and even illuminating, it does not in itself offer enough specificity for empirical confirmation beyond rather loose ideas. It seems to me more useful in explaining and even predicting the nonoccurrence of policy changes and in identifying missing factors or conditions that must exist for these changes to occur. The "garbage can" perspective can also be useful for retrospective analysis to explain those changes that have already occurred. It does not, however, enable us to make predictions about whether and when specific changes will occur or the form and substance of possible changes. As mentioned already, the very notion of "garbage can" stresses the unpredictability or randomness of the policymaking processes due to the serendipitous and contingent nature of the intersection and interaction of different streams feeding into these processes.

The conjunctive logic is evident in the discussion on the causes of World War I by Ned Lebow (2000/2001, 2003) and Willliam Thompson (2003). Lebow stresses the confluence of factors – consisting of the shock indued by the assassination of Archduke Ferdinand to present a choice opportunity, the removal of this moderate participant in Vienna's policymaking processes, and the concurrent shifts in the gestalt outlook of German, Austrian, and Russian leaders. Sarajevo (where the assassination of Archduke Ferdinand occurred) triggered a cascade of decisions in various European capitals that launched these states on a path to war. In the summer of 1914, the leaders in Berlin, Vienna, and St. Petersburg came to a new understanding of their problem and a new solution to it. German leaders were determined to seize a window of opportunity for a preventive war to crush Russia before it completed its military modernization; Austro-Hungarian leaders were determined to settle scores with the Serbs and put a stop to Slavic nationalism threatening the disintegration of their multi-ethnic empire; and Russian leaders were resolved not to yield again as they had done in prior Balkan crises lest they be humiliated again and lose their reputation as a great power. As already mentioned, Lebow argues that this confluence of conditions would have dissipated in three years, and the prospect of war occurring would thus have fallen greatly by then. Circumstances would have changed so much by 1917 that the danger of war would in his opinion have perhaps passed entirely. Thus, timing was critical. Moreover, the catalyst provided by

Sarajevo to ignite the fuse leading to war was inherently unpredictable. What if the Archduke had listened to those advising him not to visit Sarajevo, his driver had not made a wrong turn and was backing up his vehicle when the assassin struck, or the assassin (Gavrilo Princip) had misfired or missed his target? History could have taken a different turn because any of these "what if" factors could have caused a major change in the confluence of conditions by removing one of its necessary ingredients for the occurrence of the Great War – at least at that particular time and due to that particular precipitant – by disrupting the causal chain producing this conflagration. This line of reasoning is likely to gain cogency for many readers in the wake of the failed assassination attempts against Donald Trump as a US presidential candidate. Quite literally, the assassin's bullet had missed him by an inch or two on the first occasion. Imagine how history could have turned out differently. There are of course also those who argue that had the assassination of the Archduke and his wife not taken place, something else could have served as a catalyst to set Europe on fire.

Thompson (2003) also emphasized the combination of factors that had made Europe in 1914 a powder keg waiting to explode. This combination was represented by shifting balances of power, enduring rivalries among the principal contestants, intensifying armament races and commercial competition, and the bifurcation and rigidification of alliances (the Triple Alliance versus the Triple Entente). This constellation of factors made Europe ripe for conflict. Sarajevo is a streetcar in the sense that such precipitants or catalysts to ignite a tinderbox can present themselves frequently and even regularly, and leaders had already been primed by a highly tense circumstance to jump on it. Human judgments and emotions are both important in Lebow and Thompson's accounts of why World War I happened. Both also emphasize the interaction of multiple factors that formed the decision circumstances for European leaders. Lebow gives more emphasis to these leaders' cognition or perception of their respective problems and preferred solutions. He also asserts that because a catalyst is required to create a choice opportunity and because such a catalyst is inherently random, it is difficult to predict an outcome such as a war's occurrence. Thompson assigns more analytic weight to the constellation of structural factors elevating the danger of war, and he appears to suggest that Europe was primed for conflict regardless of the nature of a specific catalyst – which, if truly random and unexpected, is an elusive goal for analysts to pursue.

It is important to stress one aspect of the logic presented above. The emphasis on matching and mismatching of the four independent streams of problems, solutions, participants, and choice opportunities points to an important reason why stasis or incrementalism prevails most of the time. As Gary Goertz (2003: 141, italics in original) suggests, "One must have favorable values on *all simultaneously* for a policy shift to occur. Hence policy creation is a highly contingent event." All are necessary conditions for changes to occur. Stability or stasis is preserved, and change is forestalled if any of them is missing. The obvious implication of these remarks is that there is a strong bias in favor of maintaining the status quo. "To illustrate this, if we consider that each factor has a 50 percent chance of being favorable and that each factor is independent of all the others, then we get policy change only 1 out of 16 times (the probability of getting four heads when tossing four coins)" (Goertz 2003: 141).

This line of reasoning also suggests that there may be some important predictive value to be gained from the "garbage can" perspective of policymaking: specifically, in forecasting when change is improbable or even impossible. That is, by identifying the necessary conditions for an event, one can also forecast its nonoccurrence when one or more of these conditions is absent. From the perspective of avoiding disasters from happening, policymakers can leverage by turning the switch for one or more necessary conditions to the "off" position.

Goertz's illustration is compelling in explaining why stasis prevails most of the time and why major change happens only occasionally, even rarely because most of the time the stars fail to align. Naturally as he also points out, we may argue, "... if three of the four factors are present then we can say that a window-of-opportunity is open. Supply the last factor and the structure changes dramatically." This perspective therefore prepares us to be on the lookout for the last missing piece or ingredient to create a policy punctuation. In the next chapter, I will pick up again this discussion of conjunctive logic with an illustration on the possibility of US intervention in a conflict between China and Taiwan, thus putting China and the USA on a path to direct conflict.

Going with the Winner and Positive Feedback Loops

I continue for now the discussion about the sources and dynamics of policy punctuations. As already mentioned, the presentation of agenda setting by Kingdon (1984) and Baumgartner and Jones ([1993] 2009) owe their intellectual inspiration from the work by Cohen et al. (1972) who first introduced the "garbage can" model of policymaking, emphasizing the often serendipitous and even random way in which policy outputs emerge from the unpredictable timing of problems, solutions, participants, and choice opportunities encountering each other in a haphazard manner. Naturally, this is just one way of describing and explaining policymaking which, however, can take on different characters. As suggested in the last chapter, Baumgartner and Jones acknowledge that while they see punctuated equilibrium to provide a fruitful way of understanding policymaking, they do not claim that it exists everywhere. Similarly, Gould has argued that reality is often too complex for researchers to be dogmatic about his theory with Eldredge. Therefore, he is willing to accept that punctuated equilibrium and gradualism can both exist in evolutionary biology.

The previous chapter has mentioned Baumgartner and Jones' view that sharp policy breaks often result from the operation of positive feedback loops which can produce a self-sustaining and self-reinforcing process. Holding back change causes pressure to build up, making the eventual rupture stronger and the danger of overreaction greater. Resistance to change thus plants the seeds for a more violent eruption subsequently. Stasis is not just the opposite of change; it also becomes a source for change. In this view, the forces for change can gradually build up momentum and suddenly accelerate to culminate in a large change and sharp discontinuity.

These loops amplifying the forces for change can often be observed in human activities. They sometimes reflect people's herd instincts such as when their collective action leads to bank runs and speculative bubbles. On other occasions, people's behavior may be based on more deliberate calculations such as when states flock to join an aggressor in the hope of sharing the spoils of its conquest (Schweller 1994). This behavior has been described as "bandwagoning," and it is also shown in the tendency for states to join the winning or stronger side in interstate contests. Thus, during the Cold War most other major states, including China for a time, joined the US-led coalition even though the logic of balancing power should dispose them to support the weaker side led by the USSR. This phenomenon thus contradicts the logic behind balance of power. In his influential work introducing structural realism, Kenneth Waltz (1979: 127) has argued:

Secondary states, if they are free to choose, flock to the weaker side, for it is the stronger side that threatens them. On the weaker side, they are both more appreciated and safer, provided, of course, that the coalition they form achieves enough defensive or deterrent strength to dissuade adversaries from attacking.

That states and people in general want to be on the winning side is a large part of the explanation that membership in the victorious group often turns out to be much larger than the logic of just forming a minimum winning coalition would lead us to expect (Koehler 1975). William H. Riker's size principle (1962: 32–33) states that "... participants create coalitions just as large as they believe will ensure winning and no larger." Conditions giving rise to uncertainty are plausibly another reason why legislators and states alike create coalitions that are much larger than the bare minimum required to win a contest. Are there other reasons for this phenomenon?

People are rational conformists. They adjust their behavior based on their observation and expectation of others' conduct. Most people wait for the traffic light to turn green before crossing streets, and they also form lines waiting patiently for their turn to be served. However, should they observe others jay walking or cutting in the queue or rushing forward, they also engage in this behavior. Similarly, applauding after a public performance or speech is highly conditioned on how others are acting. If enough people applaud, people join in; if few or no one does, they also follow suit and cease to applaud. Baumgartner and Jones (2002b: 16) cite Thomas Schelling (1978) on how people's behavior hinges on others' behavior. They also recount Schelling's story about a dying seminar. After a few students cut their class attendance, others also begin to drop out – even though they continue to be interested in the course material.

Baumgartner and Jones also report the conclusions reached by many studies of fashion trends, fads, and other cultural norms. These studies show that people take cues from their neighbors, colleagues, and acquaintances. Their decisions tend to reflect other people's choices, especially choices made by those who are close to them and in whom they trust. People's decisions to join strikes, riots, demonstrations, revolutions, and political movements are strongly influenced by others' actions, including the fear of social ostracism for nonparticipation (Chong 1991; Converse and Pierce 1986). This is the gist of positive feedback in human activities. "Participation of neighbors and the expectation of success appear to be important predictors of participation in a great variety of social and protest movements" (Baumgartner and Jones 2002b: 18).

Mimicking and imitating are common. When enough people commit infractions, they provide examples for others to follow. If a critical mass or threshold is reached, the relevant normative norm can be seriously undermined by a contrary behavioral tendency such as taking bribes or cheating on paying taxes. We often encounter this phenomenon when driving on the highway. When people observe other motorists speeding, they are also likely to do so. However, frequently more than mimicking and imitating is involved. People mow their lawns, they shovel snow from the sidewalk in front of their houses, and they undertake other activities that help maintain the property value of their neighborhood. Surely, social pressure and self-interest both play a part in such behavior (Crenson 1987). Such behavior also involves the creation of a community spirit and civic mindedness that enhances generalized trust and promotes informal collective action.

We also observe neighborhoods with derelict houses where the behavior of irresponsible homeowners can also be contagious. Thus, certain behavior can spread to become social norms for good or ill. In societies with high levels of generalized trust, few people cheat on their taxes or demand bribes, whereas in other societies such behavior is common and even expected and condoned. Robert Putnam (1993) has written about such dysfunctional behavior in the culture of southern Italy. Yet even interpersonal trust (Chan 2017a) does not quite tell the whole story. As Baumgartner and Jones (2002b: 18) suggest, another critical piece of the story for political competition and policy-making is the injunction to "go with the winner." This phenomenon is relevant to the formation of positive feedback loops introducing policy punctuations.

There are good social and psychological reasons for "going with the winner." "The political advice that it is best to 'go with a winner' is an apt description of how positive feedback can affect political life" (Baumgartner and Jones 2002b: 16). This phenomenon creates a self-reinforcing cycle, such as when a political candidate is perceived as a legitimate contender, leading to more campaign donation, more media coverage, and more staff which in turn raises this candidate's perceived prospects of getting elected. We can infer from this discussion that the critical determinants on mobilizing opponents to the status quo are

(1) the strength of their preferences for an alternative, and (2) their judgment about the prospect that this alternative will prevail. The latter consideration is quite important because often people are indifferent or have only weak preferences, and their decisions are thus influenced by their expectations of how others would behave and the probability that an alternative will gain support.

As just implied, voters, officials, and states alike do not want to waste their time, effort, and political capital on a losing cause. Michael MacLeod (2002: 57, 59) emphasizes, "Like voters, policy entrepreneurs are strategic actors that do not want to waste their time on challenges that will be ignored..."; moreover, "interest groups and members of institutions are unlikely to challenge the status quo if they have low expectations of success even if they have preferences for change." He continues, "Decisions of interest groups and members of political institutions to challenge existing policies are not merely a function of their preferences, but also are heavily dependent upon their perceptions of the outcome" (MacLeod 2002: 72). Thus, even when they are persuaded that a problem exists and agree on its solution, the relevant actors must also believe that the campaign to alter the status quo will pay off. In other words, this campaign must be winnable. As this campaign gains more and more supporters, its prospects for success become brighter. Thus, there is a bandwagon effect such that increasing support for change begets further support, creating a momentum that fosters optimism about the prospects for success. I will apply this insight to the example of China's representation in the United Nations later in this chapter.

In his study of the breakup of the mighty AT&T (American Telephone and Telegraph) monopoly, Michael MacLeod (2002: 52) shows how small changes initiated by "a single institution [in this case, the FCC or Federal Communications Commission's decision to allow more competition in telecommunications] can set a cascade in motion that leads to dramatic policy changes." He also recounts Larry Bartels' (1987) research on the 1984 Democratic Party's presidential nomination race between Gary Hart and Walter Mondale. The main conclusion of this study is that in making their choices, voters' predisposition to support a candidate is a necessary condition, but another necessary condition is their perception that this candidate has a genuine chance to win the contest. He cites Mark Granovetter's (1978) model of a "threshold" or the point at which a person will decide to act based on how others have already acted. He also refers to a study by Bikhchandani et al. (1992) on the conditions under which individuals are likely to jump on a bandwagon. "The key to their model is that small shocks lead to big shifts in mass behavior only if people happen to be very close to the borderline between alternatives" (MacLeod 2002: 55). Therefore, the lack of strong preferences is a necessary condition for bandwagon, presumably because it is difficult to change the minds of those with strong opinions to switch their positions on an issue. The other necessary condition is some expectation that the alternative will succeed.

It also seems that the timing and sequence of joining should matter. In international relations as in legislative processes, the last holdout who can furnish the margin of victory should be able to extract the most concessions for her vote. At the same time, in multilateral disputes such as those involving competing sovereignty claims in the South China Sea, the first country to reach a negotiated deal with Beijing should be able to gain the most favorable terms, whereas the last holdout may have the least leverage because the other disputants might have already reached settlements that impinge on its claims, perhaps even to the point of eviscerating them.

The discussion thus far is pertinent to the "garbage can" model of policymaking presented earlier. It is a framework for which the content for each of the four factors or streams (problems, solutions, participants, and choice opportunities) will have to be specified. Thus, not any actor will do for the "participant" category. It takes at least those participants dissatisfied with the status quo as well as those sufficiently powerful and capable of organizing a coalition to bring about a major policy shift, as Colgan et al. (2012) conclude in their study of the evolution of energy-complex regimes. Indeed, even when such participants are present, it does not necessarily mean that such a shift will occur. These participants must believe that efforts to change the status quo have a reasonable probability of success.

The snowball or bandwagon effect discussed above can accelerate and create a self-sustaining momentum to overcome existing resistance to policy change. As already mentioned, policy change entails costs: information cost, decision cost, transaction cost, and cognitive cost – which combine to present institutional frictions forestalling policy change. In international relations, however, there is a further kind of cost. MacLeod is quoted saying that policy entrepreneurs do not want to commit their time and resources to a cause that will be ignored. In international relations, however, there is a far worse fate than being ignored – and that is to come into the hegemon's strategic headlight or crosshairs. There is a heavy cost to antagonizing the United States, the unipolar power. Thus, in addition to the various costs mentioned by Jones et al. (2003: 154), I add in the case of international relations the costs of suffering possible retribution or retaliation, especially from the peerless United States which has dominated the post-1945 international institutions and which has drawn the largest share of benefits from its rules. This cost of having potentially to pay a steep penalty for crossing the hegemon is one major distinction that differentiates international politics from domestic politics. Although retribution of course also exists in the domestic setting, its consequences are presumably much less severe than in the international setting. Donald Trump's penchant for going after his enemies offers an example of retribution in the domestic setting.

Put plainly, it is dangerous to anger the United States by challenging its interests or joining a coalition perceived to challenge its preponderance. Witness the fate of Saddam Hussein, Muammar Qaddafi, and Manuel Noriega. Troublemakers can be picked off and snuffed out by the unipolar power quickly and easily before any united front of opposition has a chance to form. China is a threat to Washington because it can be the center around which such an opposition can potentially develop. A countervailing coalition opposing the hegemon will either not form or form quickly for reasons just described. Lone dissenters or "troublemakers" are vulnerable to being eliminated by the United States, but there will be (greater) safety in numbers. Thus, once an anti-US coalition is perceived to be a viable alternative, its membership can expand quickly – if for no other reason than the possibility that this option can give those who have joined or who threaten to join greater bargaining leverage vis-à-vis Washington. This process is likely to resemble punctuated equilibrium. It can be hastened or hindered by the unipolar power's own policies. Conduct that is perceived to be excessive and illegitimate can accelerate this process which is, by definition, nonlinear – a protracted period of gestation and then a sudden and sharp burst of activities. Movement afoot on joint efforts to replace the dollar's dominant role provides an example of this process as does the sudden expansion of interest on the part of many countries wanting to join BRICS. The more join, the safer it is to shield oneself from the wrath of the unipolar power. This phenomenon can initially manifest itself in various forms of "soft balancing" (Paul 2018), involving passive resistance, indirect opposition, shirking, procrastinating, obstructing, or simply refusing to provide active support for Gulliver's designs. This "soft balancing" can evolve into "hard balancing" or outright resistance subsequently.

There is another factor that distinguishes international relations from domestic policymaking. The role of the US dollar as a store of value and as an instrument for the settlement of international trade can represent long-standing concerns for most countries, which would have to undertake fundamental adjustments to reduce their reliance on the dollar. Their weakness, however, means that they lack the capacity to do anything about the dollar's dominance – unless and until they can somehow effectively coordinate collective action. Yet as just suggested, such collective action would bring Washington's wrath upon them, especially putting the perceived ringleader at risk. This fear and the well-known problem of free riding (Olson 1965) thus inhibit attempts to overthrow the dollar's preeminence. Although, as mentioned earlier, shifting balance of forces (between the supporters of the status quo and proponents of change) and competing jurisdictions matter in domestic policymaking, changing interstate balance of power is an even more crucial variable in determining whether stasis will continue or whether revolutionary transformation is possible or likely. The prospect for punctuation increases as the balance of interstate power approaches a tipping point, increasing the pressure from those states demanding basic reform. Naturally, as long held by traditional realists who see a balance of power to enhance international stability and peace, a situation of greater power parity also reduces the fear of being targeted by the hegemon for retribution. Moreover, what has been said about the provision of public goods being facilitated by the presence of a preponderant power that is both willing and able to provide such goods (as suggested by the hegemonic stability theory, e.g., Kindleberger 1993) should presumably be equally applicable to the challenger to this preponderant power. That is, as this latter country, the challenger, gains increasing capabilities and acquires a larger stake in the international order, it should also presumably have more incentive and greater wherewithal to assume a heavier and disproportionate burden to support alternative institutions or rules for international relations.

Maturation, Momentum, and China's Representation to the United Nations

Although it is difficult and sometimes even dangerous to challenge a hegemon and its preferences, it is not impossible to upend a status quo preferred by the peerless United States. Until 1971, China as represented by the government in Beijing was denied a seat in the United Nations, mainly due to Washington's objection. Washington had steadfastly claimed that the Kuomintang government in Taipei was the legitimate authority representing China and thus was entitled to the China seat in the United Nations. It was able to generate enough support for its position until its preference was overturned by a vote in the General Assembly in October 1971. The resolution that prevailed stated that "the representatives of the Government of the People's Republic of China are the only lawful representatives of China to the United Nations." The history concerning the contested China seat shows a process of maturation and gathering momentum that eventually frustrated Washington's ability to amass enough support to deny Beijing's claim to represent China in this international body. New member states joining the United Nations from the Global South was the principal reason for producing this punctuation (here we encounter the phenomenon of a changing cast of participants, one of the streams feeding into policymaking in the "garbage can" model). Once the USA was shown to be unable to muster sufficient support to exploit the voting protocol for considering which government, the one in Beijing or the one in Taipei, should represent China as an "important question" and thus requiring a supermajority to pass the resolution, it had lost the battle. After many years of maintaining the status quo (continuing with the Kuomintang government in Taiwan as the legitimate representative of China – all of China), a punctuation occurred.

Table 3.1 illustrates this phenomenon, drawing on the rollcall votes in the United Nations General Assembly on the question of having the People's Republic of China in control of the Chinese mainland rather than having the Republic of China on Taiwan to represent China. In some years, this matter was framed in terms of whether it should be considered an "important question." By a simple majority, resolutions that are considered an "important question" would require a two-thirds majority for adoption. Thus, the critical vote was on

Table 3.1 *UN General Assembly votes on the question of China's representation*

Year	Anti-China	Pro-China	Abstention	Not Participating
1950	33	6	0	0
1951	37	11	4	0
1952	42	7	11	0
1953	44	10	2	4
1954	43	11	6	0
1955	42	12	6	0
1956	47	24	8	0
1957	48	27	6	1
1958	44	28	9	0
1959	44	29	9	0
1960	42	34	22	0
1961	48	36	20	1
1962	56	42	12	0
1963	57	41	12	1
1964	General Assembly Meeting Postponed			
1965	47	47	20	3
1966	57	46	17	1
1967	58	45	17	1
1968	58	44	23	0
1969	56	48	21	1
1970	51	49	27	0
1971	35	76	17	0

Sources: Bailey (1971); Bloomfield (1966); Boyer and Akra (1961); Carter (2020); Chai (1970); and Luard (1971).

whether the matter of China's representation should be considered an "important question," thereby making it more difficult for Beijing to gain its seat to represent China in the United Nations. In Table 3.1, I consider a vote to support the motion to consider this matter to be an "important question" as anti-China because it would raise the bar for recognizing the government in Beijing as the legitimate representative of China. Such a positive vote on an "important question" was tantamount in its effect to a negative vote on the substantive question of whether to recognize China. Thus, for example, the United States had voted in favor of treating the motion to recognize China as an "important question," and it had consistently voted "no" on the question of whether to have the Beijing government occupy the China seat in the United Nations. These votes are both considered to be anti-China. In contrast, a country is considered to have a pro-China stance when it voted against the motion on "important question" and in favor of recognizing China (and expelling Taiwan).

Table 3.1 shows that the US-led opposition to admitting China prevailed for about two decades, but its margin of victory became increasingly smaller over the years. By 1965, China's supporters were for the first time able to match the number of its detractors. The direction of change was clear by then, even though opponents to the Beijing government's right to represent China were able to prevail for a few more years, albeit with a smaller majority than before. The balance of the two opposing sides on this question was increasingly held by those countries that had abstained previously or by states that had joined the United Nations only relatively recently. When change finally came in 1971 favoring China's entry into the United Nations, it was swift and decisive. It was a lopsided vote with China's supporters outnumbering its detractors by a margin of more than two to one. This shift illustrates the dynamics of punctuated equilibrium. Although it was not easy to predict when exactly this change would occur, it appeared to be inevitable and only a matter of time. Perhaps this is what people sometimes mean when they say "to be on the right side of history" or a rendezvous with destiny, the inexorable progression of an ongoing process leading to a certain outcome. One need not be an expert to "read the tea leaves" in this case. Even Western countries like France and Canada had extended diplomatic recognition to China prior to the General Assembly's vote, in 1964 and 1970 respectively.

It may appear astounding to some readers today that the world's most populous country consisting of one quarter of humanity could/ should be kept out of the world's most important international organization. But that was the position of the United States, whose leaders for many years portrayed Beijing as the Kremlin's puppet regime in Asia and who insisted that "red China" was just a "passing phenomenon." Moreover, in the 1950s and 1960s Washington claimed that the Kuomintang government in Taiwan should represent China – the entire political entity called China consisting of not just Taiwan, but also the mainland which the Chiang Kai-shek government had lost to the Communists. Washington's position then was of course the exact opposite of its policy today, which argues that the government in Beijing does not represent Taiwan.

One might perhaps respond by quoting Ralph Waldo Emerson, who wrote "foolish consistency is the hobgoblin of little minds, adored by little statesmen and philosophers and divines" (Rosenzweig 2013). Ever since Nixon's visit to Beijing, the US government has acknowledged Beijing's position that Taiwan is a part of China – the word "acknowledge," however, was deliberately chosen for its ambiguous connotation to mean that the USA "takes note" of but does not necessarily agree with Beijing's claim that Taiwan is a part of China. In practice, however, the USA has tried to deter a Chinese invasion of Taiwan and has made military sales to Taiwan to enable it to better defend itself, thus perpetuating this island's de facto independence.

The four streams of problem, solution, participants, and choice opportunity converged in 1971 to produce China's representation in the United Nations. The "problem" was clear and always the same, namely, representation for the world's most populous country in the most important international organization. The "solution" was also simple and obvious: how to override the opposition led by the United States to have the government in Beijing to represent China. "Participants" was a changing variable as already remarked; the composition of UN membership changed from one that was dominated by the Western countries to a majority consisting of Asian, African, and Latin American countries that were their former colonies. This was the decisive factor that eventually altered the outcome on the question of China's representation. Finally, the "choice opportunity" was a recurrent phenomenon, indeed a regular occurrence in this case because a showdown on this question would make its annual appearance on the General Assembly's agenda.

As just suggested, the decisive difference introducing change in this case was the involvement of many new participants who were not UN members when previous votes were taken. There were also some countries that had changed their positions over time. In view of my earlier discussion, another change was an intangible but palpable feeling that the tide was turning, and the desire not to be the last holdout on a losing proposition. This perception or recognition in turn created its own reinforcing momentum, thus producing a self-fulfilling prophecy. It is difficult to quantify but this bandwagon effect was present in many political contests when the adage "go with the winner" was operating. Thus, the perception or recognition that a contest is not a lost cause but is in fact winnable can translate into a new reality which can itself create accelerating momentum and the positive feedback loop discussed earlier to bring about change.

We can all think of examples of the maturation of an ongoing process or unfolding trend, perceptions of unstoppable momentum, and seemingly inexorable forces producing an inevitable outcome – sometimes described retrospectively as a development whose time has come. One sometimes also hears the saying, "the handwriting is on the wall." Whether such perceptions or feelings are in fact justified by evidence is one thing. There is of course also the work of political entrepreneurs who try to foster, or alternatively to dampen, such perceptions and feelings. As just argued, to the extent that these perceptions and feelings are widely shared it can create its own reality. The rise of the United States to regional preeminence in the Western Hemisphere and subsequently its ascendance to become the global hegemon is a case in point. Few countries wanted to stand in the way of this rising behemoth. As negative examples from Washington's perspective, the "end games" in the protracted US wars in Vietnam and Afghanistan also come to mind. When it became clear that the USA was withdrawing from these conflicts and abandoning its allies, the "unraveling" came swiftly and accelerated quickly. Very few people would knowingly want to be on the wrong side of history or to be the last holdout in a losing or lost cause.

This said, the phenomenon just described can also cause crashes and overshooting. Investors have been known to chase stocks when the financial market is up or engage in competitive bidding that drives up stock or housing prices, leading eventually to a bubble in the stock or real estate market. In the physical world, the accumulation of pressure can produce "breaks" such as earthquakes, avalanches, landslides, and volcano eruptions.

Pivotal Actors, Turning Points, and Policy Boomerangs

To bring about a change such as that with respect to China's representation in the United Nations, it helps to have a powerful state to get the ball rolling, sort of speaking. This state leads not only in the sense of taking the initiative of starting the process of eventual change. It also serves as a nucleus around which other like-minded states can coalesce. A state with a large stake in an outcome can be the critical factor in organizing collective action. Saudi Arabia played this role in OPEC's (Organization of Petroleum-Exporting Countries) successful effort to hike the price of oil. The small number of these oil exporters and especially the concentration of production power in an even smaller number of Arab oil exporters were important considerations from the perspective of collective action (Olson 1965). These factors facilitated their gambit to raise the price of oil by lowering transaction, information, and decision costs, and skirting the challenge of free riding. This case also illustrates nicely how a perceived problem (low oil price), available solution (cutting oil production), a powerful cartel led by Saudia Arabia, and a choice opportunity created by the Yom Kippur War of 1973 converged to produce a punctuation. It was spurred by the Arab oil producers' decision to impose an embargo on the United States and the Netherlands in retaliation against their support for Israel in its conflict with its Arab neighbors (Doran 1977; Yergin 1991, 2011). This confluence of factors led to the dramatic surge in oil price caused by its scarcity due to the boycott campaign undertaken by its largest suppliers. Long periods of stagnant oil price gave way to dramatic jumps suddenly, illustrating the "garbage can" model of policymaking and the dynamics of punctuated equilibrium.

Consider another example drawn from the history of China's border disputes and its settlement of these disputes. Such disputes can linger for a considerable amount of time until the parties reach a negotiated settlement (Fravel 2008). Such a settlement broke the "logjam" to unfreeze the protracted feud between Beijing and Moscow since the 1960s. The signing of a border agreement by these countries in 2004 started a process of improving their bilateral relations. In the 1990s, the establishment of the Shanghai Cooperation Organization (see below) enhanced friendly Chinese relations with the successor states to the USSR, such as Kazakhstan, Kyrgyzstan, and Tajikistan. These developments appear to be linked and associated with a self-sustaining momentum. This institution has become one of the cornerstones in China's diplomacy (Deng 2022) attempting to overcome the vulnerability of its seaborne commerce due to its encirclement by unfriendly powers to its east and south. The resolution to this problem was to establish an alternate land route – the historical Silk Road. Beijing's westward march was also motivated by a desire to forge stronger security and trade linkages with Central Asia and to establish an important strategic position in Eurasia.

There is currently a deadlock in China's sovereignty assertions in the South China Sea and those of other claimant states. Some of the latter countries, Brunei, Malaysia, the Philippines, and Vietnam, have also overlapping claims. Although an uneasy stalemate appears to characterize the current situation, when change comes, it can arrive suddenly. The smaller claimant states can improve their collective bargaining position by presenting a united front to oppose China. At the same time, the first country to break ranks and negotiate a separate settlement with Beijing stands to gain the best terms, in part because of the (positive) advertisement value that Beijing can gain from such a settlement. Conversely, the last holdout runs the risk of ending up with little or nothing because by then its counterparts would have already divided the spoils (Chan 2016). This situation creates incentives that can foster a collective rush to settle with China, thus possibly presenting a situation reminiscent of punctuated equilibrium.

As suggested earlier, we need to supply more specific information to the various categories of the "garbage can" model to give it more substantive content for illuminating the dynamics of real-world cases of policymaking. The example just given on oil price hikes points to the importance of a pivotal actor that can play the leadership role in organizing and spearheading a campaign to promote change. It also introduces the motivation on the part of those participants in this campaign. What incentives, or disincentives, do they have for altering the status quo? In the case of OPEC, the desire for gain – higher oil revenues – is obviously a motivating factor. But even in this case, the flip side pointing to the need to avoid loss was also operating. Higher prices would naturally antagonize countries that were importing oil and might invite retaliation from them and in the long run, encourage them to develop alternative sources of energy and thus undermine the interests of those exporters that will continue to be heavily dependent on this source of foreign revenue well into the future because of their large oil reserves.

Fear of retribution can hold back participants that would otherwise benefit from altering the status quo. One example, already mentioned briefly earlier, comes from military or political coalitions. In his successive military campaigns, Napoleon was able to raise large armies with contributions from various vassal states and victims of his earlier coercion or conquest. These partners were attracted by the prospect for making gains to bandwagon with France in the hope of benefiting from the spoils of war from French aggression. Bandwagoning for profit (Schweller 1994) was not, however, the only reason. These smaller or weaker partners were also concerned about the fear of retribution by directing French hostility to themselves. Their deference to French power lasted so long as Napoleon appeared to be invincible. When the *Grande Armée* suffered military setback in the aftermath of its Russian expedition, Napoleon appeared to be vulnerable. His junior allies abandoned his coalition quickly and many in fact turned against him.

We saw the same process unfolding quickly when Adolf Hitler's foreign partners deserted him when it became increasingly evident that Nazi Germany was losing the war. Still another example of the same phenomenon was provided by the communist regimes in Eastern Europe that fell suddenly and in rapid succession when their end came, even though they had appeared to be in control not so long before their demise. When it became evident that Mikhail Gorbachev would refuse to call on the Red Army to sustain these regimes, massive and abrupt political change swept these countries in a manner befitting the dynamics of punctuated equilibrium. Mimicking and imitation were part of this story. The perception of a process gathering momentum, the idea that a situation whose time has come, and the wish to "go with the winner" also played a role. In the context of this discussion, there was the added element coming from the realization that the prospect of retribution had been removed.

These same factors had been in play in the long decline and the eventual collapse and dissolution of the USSR. In retrospect, even in the 1970s there were indications pointing to its economic decay and mounting evidence of the crushing costs of its imperial overstretch, although practically everyone either missed these signs or did not give them the credence that they deserved. So, when the end came for the USSR, it was a sudden and dramatic upheaval that caught most people by surprise. The phenomenon of a protracted period of slow but inexorable decline picking up momentum to produce a sharp break or rupture corresponds nicely with the expectation of punctuated equilibrium.

In the Napoleonic Wars, Britain was the one country that had steadfastly held out against France (Schroeder 1994). Britain played the pivotal role as a counterpoise to French power, a nucleus around which an anti-French coalition could coalesce. Saudi Arabia also played a central role in OPEC's success, and of course also the USSR in buttressing the survival of Eastern European communist regimes as demonstrated by its role in crushing Hungary's uprising in 1956 and Czechoslovakia's reform movement in 1968. Whether or not Beijing intends to upend Washington's global dominance, it seems to be the only country that is capable of serving as a counterpoise against US dominance. The Shanghai Cooperation Organization (SCO) and the BRICS group, both centered around China, can provide the basis for an incipient coalition to check US primacy.

In addition to taking advantage of a new policy image (that is, developing and propagating a new problem definition or understanding often in the wake of a focusing event heightening public awareness and concern), political entrepreneurs seeking major policy change also search for more sympathetic policy venues consisting of receptive bureaucrats and officials to promote their agenda. As in domestic politics, states can engage in forum shopping in international relations. They can moreover take the initiative to create new institutions to organize and coordinate their policies and advance their collective agenda. Even within the same organization such as the United Nations in the previous example on the question of China's representation in this international organization, states may try to move the forum for debate and decision from the Security Council to the General Assembly. In December 2023, a resolution calling for ceasefire in the then ongoing war between Hamas and Israel in Gaza was frustrated by a US veto in the Security Council, but the General Assembly took up this issue and adopted the motion with an overwhelming majority of 153 votes in favor, 10 against, and 23 abstentions.

The SCO and BRICS groups, both consisting of large, non-Western countries represent incipient coalitions that can offer opposition to US-led or European-centered organizations such as the G7, the European Union, and the North Atlantic Treaty Organization. The SCO started as a regional organization spanning Eurasia. In 2001, it succeeded the Shanghai Five (established in 1996) consisting of China, Kazakhstan, Kyrgyzstan, Russia, and Tajikistan. It was subsequently joined by Uzbekistan in 2002, India and Pakistan in 2017, and Iran in 2023. In addition to these full members, Belarus and Mongolia became observers, and fourteen other countries (including Egypt, Saudi

Arabia, Turkey, and the United Arab Emirates) joined as Dialogue Partners. From its beginning to promote economic, political, and security cooperation primarily between China and Russia, SCO has established more permanent institutions and expanded its membership. It has become the largest regional organization in geographic scope and population size, representing 80 percent of the world's area and 40 percent of its inhabitants. In 2021, its combined economic size was about 20 percent of the global total (Wikipedia 2024).

The BRICS group started with the world's largest developing economies: Brazil, Russia, India, and China, with South Africa joining this original group in 2010. It represents about 40 percent of the world's population and 25 percent of its economy. In 2023, it issued invitations to six countries to join as new members: Argentina, Egypt, Ethiopia, Iran, Saudi Arabia, and the United Arab Emirates. With its election of a conservative president (Javier Milei), Argentina has declined this invitation. Furthermore, Saudia Arabia has reportedly decided to postpone its membership. With the addition of four new members and further expansion expected in the future, this group is poised to become a more formidable coalition in both economic and political influence. Fourteen states have reportedly applied to join it, including Algeria, Belarus, Kazakhstan, Kuwait, Pakistan, Thailand, Turkey, Venezuela, and Vietnam.

The formation of groups such as SCO and BRICS offers an important policy option for non-Western developing countries. The very availability of this alternative expands these countries' policy space and creates bargaining leverage for them in their dealings with the established Western states led by the United States. Once these organizations are seen to be viable and even taking off, their expansion gains further momentum reminiscent of the dynamics of punctuated equilibrium. This perception of momentum is important as in the example introduced earlier about China's representation in the United Nations – a belief that an issue is winnable or an organization is viable. Put in terms of Albert Hirschman's (1970) well-known book, SCO and BRICS enhance the threat of exit from the established order dominated by the Western countries, amplify the voices of those demanding change, and increase the perceived value of ensuring loyalty to this established order by the current dominant state. Of course, nothing rules out states trying to be strategic by pursuing a straddling policy or hedging their bets by involving themselves with both new and old institutions and arrangements. It is not a question of binary choice for these states.

The creation and expansion of new institutions such as SCO and BRICS is pertinent to the earlier discussion that the formation of an anti-US coalition is fraught with danger. As already mentioned, prospective members recognize the costs of antagonizing Washington and incurring its wrath. The fate suffered by Saddam Hussein, Muammar Qaddafi, Slobodan Milosevic, and Manuel Noriega testifies to the risk that such "troublemakers" can be picked off and snuffed out by the USA. That Syria's Bashir Assad and North Korea's Kim Jong-un have not suffered a similar fate has been due to a significant extent to the support they have received from Russia and China respectively and the danger of a larger conflict should Washington attack them (Assad was overthrown by his own countrymen in December 2024 and fled to Russia). In the case of North Korea and Iran, US officials have also been reluctant to attack them directly because Pyongyang already has nuclear weapons, and Iran could quickly develop this capability. Thus, protection from another great power and the risk of triggering a larger conflict distinguish between Washington's policies toward Iraq, Libya, Serbia, and Panama on the one hand, and Syria, Iran, North Korea, and one might add, Fidel Castro's Cuba on the other hand (even though the USA was deeply involved in the Bay of Pigs invasion in 1961, this episode occurred prior to the consolidation of Cuban–Soviet relationship as suggested by the installation of Soviet missiles on that island after this invasion).

There is of course a double irony in the situation just described. The United States attacked Iraq probably because it knew privately precisely the opposite of what its officials were proclaiming publicly, namely, that Saddam Hussein was *not* developing "weapons of mass destruction" and he did *not* have such weapons. This perspective argues that should he in fact have these weapons, the USA would have been deterred which of course turned out to be the situation with respect to Iran and North Korea. When asked what conclusion he would draw from the attacks launched by the US-led NATO against Serbia in 1999, an anonymous Indian general reportedly quipped "Don't fight the U.S. unless you have nuclear weapons" (Chan 2008: 150). Thus, according to this perspective the US invasion of Iraq had exactly the opposite effect than the reason it gave publicly to justify this attack. It had the effect of motivating states to acquire weapons of mass destruction rather than discouraging them from doing so. Hoping to avoid Saddam Hussein's fate, Libya's Muammar Qaddafi invited international inspectors to reassure the Western countries that he did not have weapons of destruction. Once secured in the knowledge that he indeed did not have these weapons, NATO proceeded to attack Libya in the name of humanitarian intervention that eventually led to Qaddafi's brutal death.

In view of the episode involving Libya and the US invasion of Iraq, would Pyongyang or Tehran be more, or less, inclined today to give up their weapons of mass destruction or programs to develop these weapons? Moreover, even when a country does not actually have weapons of mass destruction, would it now be more inclined to pretend that it did? There is a further irony suggested by the ongoing Russo-Ukrainian War. Kyiv had agreed to give up those nuclear weapons left on its soil by the USSR in exchange for security guarantees from Moscow and Washington. As a counterfactual example, would Russia have been more, or less, likely to invade Ukraine had Kyiv kept these nuclear weapons? In retrospect, would Kyiv be better off to rely on these weapons rather than to count on Western support as there are signs pointing to waning US enthusiasm to continue this support?

President Trump has stated publicly that he wants to bring an end to the Russo-Ukrainian war, and he has had phone conversations with Vladimir Putin and Volodymyr Zelensky about ending the war. Zelensky was clearly concerned that a truce might be imposed on Ukraine without its involvement in negotiating the war's end. His misgivings were shared by other European leaders, who were told by US Vice President J. D. Vance that it is unlikely that Kyiv would gain NATO membership or fully regain its territory lost to Russia. He also ruled out US troops to enforce a ceasefire. It is ironic that Ukraine's prospective membership in NATO was the proximate cause for the Russian invasion. Kyiv felt doubly betrayed because Washington did not fulfill its promise to defend Ukraine when it sought Kyiv's agreement to remove the nuclear weapons left on its soil by Russia, as stipulated by the Budapest Memorandum of 1994.

These remarks on nuclear proliferation suggest that some policies can be self-defeating, creating a boomerang effect and chain reaction that have the exact opposite result compared to a state's professed goal. Wanton, excessive policies widely perceived as illegitimate or at least insincere would then sow the seeds of their own failure. False promises, empty threats, and contorted justifications are not likely to work in the long run. As they say, you can fool some of the people some of the time, but not all people all the time.

There is a further irony in Washington's rhetoric on weapons of mass destruction. It is of course common knowledge that the USA is interested in nuclear nonproliferation, and it has tried to coerce Iran and North Korea to give up their programs to develop nuclear weapons as well as less publicized and more successful attempts to discourage Taiwan and South Korea from pursuing these weapons. The usual argument is that we cannot take a chance to have nuclear weapons fall into the hands of unstable and even irrational leaders such as Saddam Hussein (see, for example, Mearsheimer and Walt's article in 2003 arguing against the then impending US attack on Iraq).

In actual practice, Washington had been much more restrained in criticizing and opposing India and Pakistan's acquisition of these weapons – nor Israel's possession of these weapons even though Tel Aviv has never tested these weapons or acknowledged that it has them. In connection to the brief reference to Taiwan and South Korea made just now, one would be also intrigued to ask, considering herself to be in the shoes of leaders in Taipei and Seoul, would a reader feel more, or less, secure in the knowledge that her country has nuclear weapons to defend itself rather than relying on the United States for protection? This question is especially pertinent and acute for Taipei.

Some recent news reports claim that Russia has plans to use tactical nuclear weapons in Ukraine and thus suggest a serious danger that this war may escalate to threaten European and global peace, even though there has also been considerable skepticism about such reports because earlier allegations that Saddam Hussein had weapons of mass destruction had turned out to be "phantoms" (e.g., Sciotto 2024). Recent reports about Russia sometimes overlook that during the Cold War, the USA also had plans to use such weapons as a deterrence against a possible Soviet invasion of its Western European allies (the Russians were seen to possess a large advantage in conventional forces which the USA had to offset with nuclear weapons) and if deterrence fails, to actually use tactical nuclear weapons against a Soviet assault. Washington has never agreed to reciprocate Beijing's long-standing commitment that it would not be the first country to use nuclear weapons. Much of the public discourse and popular narrative presented in the USA and the West more generally on the danger of nuclear weapons falling into the wrong hands overlook the historical fact that thus far only one country has ever used these weapons and it is the United States – and not just once, but twice against the Japanese (in Hiroshima and Nagasaki) when the outcome of World War II was all but certain.

Recently, one also hears reports that the Russians and Chinese have stepped up their efforts to weaponize the outer space and cyber space. Moscow and Beijing, however, have been largely responding to the earlier US actions that gave Washington a dominant lead in possible space and cyber warfare (see, for example, Lindsay 2014/2015 for a discussion on the threat posed by China on cybersecurity). Another example about other countries' reactions to US policies and conduct comes to mind from Washington's frequent resort to trade sanctions and financial embargoes. This practice will of course incline other countries, those on the sideline but may be concerned that they could be the future victims of US economic coercion, to take anticipatory precaution by diversifying their trade away from the USA, reducing their holdings in US financial institutions, and lessening the amount of their dollar-denominated assets. Fear of US retribution can cause countries to protect themselves in these and other ways.

As remarked earlier, in view of this fear of US retribution an anti-US coalition would either not form or if it forms, it will come about quickly. This process would then again resemble that of punctuated equilibrium. Moreover, its formation will likely develop under the aegis of another great power – just as Britain had done for an anti-French coalition to form during the Napoleonic Wars. In providing a pivotal nucleus around which Napoleon's enemies could rally, London represented a "solution" to the problem of French aggression and dominance. This point is important because in the absence of its leadership, those fearful of French retribution would chafe and endure their plight without any realistic recourse to improve their lot. Thus, even when a problem is recognized, the unavailability of a viable solution means that the status quo would persist. Even though other states' officials might grumble and complain about Washington's financial sanctions and extortions made possible by the dollar's privileged position, they could not do much about it – until and unless there is a realistic alternative, such as China's *renminbi*, to provide a secure source of funding and a reliable means for settling trade accounts.

The impetus to replace the dollar with another currency or a basket of currencies would receive a boost from a shock, such as Richard Nixon's unilateral decision to abandon the US commitment to the dollar's convertibility into gold. The Yom Kippur War, the discovery of a hole in the earth's ozone, and nuclear accidents at Three Mile Island and Chernobyl all served the role of a focusing event that draws elite and mass attention to the existence of a problem and elevating this problem's salience in people's minds, thus creating a choice opportunity to promote a new definition of an old issue and to mobilize support for an alternative solution to it. In other words, problem, solution, and willing participants may be present for a considerable amount of time waiting to be activated by a focusing event. This event can introduce a shock to jolt participants into action.

But participants with the necessary vision and power can also undertake actions to produce a breakthrough that shakes up the existing stasis or deadlock. Anwar Sadat's visit to Jerusalem in 1977 had this effect, leading eventually to the Camp David Accord for peace between Egypt and Israel. Similarly, Richard Nixon's visit to Beijing in 1972 also reversed a protracted period of Sino-American hostility and put these countries' relationship on a new footing. In these cases, leaders created choice opportunities by their decisive actions. Political entrepreneurship and leadership are the stuff that brings together problems, solutions, participants, and choice opportunities. This said, there are also important, persistent, or recurrent constraints standing in the way of leaders taking bold actions. As already mentioned, Sadat paid a heavy price with his own life for his audacity.

In conclusion, the perspective introduced by punctuated equilibrium differs from our customary logic and methodology as practiced typically in studying international relations. Instead of engaging in linear reasoning and extrapolating from current trends, punctuated equilibrium emphasizes the coexistence of stasis and change with long periods of stationarity interrupted by brief bursts of sharp transformation. Moreover, rather than privileging one factor or advancing monocausal explanations – such as power transition, balance of power, and democratic peace, the "garbage can" model of policymaking associated with punctuated equilibrium in political science stresses a conjunctive logic, suggesting that policy outcomes stem often from an accidental confluence of multiple factors. Of course, the "garbage can" model conveys a complicated and even confusing world with a great deal of uncertainty and unpredictability. It lacks the elegance, parsimony, and simple, straightforward assertions that other theoretical formulations present. In short, the policymaking process described by the "garbage can" model is messy and even chaotic – but the world "out there" *is* complicated. Simple, monocausal explanations may be beguiling but they are often wrong and can sometimes even be dangerous if they cause self-fulfilling, or self-denying, prophecies such as if leaders become persuaded that power shifts in and by themselves can cause war to break out.

Perceptions of problems and their solutions vary among different participants who are involved in the policymaking process to different degrees and at different times. A choice opportunity often emerges due to unexpected and unpredictable precipitants. The unpredictable timing and the uncertain nature of interactions among the different streams to the policymaking process suggest serendipity and even randomness. Policy outcomes depend on the matching and mismatching of problems, solutions, participants, and choice opportunities. Policies take on the appearance of sudden lurches or surges, although they are also characterized by long periods of stability or quiescence. Stationarity or stasis tends to dominate most of the time, because in the absence of new policy images and policy venues the forces favoring the maintenance of the status quo tend to prevail. The preceding discussion adds to this picture by pointing to the role of a pivotal actor providing leadership and a core around which to rally mobilization and coordinate collective action. Moreover, it points to the importance of bandwagon effect due to the perception of a "winning" issue, candidate, or strategy gaining momentum.

Political entrepreneurship and leadership are necessary to overcome those conservative forces maintaining business as usual or limiting changes to incremental adjustments. In the absence of any of the necessary conditions for change, institutional rigidity or bureaucratic resistance tends to prevail and stasis is the default option, explaining the difficulty and rarity of policy innovations. The logic of "garbage can" model points to a probabilistic rather than deterministic explanation, and its reasoning acknowledges forthrightly the difficulties in trying to make specific predictions of the timing and content of major policy transformations. It also points our analytic attention to the presence or absence of factors forcing a major policy change rather than the more customary mode of analysis in international relations asking questions about the degree or extent of pertinent factors. Thus, for example, the window of opportunity to reach a negotiated deal with a foreign counterpart is either open or closed, a binary matter.

This perspective therefore points to a qualitative rather than quantitative approach to our inquiries. Giovanni Sartori (1970) wrote some time ago that researchers should keep in mind that questions about "what kind" takes precedence over questions about "how much," because we can only measure things or undertake quantitative research about things of the same kind (i.e., after establishing that they belong to the same qualitative category). Boolean logic is an example of qualitative research inquiring about the existence of necessary and sufficient conditions. The next chapter will provide an illustration of this logic.

Finally, large consequential changes can occur from the buildup of cumulative pressure over a long stretch of time. For instance, the strains of a heavy defense burden may not be felt immediately or in the short term, but over the long haul this burden can have serious deleterious effects on a country's economy as warned by Paul Kennedy (1987) in coining the concept of imperial overstretch. These effects can manifest themselves in a country's gradual but ineluctable decline and, in the case of the USSR that was overburdened by excessive military expenditures (among other causes), a sudden, dramatic collapse. As with smoking, the harmful impact of imperial overstretch on a country's economic health takes a toll over time, and the onset of demise can happen suddenly and rapidly.

4 | Prospects of US Intervention in a Taiwan Crisis, and the Conjunctive Logic

The Chinese classic, *Romance of Three Kingdoms*, tells the military struggles among three contesting states during the fourteenth century, those among Cao Cao's Wei, Liu Bei's Shu, and Sun Quan's Eastern Wu. In the epic Battle of the Red Cliffs the combined forces of Shu and Wu faced an overwhelming invasion from Wei. Being from the north and unaccustomed to naval warfare, Wei's army was vulnerable. Zhuge Liang and Zhou Yu, the respective leaders of Shu and Wu's forces, independently reached the conclusion that they should adopt a strategy of using fire to destroy Wei's battleships. To carry out this plan, one of their generals pretended to defect to Cao Cao, the leader of Wei, and succeeded in persuading him to use iron chains to link together his ships so that his soldiers would not suffer from sea sickness. By linking these ships by chains, a fire storm can more easily destroy Cao Cao's fleet. There was one problem impeding this scheme, however. The prevailing wind at the time would blow fire in the direction of Shu and Wu's own forces. The ingenious Zhuge Liang was able to predict that this weather condition would change, which having come to pass, produced a devastating defeat for Wei's forces under Cao Cao. This account left a legacy in Chinese saying, which can be awkwardly translated to say, "everything is ready except for the missing easterly wind."

My intent for introducing this anecdote is not just to emphasize that a successful military breakthrough requires a combination of facilitative conditions, but also to show how the conjunctive logic can illuminate missing condition(s) that are necessary for such a breakthrough, thus informing us about why it often fails to materialize – and conversely, when large changes become likely and imminent if signs indicate that the missing condition(s) is coming to pass. The following discussion takes up the question of whether the USA might intervene militarily in a crisis involving Taiwan. It considers past episodes of US intervention and nonintervention in conflict situations involving China and the USSR/Russia. It is undertaken more for heuristic reasons to show the comparative method using dichotomous variables rather than the customary practice to test or confirm hypotheses.

This analytic approach exemplifies qualitative research based on binary categories to indicate whether a particular condition is present or absent – as opposed to the quantitative approach asking how much of a variable applies to a particular case and hence the difference between questions of what kind versus how much. In contrast to the statistical approach requiring a large number of cases, the Boolean logic underlying the qualitative approach usually deals with a small number of cases and applies the conjunctive logic discussed earlier (Ragin 1987), when we talked about four different streams or factors converging to produce a policy choice or output as in the "garbage can" model of policymaking. Boolean analysis has two other important advantages that are compatible with the perspective of punctuated equilibrium. It sorts out various putative causal variables as necessary, sufficient, or irrelevant. It also acknowledges equifinality, the idea that the same outcome can be produced by multiple causal paths. That is, various combinations of causal factors can produce the same outcome – such as rainy or snowy weather, a dimly lit and windy road, high speed, broken headlights, badly worn tires, and a distracted or intoxicated driver can interact in any combination to cause a traffic accident. These different pathways to an accident are not mutually exclusive.

Storm Clouds over Taiwan

This chapter's discussion focuses on how the dispute over Taiwan's status has influenced and can/will influence Sino-American relations. Taiwan's status has been the most contentious issue in these countries' relationship. It has been the cause behind several crises, including China's intense bombardment of the offshore islands Quemoy and Matus on two occasions in the 1950s. Since Nixon's visit to Beijing in 1972, cross-Strait relations have fluctuated around a new equilibrium. There were times of tension but also periods of rapprochement. As mentioned briefly earlier, tension rose in 1995–1996 when Taiwan's President Lee Teng-hui visited the USA and gave a speech at Cornell University which Beijing saw as an inflammatory attempt to promote the island's independence. Relations between the two sides of the Taiwan Strait were tense during the presidency of Chen Shui-bian

(2000–2008), who represented the Democratic Progressive Party (DPP) advocating the island's independence. Chen was succeeded by Ma Ying-jeou, who belonged to the Kuomintang. During the years of Ma's presidency, relations across the Strait improved significantly and the two sides signed several accords showing a rapprochement. Ma was followed by another president representing the DPP, Tsai Ing-wen (2016–2024). Beijing has refused to have official contact with her administration as she was perceived to be in favor of Taiwan's independence. In the most recent election in January 2024, the DPP candidate, Lai Ching-te (2024–), prevailed again.

There have thus been ups and downs in relations between Beijing and Taipei since the late 1980s when Taiwan started its democratization process. Compared to the 1950s and 1960s, however, their relations have become generally calmer and more stable even though, as just remarked in the preceding paragraph, there were times of both tension and rapprochement. The major reason for a more stable cross-Strait relationship during much of the recent decades has been Beijing's relationship with Washington which has acted as a ballast against occasional turbulence. The administration of George W. Bush, for example, had berated publicly Chen Shui-bian's pro-independence stance for destabilizing cross-Strait relations. More recently, however, the stabilizing influence of Sino-American relations has come into doubt. Donald Trump had denounced publicly various malfeasance committed by Beijing, including its alleged mercantilist economic policy, its responsibility for the spread of Covid-19 pandemic, its mistreatment of Uighurs in Xinjiang, and its suppression of protesters in Hong Kong. His administration increased tariffs on Chinese goods imported by the USA, sought to limit the operation of Chinese social media company Tik Tok, and started a technological embargo against Chinese firms such as Huawei, a large telecommunications company. Nancy Pelosi's visit to Taiwan was especially controversial. Beijing perceived this visit as another significant development in a series of US moves that have undermined Washington's pledge not to support Taiwan's independence. It lodged serious diplomatic protests in response, and as mentioned earlier, also undertook missile tests in Taiwan's vicinity to demonstrate its displeasure. There has been an evident and significant deterioration in Sino-American relations in recent years, which in turn has had a deleterious effect on stability across the Taiwan Strait. Put plainly, the state of relations between

Beijing and Taipei tends to be derivative of or dependent on relations between Beijing and Washington.

Speculation that China may resort to arms to resolve Taiwan's status has become more common in the USA, both in policy and academic circles and on popular media, and in Taiwan and China in recent days. For example, former US Commander of the Indo-Pacific, Admiral Philip Davidson, has predicted that China will attack Taiwan by 2027 (Tanaka 2023); and US Air Force General Mike Minihan has predicted that the USA and China will be at war in 2025 (Kube and Gains 2023). A third US official, Admiral John Aquilino, the current commander of Indo-Pacific Command, testified to Congress, stating that China's military will be ready to invade Taiwan by 2027 (Dress 2024). There has also been increasing scholarly attention to the danger of war over Taiwan's status (e.g., Biddle and Oelrich 2016; Erickson et al. 2017; Glosny 2004; Goldstein and Murray 2004; Mastro 2021; Mearsheimer 2014; Montgomery 2014; O'Hanlon 2000; O'Hanlon et al. 2004; Ross 2002). Since Nixon's visit to Beijing, relations across the Taiwan Strait fluctuated around a relatively narrow band – albeit with some upticks and downticks until recently as just described. War would represent a major rupture of this pattern.

Several unfolding processes and ongoing trends, however, suggest that we may have entered a more dangerous period during which the probability of war has risen. First, China's military capabilities have improved vis-à-vis Taiwan and the United States. Whereas Beijing was powerless to stop two US aircraft carrier battle groups transiting the Taiwan Strait in 1996, it now has acquired the capability to deny such access. Second, public opinion in Taiwan continues to shift with an increasing number of its people identifying themselves as Taiwanese rather than Chinese. The pro-independence Democratic Progressive Party has become the majority party, even though the Kuomintang (which is widely seen to be more accommodative to Beijing) has won electoral victories in legislative and local elections. Although Taiwan has high levels of trade with and investment in the mainland, its economic dependency has not produced a greater political affinity for China. Thus, Beijing's hopes for peaceful unification have dimmed, and its leaders' patience to resolve Taiwan's status may also have become increasingly strained. It has stated publicly that this issue cannot be postponed indefinitely from one generation to the next. Third, whereas Sino-American relations have until recent years provided a stabilizing influence across the Taiwan Strait, they have now deteriorated seriously. In Beijing's view, instead of restraining Taipei, Washington's recent statements and actions have emboldened Taipei. Public and elite sentiments in the USA have turned decidedly more antagonistic toward China. Even they do not share a common ground on most issues, Democrats and Republicans agree on a policy of getting tough on China, and there is strong bipartisan support to assist Taiwan. Finally, although there was a time when Beijing was willing to set aside the thorny issue of Taiwan to pursue its higher priority of economic development and friendly relations with Washington, it now faces a different situation whereby Washington has turned to economic decoupling and more assertive efforts to contain Chinese influence such as through its policy to pivot to Asia and to foster the Quad (the Quadrilateral Security Dialogue group consisting of Australia, India, Japan, and the United States). In combination, these developments point to an elevated danger of armed conflict over Taiwan (e.g., Chan 2021b, 2023a; for a dissenting view, see Hou 2023). The multiplicative influence produced by the conjunction of these factors is greater than the sum of their individual effect.

In the following analysis, I will try to illuminate the prospect of US intervention in a potential crisis involving Taiwan. I will compare the Taiwan case with eight other cases of US intervention or nonintervention. Wars among great powers have often stemmed from one of them intervening on behalf of an ally or quasi ally in a local conflict (Chan 2025a). Put differently, large, destructive wars among great powers usually originate from the dynamics of contagion and escalation of a local feud involving a protégé. The assassination of Archduke Ferdinand, Austria-Hungary's heir apparent, in Sarajevo in the summer of 1914 was the proximate cause for World War I, and Germany's invasion of Poland in 1939, a country that Britain and France had pledged to defend, was the casus belli for these countries' involvement in World War II. Defense of an ally or protégé has often in the past provided the fuse for igniting a larger regional and even global conflagration.

China has repeatedly and publicly declared that Taiwan's status impinges on its core interest, and Deng Xiaoping had reportedly told Gerald Ford that it was *the* issue between the United States and China (Zhang 2024: 34, 131). On the sidelines of the Asia Pacific Economic Cooperation (APEC) Leaders' Meeting in San Francisco in December 2023, Xi Jinping told Joe Biden that Taiwan is the "biggest" and "most dangerous issue" between the United States and China.

In response, Biden asserted US commitment to defend its "Indo-Pacific allies" (Hou 2023: no page number). The gist of Biden's statement is clear even though Taiwan is not a formal ally of the United States. Washington had unilaterally terminated its security treaty with Taiwan when it switched diplomatic recognition from Taipei to Beijing in 1979. Nevertheless, the exchange between Xi and Biden shows that neither is willing to give ground, and it confirms Taiwan's importance in affecting their bilateral relations.

Fareed Zakaria (2024) presented a televised special report entitled "Taiwan: Unfinished Business" on Cable News Network (CNN) on March 10, 2024, in which this island was described as the "most dangerous place in the world." It also quotes the Chinese statement that national reunification with this island is "a historical inevitability." Taiwan's unsettled status is for the foreseeable future the most likely – and perhaps even the only – imaginable cause for Beijing to accept a major war, even if it means fighting against the United States. In Beijing's eyes, Washington has been the main stumbling block preventing China's national reunification. In 2023, Joe Biden said publicly on at least four different occasions (August 2021, October 2021, May 2022, and September 2022) that the USA would defend Taiwan against a Chinese assault (Time Magazine 2022; Wingrove 2022), even though officials in his own administration tried to "walk back" his statement every time, proclaiming that the USA has not changed its position on the "One China" policy and that it opposes Taiwan's independence. The United States and China do not have any territorial dispute which has been the most common cause of interstate war (Vasquez 1993, 2009b; Vasquez and Henehan 2011), nor are these countries engaged in an ideological contest that had characterized relations between Moscow and Washington during the Cold War. It is difficult to imagine a war between the world's two largest economies over any issue other than Taiwan. Intervention by the USA in a crisis across the Taiwan Strait is *the* and only plausible cause that can put Beijing and Washington on a course of armed collision.

But Why Taiwan?

But why is Taiwan so important to both countries, such that both appear to be willing to go to war over it? Why Beijing would not "let go"? After all, it has recognized Mongolia's independence. Mongolia is the world's nineteenth largest country, occupying a territory that is about comparable in size to Alaska. Large portions of Mongolia used to be part of imperial China, but Beijing recognized its statehood after the Communists came to power. In contrast, even in the late 1980s one would see in Taipei a map of China that included Mongolia. Chinese nationalism and communist ideology cannot explain the difference in Beijing's treatment of Taiwan and Mongolia, even though foreign analysts often invoke these two variables in trying to explain why Beijing would not "let go" of Taiwan. When invoking Chinese nationalism or communist ideology, they insinuate something irrational or emotional in Beijing's stance – without, however, considering how the USA has acted toward Cuba which offers the closest parallel to Taiwan's position vis-à-vis China (Chan 2024c).

These analysts also usually overlook the other side of the coin. That is, why would the United States not "let go" of Taiwan? Why would Washington threaten to intervene on behalf of an island that it itself does not recognize diplomatically? Why make this threat to go to war for a territory that it has acknowledged in various joint statements to be part of China? Former US Secretary of State Henry Kissinger has remarked, "for us to go to war with a recognized country ... over a part of what we would recognize as their country would be preposterous" (quoted in Tyler 1999: 225). Surely, US support for a people's right to self-determination cannot by itself explain its commitment to Taiwan. After all, the USA has not threatened to go to war on behalf of the Kurds, Kashmiris, or for that matter, those who live in Crimea and Ukraine's Donbas region for their right of self-determination. Washington's endorsement of a two-state solution for Israelis and Palestinians sounds empty and trite; the Palestinians have languished in refugee camps or lived in exile in Jordan and Lebanon for over three-quarters of a century after the United Nations recognized their right to statehood. As Russia's president Vladimir Putin has remarked, "If someone thinks that Kosovo can be granted full independence as a state, then why should the Abkhaz or the South-Ossetian people not also have the right to statehood!" (quoted in Toal 2017: 154).

Biden's assertion of US commitment to defend its Indo-Pacific allies sounds like empty talk in view of his "Kabul moment" and Washington's prior abandonment of its ally in Saigon. Moreover, Taiwan is not a treaty ally of the United States. As already noted, Washington had unilaterally canceled its defense treaty with Taiwan when it recognized the government in Beijing as the legitimate representative of the Chinese people. There are clear signs of waning domestic enthusiasm for the USA to support Ukraine, with funding for its assistance being used as a bargaining chip in negotiating contentious issues such as immigration, border control, and national debt.

Moreover, the claim that the danger of war over Taiwan has risen because of China's increased military capabilities is incomplete as a solo explanation. If anything, China has become less aggressive or assertive in its resort to arms, such as in its maritime disputes in the East and South China Seas, as it has become stronger militarily in recent years (Zhang 2024). Claims based on offensive realism and Chinese nationalism do not explain changes in Beijing's resort to coercion. As China's power grew, it did not increase its use of coercion. A moment's reflection also tells us that if Chinese nationalism is a constant motivation of Beijing's statecraft, it cannot explain variations across targets and over time in Beijing's application of coercion (Zhang 2024: 126–127). Explanations based on these claims are too facile, and when they focus just on Chinese conduct, they overlook whether these claims may also apply to the United States and other countries. Would they reject similar explanations when applied to the USA, or find them wanting, strained, and even outlandish?

Washington's professed interest in protecting Taiwan's democracy is also unconvincing. US commitment to Taiwan's defense was the strongest when this island was a garrison state under martial law governed by an unelected and authoritarian regime under Chiang Kai-shek. It switched its diplomatic recognition to Beijing just when Taiwan was beginning to democratize. Indeed, it is rare for Americans to recall how they have ended their own civil war – by bullets and not ballots. Senator Frank Church (Idaho) stated forthrightly in a hearing on the Vietnam War:

had England, which favored the South, adhered to the same principle that now seems to govern American policy, and had sent troops in the name of self-determination into the Confederacy, I think the English Government would have been hard put to convince Abraham Lincoln that there should be an election to determine the ultimate outcome of the war. (Quoted in Khong 1992 : 236)

Why would China not "let go" of Taiwan? Because any Chinese leader who renounces the goal of national reunification with Taiwan will be in domestic political jeopardy. One just needs to recall how John Kennedy and his advisors had considered the domestic political implications should they fail to take decisive action against Soviet missiles in Cuba. They expected political fallout not only in defeat for Democratic candidates in the then impending Congressional elections but also in the possible impeachment of the president (Allison 1971: 184–185).

One may similarly ask why Margaret Thatcher would want to go to war against Argentina over the Falklands/Malvinas, which lacked any economic or strategic value to London and was much farther away from Britain than Argentina. A British cabinet member had supposedly confided to a reporter, saying "To be frank, I don't see how she [Margaret Thatcher] can survive [politically] if she shrinks from a military showdown" (quoted in Lebow 1985: 117).

There is another reason why China would not "let go" of Taiwan – and the United States apparently likewise. It has to do with Taiwan's strategic value (Chan 2024c; Wachman 2007). Given its location, it is the key to China's front door (Chan and Hu 2024; 2025b), and is even a dagger pointed at China with its commercial, economic, and population centers located on the east coast, China's soft underbelly, within easy reach of this island. Taiwan can be used as a strategic base to launch an offensive campaign against the Chinese mainland or, alternatively, a barrier to prevent such an attack if China controls it. In Douglas MacArthur's words, this island is an "unsinkable aircraft." It also restricts the access of China's navy and merchant fleet to the open Pacific, and it constitutes the linchpin in the so-called first island chain to contain China. This chain runs from the Aleutians in the north, to Japan and the Ryukyus, to Taiwan, and on to the Philippines. Put plainly, Taiwan is an important part of the US strategy to bottle up China's navy, to disrupt its north–south connection, and to interdict its overseas commerce in the event of armed hostilities (Green and Talmadge 2022). If China controls Taiwan, it would have succeeded in breaking out of the first island chain intended to constrict its maritime expansion. To ask why Taiwan is important to China is equivalent to asking why Britain, France, and Germany cared about Belgium's neutrality. It was Germany's violation of Belgium's neutrality in carrying out the Schlieffen plan to invade France that caused the British to finally decide to join the fray that became World War I.

Whichever country was able to control Belgium would be in a strategic position to threaten the other two.

In short, we need not invoke some vague emotional cause or nationalist impulse to explain Taiwan's importance, just as these reasons are not necessary to explain Washington's ire directed against Cuba and the Central Intelligence Agency's organization and coordination of the invasion of this island in the 1961 Bay of Pigs episode (to support plots to overthrow Fidel Castro and even to assassinate him, and to push the world to the brink of nuclear war in 1962 over Moscow's missiles installed on that island). In his testimony to the Foreign Relations Committee of US Congress, Assistant Secretary of Defense Ely Ratner stated:

Taiwan is located at a critical node within the first island chain, anchoring a network of U.S.allies and partners – stretching from the Japanese archipelago down to the Philippines and into the South China Sea – that is critical to the region's security and critical to the defense of vital U.S. interests in the Indo-Pacific. (Ratner 2021:1)

Seen in this light, Taiwan's strategic importance to Beijing far exceeds that of Cuba for Washington, because the latter island could not in any way impede US access to the Atlantic and Pacific Oceans, whereas Taiwan can serve as the linchpin for a naval blockade of China.

Although the USA has in the past adopted a policy of strategic ambiguity toward Taiwan (Bush 2005, 2013), there are signs that it is reconsidering this posture. A policy of strategic ambiguity is supposed to be motivated by a desire to practice dual deterrence (Crawford 2003) – that is, to prevent Taiwan from declaring formal independence and to also prevent an attack on it by China. By declining to pre-commit itself to any specific action in the event of a crisis involving this island, Washington reserves the discretion to decide how to act in a future crisis and by creating uncertainties in the minds of Taiwan and China's leaders about how the USA would act, this posture is supposed to have the effect of discouraging them from engaging in risky behavior. It also assigns Washington the role of a referee calling shots on supposed infractions by either Beijing or Taipei.

Recently, several important American figures have openly called for reversing Washington's policy of strategic ambiguity toward Taiwan.

For example, former US Secretary of State in the Trump administration Mike Pompeo has declared publicly that the United States should extend formal diplomatic recognition to Taiwan (Blanchard 2022). Washington's long-standing policy of strategic ambiguity has also come under scrutiny by and opposition from some other important figures. Richard Haass (Haass and Sacks 2020), the former Director of Policy Planning at the State Department and former head of the Council of Foreign Relations, has called for "strategic clarity" – that is, for Washington to pledge publicly its support for Taiwan and commit itself to come to this island's defense in the event of a Chinese attack. There is an ongoing debate about the advantages and disadvantages of changing the US policy from strategic ambiguity to strategic clarity, that is, to make a firm commitment to assist Taiwan's defense (e.g., Bosco 2023; Carpenter 2005; Georgetown University Initiative 2020; Glaser 2022; Glaser et al. 2020; Haass and Sacks 2020; Hulme 2020; Mazarr 2022; Schmitt and Mazza 2020; Zelleke 2020). The very fact that this debate is occurring communicates to Beijing a change in US thinking, a breakdown in Washington's prior policy consensus on dealing with China and Taiwan, and a possible, and even likely, revision of its prior formal agreements and informal understanding with China – all of which add up to an increase in the probability that the USA will intervene militarily in a crisis across the Taiwan Strait.

Prospect of US Intervention on Taiwan's Behalf

A possible US military intervention on behalf of Taiwan can involve it in a direct armed confrontation with China. It is the most likely scenario for this clash as the United States and China do not have any direct territorial dispute which is the most common source for interstate conflict to occur. Moreover, unlike the struggle between the United States and the USSR, China is not seeking ideological converts or military allies abroad – even though Washington is increasingly framing its relations with Beijing as a struggle between different political systems, a conflict between democracy and autocracy.

The analysis in the next section explores the possibility of US intervention in the Taiwan Strait by interrogating nine past conflict episodes that presented a "choice opportunity" for the USA to intervene against China or the USSR/Russia. Before getting to this analysis, however, this section provides a lengthy explanation about the rationale for my selection of the historical episodes for this study and important considerations pertaining to these cases.

Surely, intervening militarily in a conflict situation involving China is qualitatively different from many other past instances in which Washington has taken military actions to attack against or even invade countries like Haiti, Nicaragua, Panama, Libya, Somalia, Afghanistan, Syria, or even Vietnam, Serbia, Iraq, and Iran. China and the USSR/Russia are much more powerful than these other targets of US resort to force. They are much more capable of pushing back and the consequences of conflict escalation are much more serious in armed disputes with these countries than those involving others. Stating the point differently, it is not analytically appropriate to lump these two kinds of US military intervention in the same category, and such mingling can produce misleading conclusions because as just stated, their qualitative differences suggest it would be tantamount to mixing apples and oranges.

The cases selected for my analysis in this chapter are chosen because they are most comparable to a possible contingency involving Taiwan, and therefore can serve as precedents to instruct us about Washington's likely decision in a future crisis involving this island. The "dependent variable" is direct US military intervention, meaning the participation by US forces in sustained, coordinated and large-scale combat, and thus not isolated incidents of armed clash. These cases are Washington's interventions on behalf of South Korea and South Vietnam and its nonintervention against Fidel Castro's Cuba and in the ongoing Russo-Ukrainian War, the Russo-Georgian War in 2008, the Hungarian Uprising in 1956, and the Sino-Indian War in 1962. In addition, I include two past occasions involving Taiwan when China initiated intense bombardment of the offshore islands of Quemoy and Matsu under Taiwan's control (e.g., Chan 1978; Stolper 1985; Whiting 1975). In these latter cases, Washington provided military support for Taiwan, such as escorting its supply ships to these offshore islands without, however, deploying its armed forces in such a way that could involve them in a direct fight with China. The highly qualified nature of US support in these cases led me to indicate "no" on the question of whether Washington intervened militarily on behalf of its protégé, Taiwan. The US involvement in these two episodes did not reach the level of direct combat support for Taipei. This said, it is also pertinent to consider that Beijing decided to deescalate these episodes and thus to pull back from a direct confrontation with Washington. In other words, Beijing's actions to defuse tension in these two cases prevented them from escalating to the point where the United States would feel compelled to consider whether to intervene more directly.

A few words of explanation are also necessary for US policies toward Cuba. Washington did undertake various covert operations against Castro's regime, being even involved in plots to assassinate the Cuban leader. Moreover, Washington was complicit in organizing and financing the Bay of Pigs invasion in 1961. This invasion was undertaken by anti-Communist Cuban exiles trained and organized by the Central Intelligence Agency, and the USA tried to conceal its role in planning, coordinating, and supporting this invasion. More importantly, when this invasion failed, the Kennedy administration decided not to intervene directly by attacking Castro's forces. The invaders were taken prisoner by Castro's forces, and Washington had to subsequently provide food and medicine to Cuba in exchange for the release of these prisoners. In 1962, the USA also refrained from attacking Soviet missiles installed in Cuba, choosing instead to impose a naval blockade to pressure Moscow to remove these missiles. When Nikita Khrushchev agreed to do so, the crisis abated. In a secret deal with the Kremlin, the USA promised never to invade Cuba again – and it has not done so since then even though it has continued to apply economic and political pressure against its communist government. The USA also withdrew its missiles in Turkey as a part of the bargain for the USSR to remove its missiles from Cuba. For reasons that I have just given, I coded the case of Cuba as an instance of US nonintervention (again, intervention in this analysis refers to direct involvement of US armed forces in organized combat).

I do not include in this analysis two other cases involving Taiwan in 1995–1996 (Ross 2000), and more recently in 2022 when Beijing undertook missile tests around the island to signal its displeasure with the pro-independence stance of Taiwan's then President Lee Teng-hui, and Nancy Pelosi's (who was then Speaker of the US House of Representatives) visit to Taiwan, respectively. The reason for excluding these two cases from the following analysis is that they did not escalate to a point whereby Washington was faced with a choice opportunity to decide whether to intervene militarily in an ongoing armed conflict.

But why select the other cases, such as those past armed conflicts involving Korea, Hungary, Cuba, India, Vietnam, Georgia, and Ukraine for comparison with Taiwan? My rationale is that in addition to these cases offering the closest parallels to Taiwan, they present variation in our dependent variable, namely, Washington's decision on whether to intervene militarily. In other words, they differ from each other in that the USA intervened in Korea and Vietnam but did not in the other conflict episodes involving Hungary, Cuba, India, Georgia, and Ukraine.

In what sense are these cases comparable to Taiwan? All of them except Cuba took place on China and the USSR/Russia's doorstep. Of course, the USA has resorted to force on many other previous occasions such as when it intervened militarily in the Caribbean (e.g., the Dominican Republic, Grenada, Haiti), Central America (e.g., Nicaragua, Panama), and even distant countries such as Afghanistan, Iraq, Kuwait, and Lebanon. Washington's interventions or invasions in these cases, however, did not run the risk of having to fight the Chinese and Russians directly. Therefore, they are qualitatively different from those other cases just mentioned involving China and the USSR/Russia directly (or the potential to do so in Korea and Vietnam). The case of Cuba is instructive. In contrast to the other cases, this island is located in the USA backyard with Washington enjoying a huge military advantage and backed by strong domestic support to take decisive action. That the USA had decided not to intervene militarily in this instance should tell us something about whether it is likely to do so in less favorable or rather, less conducive circumstances.

The preceding discussion argues that we need to select cases carefully to ensure that we are comparing apples with apples, or cases belonging to the same category. As Giovanni Sartori (1970) pointed out some time ago, we can only compare things that are comparable. He warned us not to engage in concept stretching in trying to expand an idea's connotation at the expense of obfuscating its denotation; that is, engaging in quantitative measurement of things that are qualitatively different. All the cases being studied here belong to the same class in that they all refer to potential collision with another major power, the USSR/Russia or China. Moreover, as already mentioned, all except the case involving Cuba were located far from the USA, and where the other great power, its potential adversary, enjoyed a "home court" advantage. Moreover, aside from Cuba all the cases are also similar in that they presented "choice opportunities" for Washington to decide whether to intervene militarily after war or armed conflict has already commenced. In the absence of this occurrence, the choice opportunity for US military intervention would not have happened. Therefore, the logic of case selection reflects that of the "most likely" cases that are comparable to Taiwan. The cases in Table 4.1 all share the common feature that military intervention by the USA would put Washington in a direct military contest with Moscow or Beijing. Although the case of Cuba also has this characteristic, it shows an important difference from the other cases. As already mentioned, if the USA did not resort to armed force in this instance when and where it enjoyed a "home court" advantage, a large military edge in conventional forces, and strong domestic support for a hard-line stance, it should be less inclined to intervene militarily in other less advantageous situations.

As explained later in this chapter, it is important to stress that there has not been any war involving a formal US ally (that is, a country that Washington has pledged to defend by its formal treaty commitment) against either the USSR/Russia or China. The absence of such cases is clear, remarkable, and significant. This situation has not happened since the end of World War II – an important phenomenon pointing to self-selection. That is, neither Moscow nor Beijing has targeted a formal US ally as the target of its aggression (except China's shelling of the two offshore islands, Quemoy and Matsu in the 1950s), and US allies have also avoided getting into a direct armed conflict with either Russia/the USSR or China in a hot war. Whether this phenomenon suggests effective self-restraint by the countries involved or effective restraint (or in other words, deterrence) enforced by Washington on both its allies and adversaries, history has thus far provided us with a record absent of any such episodes (except, as just mentioned, crises involving the offshore islands of Quemoy and Matsu in the 1950s before Washington terminated its defense treaty with Taipei) presaging a US military clash with the USSR/Russia or China. The world did come close to the brink of such a clash in the 1962 Cuban Missile Crisis and American and Chinese soldiers did clash directly in Korea in the early 1950s. Note, however, that South Korea (and South Vietnam, we might add) was not a formal US ally at the time when Washington decided to intervene, and during the Korean War China was not nearly as strong as it is today as an adversary for the USA – important differences that deserve our attention when comparing then and now.

Several other important clarifications are in order. As just remarked, China at the time of the Korean War, its border war with India, and even during the Vietnam War was much weaker than the United States, whereas it is today a much more formidable adversary for Washington. Certainly, the USA commanded a huge advantage in its capabilities compared to the North Koreans and the North Vietnamese. It should also be noted that in Table 4.1 the level of domestic support refers to when the US decision on whether to intervene was made, and not subsequently after its involvement in a war that became protracted and American casualties began to mount.

It is also pertinent to recall that after both wars in Korea and Vietnam, there was a strong sentiment among American officials to never again fight another land war on the Asian continent. Thus, to the extent that historical memory, or learning from the past and path dependency influence Washington's thinking, its potential involvement in a future crisis involving Taiwan will reflect these experiences. Parenthetically, Taiwan is of course an island but there is no guarantee that a conflict involving it will be limited to the maritime sphere, such as possibly if Beijing "pushes back" in other conflict arenas on land, the most obvious one being the Korean peninsula, especially if the USA uses its military assets based in South Korea in a contingency involving Taiwan.

Finally, had the USA intervened militarily in episodes involving Hungary, Georgia, and Ukraine, it would have immediately put itself in a direct fight against the USSR/Russia's armed forces, whereas in Korea and Vietnam Washington's initial adversary was the North Koreans and North Vietnamese. In these cases, the risk of Chinese involvement would only come to pass if the US forces crossed the 38th parallel in Korea and the 17th parallel (dividing North and South Vietnam) in the Vietnam War to invade North Vietnam (or some other serious escalation such as bombing the Red River dikes in North Vietnam).

This is an important difference that is likely to have been responsible for Washington's decision not to intervene in Hungary, Georgia, and Ukraine, but to intervene in Korea and Vietnam. Significantly, a possible war between the USA and China in a contingency involving Taiwan is more comparable to Washington's choice opportunities regarding armed conflicts involving Hungary, India, Georgia, and Ukraine, setting it apart from its interventions in Korea and Vietnam which only challenged the Chinese indirectly. I consider the USA to have enjoyed a lopsided military advantage over its immediate opponent in Korea and Vietnam (the North Koreans and North Vietnamese), but not in Hungary, Georgia, and Ukraine, cases for which its intervention would have put it in a direct and immediate armed conflict with the USSR/Russia.

Moreover, on questions about whether the USA has an important economic and security stake in these cases, my benchmarks are Kuwait/Iraq (1990) and Cuba (in the early 1960s) respectively. I consider these two cases to have impinged respectively on important US economic and security interests, and I use them to compare with the other episodes. In the case of Korea, US Secretary Dean Acheson had placed this peninsula (and the island of Taiwan) outside the US defense perimeter in East Asia in a public speech shortly before North Korean forces invaded the South. As for Taiwan, all signals from the USA prior to the onset of the Korean War indicated that it had decided to abstain from any further involvement in the Chinese Civil War. Therefore, Washington's own assessment had indicated that the USA had a low stake in Korea and Taiwan's future, and I have coded these variables in Table 4.1 accordingly. These and other variables are presented in a binary form in this table. Readers who disagree with my judgment can alter my coding and decide for themselves whether and how this alteration changes the conclusion.

The Boolean Logic and Extended Deterrence

Naturally, dichotomizing the pertinent independent variables into binary categories of "yes" and "no" means a loss of information should more sensitive scalar data be available and appropriate. Yet, in many aspects of life people act on their binary judgments. Whether a protégé is a formal ally of the United States is a binary question even though analysts may resort to quantitative measures such as the value of arms sales and the volume of bilateral trade to provide interval measures to gauge the importance of US stake in its protégé's security and the strength of its commitment to this protégé. The Boolean logic is especially appropriate for the analysis of dichotomous variables. It seeks to understand which of these variables represent necessary conditions for an outcome to occur, which of them are sufficient conditions, and which ones are irrelevant. It can also help us to discern multiple combinations of factors that can produce the same outcome.

The last point is important to stress. In social science research, the idea of equifinality suggests that there can be different pathways to the same outcome. For example, there can be many reasons for a child to perform poorly at school. Possible reasons can include parental neglect and even a dysfunctional family environment, lack of resources due to the student's socioeconomic circumstances, her chronic truancy or attention deficit, a hostile school environment, and inadequate school facilities, large class sizes, and unmotivated teachers. Any of these factors, or combinations of them, can cause poor academic performance.

Gary Goertz (2003: 191) has argued counterintuitively that necessary conditions can be treated as continuous variables. To support this view, he introduces a machine metaphor and fuzzy logic. He points to a car with a spark plug that fires only sporadically but one that can still turn on the engine albeit only occasionally. He reasons that when a component's failure rate is close to 0, it is practically useless, but at values significantly higher than 0, the car can still operate although not optimally (Goertz 2003: 202). Presumably, we need a large sample of observations to establish relative frequency or in this illustration, the spark plug's failure rate.

Goertz (2003: 201, italics in original) also points to fuzzy logic, stating that "instead of saying that a necessary condition variable can only take 0 or 1 values I propose that it can take on *all* values in the [0, 1] continuum." Fuzzy logic was introduced by Lofti Zadeh (1965), a mathematician, computer scientist, and electrical engineer. In contrast to classical logic which deals with absolute truths such as whether a statement is either true or false, fuzzy logic mimics human judgments that are subjective and vague such as a person being "nice" or "good looking" or a state being "powerful" or "compassionate." In fuzzy logic, truth values can be any value between zero and one. Claudi Cioffi-Revilla (1981, 1998a) has written about fuzzy sets in the context of international relations. The initial values taken on by fuzzy logic are never optimal. They are approximations to be updated and revised subsequently in future iterations of analysis, or to use Goertz's word, that the analysts can "fiddle" with.

Without a large sample and given uncertainty about assigning initial values, I have decided to treat the dependent variable being discussed here, namely, whether the USA decided to intervene militarily in a foreign conflict, as a binary choice. Sometimes, "A binary treatment is preferable because decision-makers do not operate in a complex mathematical world" (Zhang 2024: 33). For example, theft, incompetence, and absenteeism can all get one dismissed from a job. These reasons may be based on quantitative matrices, but they are usually presented in dichotomous terms and the outcome in question – job dismissal – also involves a dichotomous decision. Moreover, the example just cited illustrates nicely the idea of substitutability, that is, any number of causes (e.g., theft, incompetence, and absenteeism) can produce the same outcome (job dismissal). The various forms of misconduct warranting dismissal are therefore substitutable. There can be multiple causal paths leading to the same result. Although the Boolean approach has its own limitations, I have argued that it is more appropriate for "situations with a relatively small number of cases and variables and when concerns for context sensitivity and causal substitutability are more germane" (Chan 2003a: 57).

It is also important and pertinent to note that dichotomization of the dependent variable is the appropriate approach to studying punctuated equilibrium, which refers to one state of affairs prior to the punctuation and another after it. In other words, punctuated equilibrium is about a qualitative, not quantitative, change. Thus, for example, although we can count the number of votes in favor of or against the government in Beijing being recognized as the legitimate representative of China to the United Nations in the example introduced in the last chapter, we are ultimately interested in the outcome of these votes which is a binary choice to either recognize China or not.

Studies on military intervention have often been couched in terms of deterrence, referring to a country's threat to retaliate or respond forcefully if the target of this threat undertakes some unwanted action. For instance, the USA threatens to intervene militarily to aid any of its allies that are members of NATO if the USSR/Russia invades them. This example points to an instance of extended deterrence, whereby A threatens B with decisive action and punitive damage if B attacks C, which is A's ally or protégé. The question taken up in this chapter pertains to extended deterrence. It seeks to discern whether the USA would intervene militarily to defend Taiwan in the event of a Chinese attack against this island.

Extended deterrence differs from direct deterrence, which refers to A's threat to defend itself should B attack it. Whereas A's determination to defend and fight for its home territory is inherently believable, its resolve to go to war on behalf of a third party is more questionable. If Paris were attacked by the USSR, would Washington respond in kind by attacking Moscow or Leningrad/St. Petersburg, thus risking the destruction of New York or Los Angeles in a Soviet counterstrike? This question shows doubts about A's pledge to defend C in comparison to its commitment to defend itself. It captures former French President Charles de Gaulle's rationale for insisting on an independent force de frappe for France rather than relying on US protection or in other words, Washington's promise of extended deterrence. Thomas Schelling (1966: 36) has stated succinctly, "the difference between the national homeland and everything 'abroad' is the difference between threats that are inherently credible, even if unspoken, and threats that have to be made credible."

There is a considerable literature on deterrence, including extended deterrence (e.g., Danilovic 2001a, 2001b; Fearon 1994, 2002; Huth 1984, 1988a, 1988b; Huth et al. 1993; Huth and Russett 1993; Lebow and Stein 1990; Russett 1969). In attempting to understand whether efforts at extended deterrence succeed or fail, researchers have tried to determine the influence of variables such as whether C is A's alliance partner, whether it shares similar regimes or ideology with A, how much do these countries trade, and the physical distance separating them in order to gauge the strength of ties between A and C and A's stake in C's security.

Rather than pursuing my question about the prospect of US military intervention using statistical analysis as many of the studies mentioned above have done, I adopt the comparative method based on Boolean logic (Ragin 1987). The small number of cases for my purpose suggests that statistical methods requiring a large sample are inappropriate. The number of cases pertinent to my interest is small because I want to study how the USA has decided to act in past episodes involving another major power, which means that I should limit my cases to those situations involving the danger of conflict with either the USSR/Russia or China. Although the USA has resorted to the use of force abroad frequently in the past, it is one thing for it to attack Libya, Serbia, Iraq, Syria, or Iran's proxies in the Middle East, but it is quite another matter when it comes to putting itself in a conflict situation that can cause it to collide directly with the USSR/ Russia or China.

Seeking to understand the reasons behind Washington's decisions on whether to intervene militarily in past conflict situations involving the USSR/Russia and China, I ask the following questions eliciting binary answers of "yes" or "no":

A. Does the USA have a formal alliance with the protégé in question?
B. Is the military balance lopsidedly in favor of the USA vis-à-vis the USSR/Russia or China in the pertinent episode?
C. Does the USA have a large economic stake in this protégé's survival?
D. Does the USA have a large security stake in this protégé's survival?
E. Are public opinion and congressional sentiment strongly supportive of US intervention on behalf of this protégé?

I give my answers to these questions in Table 4.1, and Boolean logic is used to analyze this evidence. This method is especially suitable for qualitative studies of binary data from a small number of cases. In contrast, quantitative (statistical) analysis is more appropriate for interval or ratio data from a large sample of cases. Statistical tests of significance would not be meaningful when a dataset encompasses an entire population, and when multiple causal connections may be at work in conjunction. Boolean algebra focuses on logical structures (e.g., Goldstein et al. 1995; Kemeny et al. 1974), and its application has become more popular since Charles Ragin's (1987) influential book seeking to bridge the traditional gulf between qualitative and quantitative scholarship. A small number of cases, dichotomous variables, and skewed distribution pose problems for standard regression approaches, but Boolean analysis does not suffer from these same limitations. As I have argued elsewhere (Chan 2003a: 58):

[Boolean analysis] provides a way of testing all possible causal combinations and, by way of logical deduction, eliminates irrelevant factors and differentiates the status of the relevant ones as necessary, sufficient ... for the realization of the outcome of interest. Perhaps the most important advantage of the Boolean approach is that it addresses explicitly the idea that there can be multiple causal mechanisms producing the same outcome. That is, the same outcome can result from different combinations of factors.

The last point is worth repeating. Boolean logic accepts and even expects multiple causal paths producing the same outcome. It does not consider these alternatives to be mutually exclusive. Moreover, its logic introduces the idea of substitutability. Different variables can play a similar role in these alternative paths leading to the same outcome. It can also separate variables that may appear to be a plausible cause but turn out to be in fact irrelevant. Charles Ragin (1987: x) explains in these words, "causation is understood conjuncturally. Outcomes are analyzed in terms of intersections of conditions, and it is usually assumed that any of the several combinations conditions might produce a certain outcome" (quoted in Goertz 2003: 188).

It is also important to bear in mind that under different circumstances, the same factors can have different effects. Conversely, different factors can produce similar effects. Thus, situations presenting a choice opportunity to US officials might have changed significantly over time. Just as a quick example, although previous crises in the Taiwan Strait in the 1950s and even 1990s might suggest important parallels to a possible future contingency involving Taiwan again, an important change has occurred in the intervening years: Namely, China has improved its relative military position significantly vis-à-vis the United States, thus possibly altering the effects that a factor had in the past (such as whether stronger domestic legislative and public support would now be required for deciding in favor of US intervention, especially if this situation involves supporting a protégé that is not a formal US ally for which Washington is bound by treaty obligation to assist).

The application of Boolean logic typically requires the construction of a truth table, but I will skip this step for now and introduce this formality only briefly later. The data in Table 4.1 are simple and straightforward. The most immediate impression given by this table is that formal alliance commitment is *not* a requirement for US military intervention to occur. Washington did not have a treaty obligation to intervene on behalf of South Korea and South Vietnam, nor in the case of present-day Taiwan. This formal alliance tie is therefore not a necessary condition for US military intervention.

With the exceptions presented by the two crises involving the offshore islands of Quemoy and Matsu in 1954–1955 and again in 1958, the absence of any formal ally of the United States being involved in an armed conflict with either China or the USSR/Russia is itself a significant phenomenon as already noted earlier. This is so because the cases reported in Table 4.1 constitute practically the entire population of

Table 4.1 *Exploring possible US intervention in Taiwan: The conjunctive logic*

	Korea 1950	Quemoy/Matsu 1954–55	Hungary 1956	Quemoy/Matsu 1958	Cuba 1962	India 1962	Vietnam 1964	Georgia 2008	Ukraine 2022	Taiwan ?
A. Formal Ally?	no	yes	no	yes	no	no	no	no	no	no
B. Lopsided Military Advantage?	yes	yes	no	yes	yes	no	yes	no	no	no
C. Large Security Stake?	no	yes	no	no	yes	no	no	no	no	no
D. Large Economic Stake?	no	no	no	no	yes	no	no	no	no	no
E. Domestic Support?	no	no	no	no	yes	no	yes	no	no	yes
Did the USA Intervene?	yes	no	no	no	no	no	yes	no	no	?

foreign armed conflicts involving Beijing and Moscow in the past three-quarters of a century. I say "practically" because Table 4.1 does omit a few unusual cases for which US military intervention is highly implausible, such as the Kremlin's crackdown on the Prague Spring in 1968, the Sino-Vietnamese border war in 1979, and the Sino-Soviet clash along the Ussuri River in 1969.

As already stressed, that except for the two episodes involving the offshore islands (Quemoy and Matsu) under Taiwan's control in 1954–1955 and 1958, there has not been an armed conflict between a formal US ally on the one hand and China or the USSR/Russia on the other is a highly significant phenomenon, pointing to self-selecting on both sides. One may interpret this phenomenon as evidence of Washington effectively restraining its allies from getting into an armed conflict with Beijing or Moscow, or its allies exercising self-restraint to avoid such a conflict with Beijing and Moscow – and/or reciprocally, China and the USSR/Russia engaging in similar behavior to avoid an armed conflict with a formal US ally lest Washington intervenes militarily.

This being the case, we do not have past episodes to help us shed light on the escalatory potential of a prospective conflict involving a formal US ally, say, Japan or the Philippines becoming embroiled in an armed clash with China in their respective dispute with Beijing in the East China Sea and South China Sea. Parenthetically, Washington's public posture in the two episodes involving Chinese shelling of Quemoy and Matsu was to support Taiwan but privately it pressured Taipei to withdraw from the Dachen archipelago to avoid a confrontation with China, and it provided naval support for Taiwan to evacuate its personnel from these islands in 1955. Of course, the USA had unilaterally abrogated its defense treaty with Taiwan when it switched its diplomatic recognition from Taipei to Beijing in 1979, and thus from that time on, Taiwan was no longer a formal US ally and is still not today. It should also be noted that even when Washington's defense treaty with Taipei was in force, it deliberately excluded the defense of the offshore islands from this treaty's provision for US military support.

Significantly, in the 1954–1955 and 1958 offshore crises, the USA did not interject itself directly in combat on Taiwan's behalf. These earlier episodes happened at a time when Taiwan was a formal treaty ally of the United States, and when Washington commanded a huge military edge over China – two factors that should have facilitated a decision in favor of US military intervention. That Washington did not decide to intervene directly in these earlier episodes would suggest that it would be even more reluctant to do so today – because it no longer has a treaty obligation to come to Taiwan's aid in a military contingency involving China, and because China is militarily much stronger today so that the USA no longer enjoys a lopsided military advantage as it did in the 1950s. Both considerations would reduce the prospect of US military intervention today.

Furthermore, the pattern shown in Table 4.1 is unambiguous in pointing out that the USA had never intervened militarily in a situation that would put it in direct conflict with either the USSR/Russia or China – except for the two episodes involving China's offshore islands mentioned above. In Korea, the US intervention came before China's decision to enter into the war. It was only when General Douglas MacArthur's troops crossed the 38th parallel in pursuit of the North Koreans to unify the peninsula under a pro-Western government that Beijing was confronted with a choice opportunity to decide whether to undertake counter-intervention. As for the USSR/Russia, there has yet to be a case indicating US military intervention on behalf of a client or protégé that would place Washington possibly in a direct collision with Moscow. The Cuban Missile Crisis in 1962 was the closest encounter that could have pushed Washington and Moscow into such a collision. This is a significant case, because it differs from the rest of the cases in that it was not a situation whereby the US came to the defense of a beleaguered junior partner.

Washington has of course expressed verbal support for the victims of Soviet aggression, and it has in some cases such as the ongoing war in Ukraine provided substantial material aid to these victims. But it has never undertaken direct combat to extend support to those countries that had taken up arms against the USSR/Russia. From the outset, the Biden administration had stated publicly that direct US military intervention was not among the options being considered in the case of the then prospective war between Russia and Ukraine. By taking this option off the table, Washington's attempt at extended deterrence was less forceful than, say, what it had pledged to do if one of its NATO allies were to come under attack.

Just as being a formal US ally is not a necessary condition for US military intervention on behalf of a third party, being such an ally is not a sufficient condition for this intervention. Taiwan was Washington's formal ally in the 1950s but as already remarked, the USA eschewed direct military intervention and took precautionary measures to lower the risk of its involuntary involvement in an escalating military situation involving China.

As noted already, the case of Cuba is especially informative. It is located close to the USA, thus providing Washington a "home court" advantage. Moreover, the USA also had in my view a large economic and security stake in Cuba's status although, as already mentioned, Castro's Cuba was of course not a US ally. Finally, among all the cases included in Table 4.1, there was the strongest domestic support for Washington to take decisive action against Castro's Cuba even before the Cuban Missile Crisis in 1962. The case of Cuba is informative in that none of the factors just cited alone or in combination was sufficient for Washington to take military intervention that would risk a direct clash with the USSR even in the US backyard. In July 1962, Havana and Moscow reportedly signed a mutual defense pact, including the installation and deployment of Soviet missiles in Cuba (Operation Anadyr). According to Tomas Diez Acosta (2002), Nikita Khrushchev had insisted that the treaty be kept secret. It is possible that Washington did not know about this treaty, but in the missile crisis that ensued the Kennedy administration chose to pursue a naval blockade rather than to launch a surprise airstrike to destroy Soviet missiles installed in Cuba that could have resulted in Soviet casualties. Washington might have proceeded with an attack on the island if Khrushchev had refused to remove the missiles. This action was not necessary in the end. Nevertheless, Curtis LeMay, Chief of Staff of US Air Force, advocated undertaking this strike even after Khrushchev had agreed to remove the missiles. These missiles were removed from Cuba in exchange for the USA removing its missiles from Turkey and for it to pledge not to invade Cuba again (Allison 1971). The main point of this discussion is that Washington's policy was prudent in this episode, seeking to avoid a collision with the USSR, even in circumstances that were most conducive for it to take decisive military action.

A decisive US military advantage appears to be a necessary but not sufficient condition for US intervention. In Korea and Vietnam, Washington enjoyed this advantage, and it intervened. In the cases involving Cuba and Quemoy and Matsu off China's coast in the 1950s, the balance of military capabilities also favored the USA, but

Washington did not undertake direct military intervention. Strong domestic support for intervention was also neither a sufficient nor a necessary condition for US military intervention to occur. This intervention happened in Korea and Vietnam even though there was not any strong domestic support or demand for this course of action. Weak or lukewarm domestic support for intervention did not rule out this action for US leaders in these episodes. Conversely, strong domestic support or demand for decisive action also did not push US leaders to intervene more aggressively against Cuba.

The physical location of a conflict also does not appear to make an important difference in Washington's decision on whether to intervene. It chose to intervene in Korea and Vietnam, but not against Cuba which is much closer geographically. Naturally, the USA has often undertaken military actions in Central America and the Caribbean, but it has also resorted to arms in more distant theaters such as Korea, Vietnam, Iraq, and Afghanistan.

One variable appears to matter, and it pertains to US military advantage. In those conflict episodes that Washington had intervened directly, it held a large military edge. This variable, however, points to a necessary rather than sufficient condition for US intervention. Washington did not intervene in every instance when it had such an edge.

The larger pattern emerging from Table 4.1 suggests that US leaders have acted cautiously in situations fraught with the danger of a possible clash with the USSR/Russia or China. In 1950, fighting between Chinese and American soldiers came about more due to US leaders' underestimation of Beijing's resolve to intervene rather than a risk of confrontation that they accepted with their eyes wide open. Harry Truman's dismissal of Douglas MacArthur as the general in charge of UN forces in Korea was a telltale sign that he disagreed with MacArthur's bombastic style and threats to invade China. Incidentally, Washington also turned down Chiang Kai-shek's offer to send Nationalist forces to join the Korean War. This action is also informative about US intention not to further expand its war with China.

With their Korean experience in mind, US leaders avoided escalatory moves in the Vietnam War, such as invading North Vietnam or bombing the Red River dikes, actions that could have provoked direct Chinese military intervention. Washington was aware that the Chinese had sent logistic troops and personnel manning anti-aircraft batteries to

North Vietnam (Whiting 1975). In one of the most thoughtful and thorough analyses of US policymaking in the Vietnam War applying both documentary analysis and process tracing, Yuen Foong Khong (1992) provides strong support for this chapter's proposition that Washington has been very cautious in avoiding putting itself in a potential conflict with China. Remembering their experience in Korea, top officials in the Johnson administration had consistently chosen military options that they knew to be less effective in coercing Hanoi but that were in their mind more prudent in reducing the risk of Beijing's intervention – even when their intelligence services were telling them that short of a direct US invasion of North Vietnam, this risk was low. Khong (1992: 116, 136) states that "the salience of this lesson [from the Korean War that the USA must avoid Chinese intervention] for [Dean] Rusk and the president [Lyndon B. Johnson] cannot be overemphasized," and that ". . . one of the things about which there is a strong consensus among Johnson's former military and civilian advisers is that this . . . lesson of Korea, the specter of Chinese intervention, constrained American strategy in Vietnam decisively."

As mentioned previously, US military intervention in Korea and Vietnam had the North Koreans and North Vietnamese forces respectively as its immediate target and not China. These cases are different from the other episodes in Table 4.1 for which the USSR/Russia or China was already directly involved. The two crises involving the offshore islands (Quemoy and Matsu) in the 1950s would be more comparable to a possible future military contingency in the Taiwan Strait – except that Beijing is in a much stronger military position today compared to those earlier times. The general conclusion I draw from Table 4.1 is that US leaders have been quite prudent in situations involving the possibility of military escalation with the USSR/Russia and China in the past. Although there is the danger of China and the United States clashing directly over Taiwan, evidence from the past suggests that this risk is not very high. Washington has thus far refrained from actions that could possibly put it in a direct collision course with Moscow or Beijing.

I mentioned earlier the ideas of equifinality and substitutability. It turns out that there are not enough cases and enough variations among the cases presented in Table 4.1, thus limiting what can be said about different paths leading to a US decision to intervene militarily against China or the USSR/Russia. The two cases of US intervention (in

Korea and Vietnam) display the same pattern of variables. The coding convention for Boolean analysis calls for using an upper-case letter to indicate the presence of a pertinent independent variable and a lower-case letter to indicate its absence. Thus, for the two instances of US military intervention in Korea and Vietnam, they share an identical combination of *aBcde* – indicating the presence of lopsided US military advantage but the absence of the other four factors. This combination can also be written as *~formal ally, lopsided military advantage, ~large security stake, ~large economic stake,* and *~strong domestic support* (with ~ indicating that the pertinent factor is absent). These expressions indicate that a lopsided military advantage is perhaps a necessary condition for Washington to decide in favor of intervention, whereas none of the remaining factors is necessary for this decision to occur. Put differently, lopsided US military advantage can override the influence from an absence of the other four variables which should restrain intervention. That the protégé in Korea and Vietnam was not a formal US ally or that these protégés did not engage vital US security or economic interests did not stop Washington from intervening. Nor was the absence of strong domestic voices demanding intervention.

If we turn our question from why the US intervened to a question about why it decided *not* to intervene, we can see three paths leading to this decision.

Nonintervention = ABcde (the two Offshore Island crises) + *aBCDE* (Cuba) + *abcde* (India, Georgia, and Ukraine)

When expressed in these terms, we see immediately a seeming paradox. In the two crises involving Quemoy and Matsu in 1954–1955 and again in 1958, the US held a decisive military advantage. Moreover, Taiwan was at that time a treaty ally of the United States. When juxtaposed against the result just reported above – namely, US intervention in Korea and Vietnam, even though these countries were not US allies at the time of Washington's decision to intervene – we naturally face a puzzle. Why did the USA not intervene in the two crises involving the offshore islands? Part of the answer is that the USA *was* involved in these latter cases, but its role did not escalate to the point of engaging in direct combat as in Korea and Vietnam. I have remarked earlier that Beijing decided to deescalate the conflict before these crises reached this point. Thus, it is possible – although we do not know for sure – that the USA would have become involved in a direct and active combat role should these crises continue to escalate. I have made a similar observation for the Cuban Missile Crisis in 1962. Washington had chosen to impose a naval blockade rather than launching a direct and surprise air assault on Soviet missiles on that island. Had Nikita Khrushchev not agreed to remove these missiles in exchange for Washington's promise to withdraw its missiles from Turkey and to not invade Cuba again, it is quite likely that the Kennedy administration would have ordered US forces to attack Cuba, thus putting US forces in a direct armed conflict with the Cubans and Soviets. As in the two cases of Quemoy and Matsu, the 1962 crisis did not reach this point, and a direct armed clash between the USA and USSR was averted. Of course, we can never be certain whether Washington would have intervened if these episodes had continued to escalate.

There is in my view a stronger explanation for the seemingly discrepant result mentioned in the above paragraph – specifically, why did the USA intervene in Korea and Vietnam but not in Quemoy and Matsu, even though it had a lopsided military advantage in all these four cases; and moreover, it should have a stronger reason to intervene in the latter two cases because, unlike Korea and Vietnam, Taiwan was at the time of these episodes a formal US ally. The main difference between these two sets of cases is that whereas in Korea and Vietnam US military intervention took on the North Korean and North Vietnamese Communists respectively, China was directly involved in the two episodes involving the Taiwan Strait. This fact made all the difference in my view. Beijing's role as a direct participant in the latter two episodes had a restraining effect on Washington, making it more cautious and limiting the extent of US participation in these cases.

The same argument can be applied to the 1962 Cuban case in which the USSR was directly involved. In this episode, a large US advantage in conventional military forces, a strong security and economic stake in Cuba's status, and strong domestic political support for decisive action were not in combination enough to persuade the Kennedy administration to launch a military assault – at least not as Washington's initial move in this crisis. In this view, the case of Cuba might have appeared to be anomalous at first glance. Even though most of the variables seem to have been aligned to encourage, or at least not to inhibit, US intervention, it did not happen. Of course, we do not know whether Washington would have used force if the USSR had not agreed to remove its missiles. It would also appear that had Beijing escalated the two cases involving Quemoy and Matsu to the point of attacking Taiwan itself (as opposed to these two offshore islands), Washington might also have intervened militarily. As mentioned already, we would never know for certain how these cases would have turned out if Moscow or Beijing had decided to act differently.

This last remark is important to keep in mind because war requires two actors to become entangled. Thus, to repeat the obvious, Moscow and Beijing had played a role in determining how the various episodes had turned out. This said, it is also important to acknowledge that Washington had also played its part in deescalating the Cuban Missile Crisis. It had agreed to exchange Soviet missiles in Cuba for US missiles in Turkey, and it had pledged never to invade Cuba again. Thus, although popular narratives in the US typically claim that the USSR "folded" under strong US pressure to dismantle its missiles in Cuba, they do not tell the full story also involving US concessions to bring about de-escalation.

Compared to Quemoy, Matsu, and Cuba, the other cases of US nonintervention are easy to explain. All these other cases showed a combination ~*US ally*, ~*US lopsided military advantage*, ~*a large US security* stake, ~*a large US economic stake*, and ~*strong domestic political support for military intervention*. Indeed, in the parlance of statistical analysis, the outcomes of these cases were "over-determined" – that is, even some lesser combination of these inhibiting factors would have probably sufficed to produce US nonintervention. In all these cases, US military involvement would put the USA on a collision course with the USSR/Russia or China, which was a direct party in these conflict situations. Thus, even if there were strong domestic support for Washington to get involved militarily, my intuition is that it would choose not to do so – at least not putting itself in a direct combat role.

As already mentioned earlier, prior to Russia's invasion of Ukraine in 2022, the Biden administration had signaled publicly that the option of putting "US boots on the ground" was "off the table." This most recent conflict should be more pertinent and analogous to a possible contingency in the Taiwan Strait, hinting that although Washington might give significant indirect aid to Taiwan in the form of supplying money and weapons, it would be reluctant to get directly involved in military combat on Taiwan's behalf. Another way to think about the possibility of a future US intervention in a situation involving Taiwan is to engage in a *Gedanken* experiment, asking what has changed or not changed in the years since the crises of the 1950s and even 1990s, and whether these developments would have made Washington more or less inclined to undertake direct, overt and large-scale military action in a war against China. If not in 1954–1955, not in 1958, and not in 1995–1996, what could make the USA become more acceptant of the costs and risks of an armed collision with China in 2025, 2030, or 2035?

Some additional comments are necessary to expand on the discussion in the previous paragraph. First, it is conceivable that we may encounter a future situation featuring *abCdE*, say, involving North Korea or Iran, backed respectively by Russia and China. Should Washington eschew direct military intervention in this hypothetical scenario, it would help us to understand how decisive a perceived large military stake (C) is in influencing its policy decision. Moreover, if Washington decides not to get itself directly involved in large-scale combat, this combination of factors would present another path to nonintervention. As already mentioned, multiple paths could lead to the same decision outcome. When these words were being written, the USA undertook retaliatory strikes against various Iran-backed militia groups in the Middle East in the wake of drone and missile attacks launched by Yemen's Houthis on shipping in the Red Sea. The USA has refrained from attacking targets inside Iran, and it has stated publicly and repeatedly that it does not wish to widen and escalate the conflict to involve Tehran. Significantly, neither Russian nor China was directly involved in this episode, but Washington still showed an abundance of caution.

Second, that the USA intervened militarily on behalf of the two non-allies in Korea and Vietnam suggests that as already mentioned, being an ally is not a necessary condition for the USA to intervene militarily in foreign war. This observation can be stated even more strongly by advancing the proposition that a formal alliance relationship with Washington is in fact *irrelevant* for this consideration. The Boolean analysis implies this conclusion. A moment's reflection suggests the plausibility of this claim. After all, Israel does not have a formal alliance relationship with the USA, which has provided Tel Aviv with massive aid – albeit not assisting it in direct combat which Israel had not needed or requested thus far in its various military conflicts with its Arab neighbors. Naturally, the popular topic discussing whether

Washington would come to Taiwan's defense acknowledges implicitly that the lack of a formal security treaty in this case does not rule out the possibility of US military intervention.

Moreover, further reflection suggests other factors should be considered in interpreting the contents of Table 4.1. As mentioned earlier, the initial criterion for selecting those cases included in this table was conflict situations involving either the USSR/Russia or China. However, notwithstanding this common feature, important differences also separate these cases. Although I mentioned earlier the literature on extended deterrence, this concept is not, strictly speaking, applicable to all cases other than the two crises involving the offshore islands in the Taiwan Strait – and one can even quibble about the latter two cases because the USA had deliberately excluded Quemoy and Matsu from its defense treaty with Taiwan. Similarly, the USA had not pledged to defend adversaries of the USSR/Russia and China in the other conflict episodes – at least not threatening to undertake direct military intervention – in its attempt to deter an attack by Moscow or Beijing on them, such as those cases involving Hungary, Georgia, and India in Table 4.1. Indeed, armed hostilities had already broken out in these cases prior to Washington coming to a choice opportunity on whether to intervene militarily. Therefore, these other cases were not instances of Washington's failed attempts at extended deterrence, and strictly speaking, not even the two crises involving Quemoy and Matsu because they were not covered by Washington's defense treaty with Taipei.

In the case of Cuba, compellence would be a more accurate description than deterrence. In the missile crisis of 1962, Washington had insisted that Kremlin remove its missiles already in Cuba, a demand for the other side to change its ongoing behavior as opposed to preventing it from undertaking some unwanted behavior before it has begun to do so. We typically use compellence to characterize the former situation and deterrence for the latter situation. Prior to the missile crisis, the USA had sought to overthrow Fidel Castro's government such as in the Bay of Pigs episode in 1961. In this situation again, US action was not motivated by a desire to defend a protégé or ally from an attack from a third party. It was not a case of extended deterrence. Nor were some of the other cases included in Table 4.1 such as the Sino-Indian border conflict in 1962, the Soviet suppression of the Hungarian Uprising in 1956, and Russia's war against Georgia in 2008. Moreover, by excluding the involvement of US troops in the Russo-Ukrainian conflict, one can debate how seriously Washington had undertaken extended deterrence in this case.

A moment's reflection suggests that Washington's role in the case of Cuba in 1961–1962 would be comparable to Beijing's role today vis-à-vis Taiwan, seeking to prevent an extra-regional power to support an "errant" neighbor in its backyard. The USA would be playing, in Taiwan's case, the role of the USSR in the Cuban case – that is, acting in a situation of extended deterrence to prevent a protégé from being attacked by another major power. One may engage in an analysis similar to the one undertaken in this chapter to discern under what circumstances Beijing would choose to select itself into a direct military confrontation against Washington.

Finally, it bears repeating that in the two instances of US military intervention in Korea and Vietnam, these were also not instances of failed extended deterrence. These cases came closer to examples of compellence: to repel the North Korean forces and subsequently to unify Korea under the control of a pro-Western regime, and to compel Hanoi to cease its support of the communist guerrilla forces (the National Liberation Front) fighting against the Saigon government in South Vietnam. Neither the South Korean nor the South Vietnamese government on whose behalf Washington intervened was a formal US ally. In these two episodes of direct and massive US involvement actual large-scale combat support for Seoul and Pyongyang occurred after the fighting had already started and as pointed out earlier, the immediate target of US military intervention was the North Koreans and the National Liberation Front (and subsequently the North Vietnamese) – and not Beijing. In reviewing the cases included in Table 4.1, this last observation stands out as perhaps the most important takeaway – Washington's military intervention occurred in these two cases and not the other cases because it was not intervening directly against Moscow or Beijing.

Reflecting further on these past episodes of US intervention and nonintervention, one conclusion emerges. Washington, as I have said before, has been quite prudent in avoiding situations that would or could put it directly on a collision course with the USSR/Russia or China. My review of these cases suggests that the most plausible case for US escalation against either one of these two countries would be in the Cuban Missile Crisis of 1962 – if Khrushchev had decided not to remove the Soviet missiles that had been installed in Cuba. In this case again, Cuba was not a formal ally (and therefore this case would not be an instance of Washington coming to an ally's assistance), and the USA was engaging in compellence rather than deterrence. The "stars were aligned" for the USA to undertake decisive military action in this case, because it not only commanded a large military advantage in conventional forces, but the Kennedy administration also felt that it had a large political, security, and economic stake in Cuba and strong domestic support to act decisively.

The reader may recall that the purpose of this analysis is to discern the prospect of a US military intervention in a future contingency involving Taiwan's status. Given the caveats and qualifications discussed thus far, it appears that the most comparable cases from the past would be the two episodes involving the two offshore islands. In these two instances, tension dissipated after Beijing refrained from military escalation, when it in fact reduced and then stopped its bombardment of Quemoy and Matsu. But there are also important differences between these cases from the 1950s and now. At that time, Taiwan was a formal ally that had signed a defense pact with the United States. Moreover, Beijing was in a much weaker military position at that time than now. More recent episodes involving Moscow in its war against Georgia and Ukraine suggest that Washington was not interested in putting itself in a direct military confrontation with Russia that had become much weaker than its heydays during the Cold War.

Since the outbreak of the Russo-Ukrainian War in 2022, there has also been a surge in popular, journalistic, and academic attention to and concern about possible parallels between that conflict and a possible war over Taiwan – but less awareness about important differences between these two cases (e.g., Chan 2022; Chan and Hu 2024, 2025b). The pertinent differences include their geographic location with Ukraine having land borders with sympathetic neighbors, whereas Taiwan is an island, thus making it more challenging for an outsider to supply assistance to it. Other obvious differences include considerations such as China has much deeper economic relations with other countries than Russia (therefore making it much more difficult and costly for the USA and Western European countries to sanction it than Russia), a much larger economy than Russia, and moreover, there is obviously no NATO (a multilateral military alliance) in Asia. Finally, although not mentioned frequently in popular narratives, an overwhelming majority of states in the world do not recognize Taiwan as a sovereign state and instead acknowledge it to be part of China, including Washington in its formal agreements signed with Beijing. Taiwan's status is considered by them to be a matter of China's internal affairs. This statement obviously does not apply to Russia's invasion of Ukraine, an independent, sovereign country recognized by the rest of the world

The Russo-Ukrainian War implies strongly that a direct military intervention by Washington is less likely in a contingency involving Taiwan than popularly believed. The reader need not, however, agree with this conclusion. She can alter my coding in Table 4.1 to decide for herself what changes would have to occur to alter Washington's calculus to intervene on Taiwan's behalf. In addition to undertaking such *Gedanken* experiment by asking "what if" questions, she can add other variables to Table 4.1 that might be pertinent to Washington's decision to discern their likely impact, if any, on this decision.

Concluding Reflections

A possible US military intervention in a contingency involving Taiwan will of course constitute a punctuation of the current state of relations between Beijing and Washington. If this happens, it will undoubtedly reset this relationship for the next few decades, if not longer. The preceding discussion suggests that Washington has been prudent in avoiding the danger of a direct military encounter with Moscow or Beijing in the past. This history would suggest that this danger is not very high – although obviously, we cannot rule it out. Some changes have occurred since the time of the two crises involving the offshore islands and even the 1995–1996 Taiwan episode. For instance, domestic politics seems to be playing a larger role in the formulation and conduct of foreign policy in both Beijing and Washington. Despite popular suggestions that Xi Jinping has consolidated and elevated his power in China, my sense is that leaders in both countries appear to face more domestic constraints and less policy space to maneuver than at the time of the earlier cases – or when Mao Zedong decided to intervene in the Korean War and Richard Nixon decided to visit Beijing (which would also require Mao's support and approval). Moreover, I have suggested earlier that Beijing took steps to deescalate tension in the previous cases involving the offshore islands, thus pulling back from confronting the USA. If so, one would naturally be inclined to ask why would it want to challenge the status quo again? That is, why would it want to start another crisis in view of its previous setback? One plausible answer would be that should Beijing initiate another confrontation in the Taiwan Strait, this would mean that it has become more resolved to have its way this next time, or that it would have reason to be more optimistic in succeeding in its gambit this next time. That is, each failure to change the status quo in its favor on prior occasions should make Beijing more reluctant to start another round of confrontation. However, if it does decide to do so, this action would imply that in its belief the outcome would be more positive for it the next time.

In many situations in life, multiple causes or multiple paths can produce the same outcome. I have cited earlier the example of a student's poor academic performance due to any combination of factors such as a dysfunctional family environment, disadvantageous socioeconomic circumstances, personal disabilities, poor school facilities, and unmotivated teachers. Similarly, a person's risk of suffering a heart attack can be due to the interactions of several factors such as obesity, lack of exercise, unhealthy habits (e.g., smoking), and genetic inheritance. In their study of the potential for interstate militarized disputes to escalate, Paul Senese and John Vasquez (2008: 197) reported that when two states quarrel over contested territory, they have 0.165 chance of going to war in the next five years. When these states have alliances with other countries, the danger of a war between them in the next five years jumps to 0.486. Add to this mix the fact that these countries have had recurrent confrontations in the past, the danger of war rises even more to 0.692. Finally, if there is an arms race between them in addition to the other factors just mentioned, the odds of war breaking out between them is 0.921; in other words, more than nine out of ten times. This example illustrates nicely the compounding effects of the pertinent variables. Their joint effect is greater than the sum of each individual factor.

Boolean analysis also applies the conjunctive logic to study which combination(s) of factors can produce the occurrence – or nonoccurrence – of an outcome, in this case, US military intervention that would put it potentially in a direct confrontation with Moscow or Beijing. The logic for Boolean analysis accepts equifinality, that is, the idea that different combinations or paths can lead to the same outcome.

Therefore, that one causal chain has produced a certain outcome in the past does not rule out the possibility of other such chains producing the same outcome. In the cases included in this chapter's analysis, different combinations have accounted for the same outcome of Washington deciding *not* to intervene. This analysis points to the conclusion that the main tendency of past US decisions has been nonintervention in situations suggesting the potential danger of a direct collision with the USSR/Russia or China. In the two crises involving Quemoy and Matsu in 1954–1955 and 1958, the USA avoided direct actions against Chinese forces, choosing to provide indirect support to its ally, Taiwan. In the two cases of the USA taking on a direct and large combat role, the immediate targets were the North Koreans and North Vietnamese. One of the advantages of the Boolean analysis is that if a reader disagrees with my coding of any independent variable, she can easily alter it and determine for herself whether and how the result of any analysis may be changed.

The Boolean approach is not, however, without its limitations or weaknesses. It assigns the same weight to all cases. Thus, a minor episode is given as much analytic importance as a major episode. Moreover, just one or two deviant or exceptional cases can alter the observed patterns significantly, thus affecting the conclusions that analysts would draw from their study. Finally, the Boolean analysis is insensitive to the relative frequency of cases supporting the various patterns observed. In the analysis reported earlier, a combination of factors shown by just one case (that of Cuba: *aBCDE*) can assume as much importance as another combination that characterizes more cases (e.g., *abcde* for India, Georgia, and Ukraine). Finally, this type of analysis does not provide estimates of statistical significance. Furthermore, it can become rather unwieldy when a study has to attend to many cases. Conversely, when the number of cases is too small, as in the preceding analysis, there may not be enough variations in the data for us to establish the robustness of the observed patterns or to really go after interesting questions such as substitutability and equifinality.

The preceding analysis also shows that first, being a formal US ally is *not* a necessary condition for US military intervention on behalf of a protégé. In the two cases of US direct intervention included in Table 4.1, neither South Korea nor South Vietnam had signed a security treaty with the USA for Washington's military protection. The causal arrow points in the reverse direction, that is, Washington entered into a formal defense arrangement with Seoul only *after* its military intervention, and even after the USA took up the role of direct combat in South Vietnam, that country did not become a formal member of the Southeast Asian Treaty Organization (SEATO) although it was extended military protection by a SEATO protocol. The matter of alliance status is of course pertinent to the prospect of US military intervention on Taiwan's behalf, because Washington had unilaterally abrogated its defense treaty with Taipei even though US Congress had (unilaterally) passed the Taiwan Relations Act, which as a piece of domestic legislation, and not a foreign treaty entailing international legal obligation, does not necessarily commit Washington to Taiwan's defense.

Second, the matter of alliance relationship is also pertinent to the ongoing Russo-Ukrainian War. The proximate cause of this war from Moscow's perspective is of course Kyiv's reorientation toward the West, or more specifically, NATO's open invitation to it and Georgia to join this organization (McFaul et al. 2014). Russian President Vladimir Putin had angrily denounced NATO's expansion right up to his country's border, proclaiming, "We view appearance of a powerful military bloc on our borders ... as a direct threat to the security of our country. The claim that this process is not directed against Russia will not suffice. National security is not based on promises" (quoted in Toal 2017: 125). Thus, alliance membership would represent at least in the minds of Russian leaders one of the important causes of the current war. It is ironic that US Vice President J. D. Vance has recently (February 14, 2025) stated publicly in a meeting with European allies that NATO membership is unlikely for Ukraine, nor is it likely that Kyiv will be able to recover all its territories lost to Russia.

Third, what may be relevant may become irrelevant (or vice versa) when a factor is in the presence or absence of another factor, that is, when it interacts with another factor. Thus, regarding the US resort to force abroad in general, whether a situation impinges on vital US security or economic interest and/or whether there is strong domestic support may be secondary concerns and even irrelevant in situations when the danger of Soviet/Russian or Chinese involvement is small. Washington's use of military force against Grenada, Nicaragua, and Panama are examples that come to mind representing such situations. Another way of stating this proposition would be to argue that the identity of potential US adversary is the master variable. If this adversary is the USSR/Russia or China, it can trump other considerations in its importance in US policymaking on whether to intervene militarily abroad. In other words, a direct armed conflict with Moscow or Beijing would be in a different league or kind of encounter, distinguishing it from the "round of mill" cases involving minor states.

Fourth, although we do not encounter clear examples of substitutability in the cases studied in this chapter, other plausible situations may help us to illuminate its presence or absence. When Saddam Hussein invaded Kuwait in 1990, one might plausibly argue that the USA had a vital economic interest to protect due to the prospect of Baghdad coming to control a large portion of the world's oil reserve. Washington used force in this case to evict Iraqi forces from Kuwait, even though Iraq did not pose a serious security threat to the USA – notwithstanding Washington's public rhetoric claiming that Iraq had weapons of mass destruction and ties to Al Qaeda. Imagine a situation involving North Korea whereby important US security, but not economic, interests were engaged. Would Washington use force against Pyongyang? In other words, would its security and economic stakes be substitutable – or in this comparison the key difference would have to do with China's close ties with Pyongyang whereas Saddam Hussein's Baghdad lacked a powerful foreign ally or patron?

Moreover, having a large security and economic stake in a protégé's survival was not a necessary condition at least at the time of Washington's intervention in Korea and Vietnam. This consideration, however, was more than likely offset by the vast military advantage it enjoyed over its immediate adversaries in these two cases. When matched against another nuclear-armed country in the Cuban Missile Crisis in 1962, the Kennedy administration chose a more cautious course of action by relying on a naval blockade rather than opting for a surprise air attack on Soviet missiles. This experience is instructive because of the prudence shown by Washington even in a location where it enjoined a decisive advantage in conventional forces, when it had strong domestic support to take decisive action, and when the security and economic stakes were greater for it than the other episodes examined here. This case in turn suggests an important difference between prior cases involving Taiwan in the 1950s and even the 1990s because Beijing has improved its military position relative to the USA considerably in the intervening years, a factor that should diminish Washington's enthusiasm to engage China militarily on Taiwan's behalf.

Indeed, regarding the last point just made on the shifting balance of military capabilities, Fareed Zakaria (2020: 68) notes "The Pentagon has reportedly enacted 18 war games against China over Taiwan, and China has prevailed in every one." Richard Bernstein (2020), Jean-Pierre Cabestan (2024: 83–86), and Bonnie Glaser (2020) have made similar observations. Beijing controls the timing of the next episode it initiates, and it is favored by geographic proximity to Taiwan, although the USA does have military bases and personnel stationed in Japan and South Korea.

Finally, the USA has of course taken military action abroad on many occasions, but they do not always involve extended deterrence. It is sometimes even difficult to describe these actions exactly even as instances of compellence such as in its invasion of Grenada, Panama, and Afghanistan. Washington ended some of its military involvements abroad without accomplishing what it sought initially to accomplish. One reason was the turning tide of public opinion at home. As a conflict becomes protracted and casualties begin to mount, the American people are likely to turn negative on the war. Thus, even though there might have been a situation pointing to the syndrome of rallying around the flag at the start of US involvement abroad, support for it could decline precipitously, causing Washington to reverse its intervention quickly in some cases such as in Somalia after the downing of a Blackhawk in 1993 and in Lebanon after the bombing of the marine barracks in 1983. In other cases, such as Vietnam, Iraq, and Afghanistan, it took much longer for Washington to extricate itself. The main takeaway of this discussion, however, is that officials are forward-looking and try to anticipate the future. If they can foresee a protracted conflict abroad and declining domestic support for this conflict, they would be less inclined to enter into such a situation in the first place. Of course, a fight with Moscow or Beijing would be a nasty, prolonged, and costly affair in contrast to even Washington's experience in Vietnam and Afghanistan.

The relevance of these remarks for a potential conflict over the Taiwan Strait points to time as a consideration. Such a conflict is unlikely to be resolved quickly and conclusively – even if the USA manages to prevail militarily. An analogy from the Falklands/ Malvinas comes to mind. Even though Britain had won the battle against Argentina to retake these barren, distant islands, how long would London be willing to bear the costs of defending them? The Falklands/Malvinas episode offers another important lesson. As observed earlier, Margaret Thatcher's decision to retake these islands from Argentina was motivated primarily by domestic considerations and not due to their strategic or economic importance (Lebow 1985).

Singapore's former Prime Minister Lee Kuan Yew was once asked whether the United States would intervene militarily on Taiwan's behalf in a crisis involving China. His answer was quick and to the point. He said "no." His reason? The USA might prevail the first time. But what about the next time, the time after that, and then an even later one (Singapore Now 2011)?

Put simply, there is a basic asymmetry in Beijing and Washington's stake in Taiwan's status. In a more recent rendition of Charles de Gaulle's remark seeking to justify France's independent force de frappe introduced earlier, Cabestan (2024: 91) quotes a Chinese general saying, "you [the United States] care more about Los Angeles than Taiwan!"

China is more committed to its cause, and it will be willing to play the long game while the USA is more likely to become impatient, distracted, or disillusioned. It can always "go home," whereas Taiwan, like the Falklands/Malvinas, will be "stuck with" its larger, more powerful neighbor. In terms of policy attention which, as remarked on several occasions already, is always in short supply, Washington has many items on its agenda, whereas Beijing's focus is on its immediate neighborhood and Taiwan is its top priority. In their classic work on complex interdependence, Robert Keohane and Joseph Nye (1977: 207–208) point to asymmetry in Australia and Canada's relative cohesion and attention in explaining why these countries managed to obtain more favorable outcomes in their respective disputes with the United States than one would have expected from the asymmetry in these countries' relative power in these words:

Governmental cohesion is important in determining [dispute] outcomes, and in general, the United States was less cohesive than Canada and Australia. In part this lack of cohesion is a function of sheer size and of presidential as contrasted with parliamentary government, but it is also a function of asymmetry of attention. The United States government does not focus on Canada and Australia the way that Canada, or even Australia, focuses on the United States. Greater cohesion and concentration helps to redress the disadvantage in size.

Taiwan occupies an unenviable position, like Ukraine, as a proxy, or the Chinese would call it, a pawn, in US grand strategy. Washington had pretty much decided to wash its hands of Chiang Kai-shek's regime in the late 1940s until the Korean War broke out, and it had "de-recognized" Taipei in favor of Beijing and abrogated its defense treaty with Taiwan in 1979. Not to put too fine a point on it, Taiwan has been "abandoned" by the United States on prior occasions. Taiwan's leaders do not have a short memory, nor are they unaware of how the US intervention in Vietnam and Afghanistan had turned out. The Taiwanese are also not unfamiliar with the saying, "fool me once shame on you, fool me twice shame on me." They understand that their importance to Washington is derivative of Beijing's importance to Washington. Put bluntly, when push comes to shove, they are of secondary importance to the United States which cares more about its relations with Beijing than its ties with Taipei. As these words were being written, funding for US assistance to Ukraine was in limbo because Congress had rejected a bipartisan bill linking legislation on US border security to this appropriation. James Fearon (1994, 1995) has written extensively about distinguishing between credible commitment on the one hand and "hot air" and "empty talk" on the other. US congressional action – or rather, inaction – indicates the legislators' political priorities.

This said, domestic considerations could also play a part in encouraging US military intervention abroad. Public and elite opinion after the September 11 terrorist attack had a large influence on George W. Bush's decision to invade Iraq. It increased domestic support for this intervention (the rally-around-the-flag syndrome), enabling this US president to capitalize on surging patriotism to carry out a course of action that he and his entourage were already inclined to undertake (Birkland 2004; Kaufman 2004; Mazarr 2007; Mearsheimer and Walt 2003).

5 | War, Uneven Economic Growth, and Trees Don't Grow to the Sky

Changes in international relations reflect several stylized facts. "In social sciences, especially economics, a stylized fact is a simplified presentation of an empirical finding. Stylized facts are broad tendencies that aim to summarize the data, offering essential truths while ignoring individual details" (Wikipedia 2025). Stylized facts therefore refer to general patterns based on empirical evidence, such as statements like "education contributes to a person's income," "smoking causes cancer," or in international relations, "democracies do not fight each other" and "boundary disputes produce militarized disputes." Of course, there can be relatively rare, isolated, or borderline cases that contradict these statements. Some individuals with a high level of education have low income, and some smokers never develop cancer. These cases, however, do not invalidate the basic truths articulated by stylized facts which refer to the central tendencies of empirical phenomena.

China's economic growth in recent decades has shaken international relations or more specifically, the distribution of power among members of a small elite group of great powers. Power shifts among these countries affect the prospects of war and peace, and they are derivative of the relative economic performance of this handful of leading states. Put in another way, different rates of economic growth are responsible for interstate power shifts, which in turn have a profound influence on the stability or instability of the international system (e.g., Gilpin 1981, 1987; Organski and Kugler 1980; Rasler and Thompson 1985, 1991; Thompson 1983). Changing power distribution augurs an elevated danger of war also according to Graham Allison's (2015, 2017) formulation of Thucydides' Trap. Economic growth is influenced by a country's capacity to invent and innovate and its ability to pioneer leading industries that pull the rest of its economy along and confer upon it a competitive edge to advance and secure its global standing. In the views of those authors just cited, this

150

standing and the security implications that stem from it are the main reason motivating states to go to war, and war in turn introduces a new interstate hierarchy and order in its wake.

Except for the specific reference to China's economic growth in the preceding paragraph, the other statements represent stylized facts that most scholars of international relations would concur. These other observations pertain to the states' uneven rates of economic growth, the effect of this unevenness on the interstate pecking order, the role of inventions and innovations in spurring economic growth, and the putative causes and consequences of war. Significantly, all these phenomena are characterized by punctuated equilibrium in one way or another. Terms such as phases, stages, or cycles are often used to describe the relevant processes. Moreover, countries go through protracted periods of economic stagnation or slow growth, but they also sometimes experience growth spurts that enable them to reach a new plateau of economic production. We call this phenomenon industrialization or modernization. Their processes resemble punctuated equilibrium whose characteristics should by now be familiar to the readers. This chapter applies the perspective of punctuated equilibrium to illuminate them. Britain became the leading industrial power because of a fortuitous confluence of factors; it was able to successfully harness a cheap and reliable source of energy (namely, coal) to power new technological innovations (particularly the steam engine), a *combination* that launched the industrial revolution. The readers will also hear about the role played by a shock or jolt to present a challenge or opportunity to initiate a country's economic take-off. This stimulus or catalyst presents the functional equivalent of a focusing event or choice opportunity that mobilizes public opinion and engages the policy elite's attention to take action. The readers may recall the role played by the accidents at Three Mile Island and Chernobyl in energizing the movement against nuclear plants to provide electric power and the discovery of a hole in the earth's ozone in mobilizing collective efforts to curtail the emission of greenhouse gases.

The history of inventions and innovations shows a protracted period of gestation during which improvisation, experimentation, and "fiddling" on shop floors and in garages take place. This period is followed initially by a gradual and halting introduction of new techniques and technology (such as the steam engine and cotton gin) to production processes. Diffusion of this knowledge then picks up speed with widespread adoption, scaling up to mass production, and the creation of new leading industries (such as in successive waves of industrial or technological development led by textiles, then steel and railways, industrial chemicals and electrification, automobiles, electronics and semiconductors, and most recently, robotics, bioengineering, electric vehicles, and artificial intelligence) (Modelski and Thompson 1996; Mokyr 1990; Rasler and Thompson 1985, 1991; Thompson 1983, 1990, 2020, 2022). The relevant processes typically involve a long period of seeming stasis or stagnation, then a slow initial start, then a sudden burst, and finally leveling off at a new plateau until the next round started by a renewed cycle repeating the same steps. The general pattern of economic growth just described follows an S-curve (Organski 1968: 341) – depicting a slow start, a rapid take-off, and a new "normal." Indeed, in his well-known book on stages of economic development, Walt Rostow ([1960] 1971) describes industrialization in general as a process following this S-curve. The metaphor of take-off conjures up images of a long runway, gathering momentum, a steep ascent, and eventually gaining cruising speed at a high altitude – until deceleration prior to landing an aircraft and its coming to a stop. This analogy is inexact but the general ideas behind it should be easy to grasp.

Rostow's *Stages of Economic Growth*

Published originally in 1960, Rostow's book, *The Stages of Economic Growth*, predated the advent of punctuated equilibrium popularized by Niles Eldredge and Stephen Gould in the early 1970s. Rostow's analysis, however, foreshadowed independently the many hallmarks of punctuated equilibrium introduced by these paleontologists and addressed in the research on public policymaking by Frank Baumgartner and Bryan Jones and others reviewed earlier. The very idea of stages-of-growth suggests periodicity in the history of economic development – a feature also shared by various schools of international relations scholarship cited earlier, such as those stressing the cyclical nature of or transitional frictions in these relations (e.g., studies by Modelski and Thompson on long cycles, Doran's power cycle theory, and works on interstate power transitions by Gilpin, Organski, and Kugler, and most recently, Allison). Implicitly or explicitly, all these studies of biological evolution, economic history, public policymaking, and war and peace in international relations refer to recurrent patterns characterized by lulls and lurches, or in other words, alternating phases of quiescence and hyperactivity, calm and turmoil, seeming stagnation and sharp breakthrough.

Rostow describes the history of economic development in terms of five major stages: a protracted period of stagnation, a period when the preconditions of economic development are instituted, a period of rapid growth indicating economic take-off, a period representing transition to economic maturity, and finally the arrival of the age of affluence when the economy turns to satisfying high mass consumption. He locates various countries (e.g., Britain, France, Germany, the USA, Canada, Argentina, India, China, and Turkey) at different points or stages in this general model of economic development. Words such as gestation, shocks, breakthrough, surges, discontinuity, "a critical level," transformation in "kind [rather] than merely in degree," and overreaction (such as in "overdone" in investment or "over-reach" in production) are sprinkled throughout his discussion (e.g., Rostow [1960] 1971: 40, 62, 80). He uses "compound interest" to describe the geometric progression of economic growth propelled and characterized by successive waves of leading sectors (Rostow [1960] 1971: 14, 18). He explains why Britain was the first country to launch industrialization in a language that corresponds nicely with the ideas of conjunctive causes and serendipitous timing emphasized earlier in the discussion of the "garbage can" model of policymaking.

"[The] *combination* of necessary and sufficient conditions for take-off in Britain was the result of the *convergence* of a number of quite *independent* circumstances, a kind of statistical *accident* of history..." (Rostow [1960] 1971: 31; my italics). Timing was important in the (accidental) convergence of two major historical occurrences: the discovery or rediscovery of regions beyond Western Europe, and the advent of and subsequent acceleration in the development of modern scientific knowledge and attitudes. Compared to other countries, Britain was more successful in seizing the opportunities created by these macro-conditions. "... Britain alone was in a position to *weave together* cotton manufacture, coal and iron technology, the steam-engine, and ample foreign trade to pull it [industrialization] off" (Rostow [1960] 1971: 33, my italic). Successful economic take-off came about not because of any single factor; it was rather the result of a combination of factors that gave Britain an edge over other countries such as the Netherlands and France. An important part of this "pulling off" was due to its ability to harness a cheap and reliable source of energy (coal) to power new production processes introduced by inventions and innovations (Thompson and Zakhirova 2019). The integration of these two factors enabled Britain to establish the leading sectors of its day (initially the textile industry, and subsequently railroads and steel). As Modelski (1987a, 1987b) and Modelski and Thompson (1996) have pointed out, Britain managed to "pull it off" not once but twice, as it had two growth spurts with the second one enabling it to maintain its top-dog status in international political economy until about the last two or three decades of the nineteenth century.

Furthermore, Rostow points to the effects of catalysts, shocks, and interventions introduced by history such as the US Civil War, the Great Depression, and the two world wars. These events caused shortages, inflation, surging or plunging exports, massive lay off or full employment, a precipitous fall in consumption or alternatively, pent-up demand, all of which have an impact on a country's economic performance. They presented challenges or opportunities, sometimes critical junctures, affecting the course of its economic and even political history. The Great Depression's effects on the downfall of Germany's Weimar Republic and the rise of the Nazi Party, and the role played by pent-up demand in stimulating the US economic boom after World War II come to mind as examples. In Rostow's ([1960] 1971: 36) view:

The beginning of take-off can usually be traced to a particular sharp stimulus. The stimulus may take the form of a political revolution which affects directly the balance of social power and effective values, the character of economic institutions, the distribution of income, the pattern of investment outlays and the proportion of innovations applied.

The arrival of Commodore Matthew Perry's "black ships" in Edo Bay in 1853 was such a stimulus or catalyst, setting off a cascade of events including the collapse of Japan's ruling Tokugawa Shogunate, the Meiji Restoration, and this country's impressive efforts to achieve national rejuvenation and rapid industrialization. Of course, a country may also fail to seize a fleeting opportunity. Prime Minister Robert Salisbury lamented Britain's missed opportunity to check a rising US behemoth in these words:

It is very sad, but I am afraid America is bound to forge ahead and nothing can restore the equality between us. If we had interfered in the Confederate Wars [on behalf on the South] it was then possible for us to reduce the power of the United States to manageable proportions. But two such chances are not given to a nation in the course of its career. (quoted in MacMillan 2013: 38)

Here I interject that Ned Lebow (1984) questions the very idea of "window of opportunity," arguing that states often do not jump through them. For example, Germany could have but did not start World War I at an earlier and more propitious time when it was stronger rather than going to war in August 1914. Moreover, Lebow (2000/2001) claims that World War I could very well have been avoided if the catalyst provided by Sarajevo (where the assassination of Austria-Hungary's heir apparent, Archduke Ferdinand and his wife, occurred) were delayed for just three years. In his view, by 1917 the window for war would have become shut. I mention Lebow's argument to point to historical contingency, that is, to underscore the importance of chance or fortuitous timing that is an important part of the "garbage can" model of policymaking. Of course, shocks or focusing events also have a prominent analytic place in Baumgartner and Jones' explanation of the genesis of policy punctuations or disruptions.

Rostow ([1960] 1971: 95) also argues that Russia's take-off had already started in the 1890s, and the Bolshevik Revolution occurred toward the tail end of this country's vulnerability to political upheaval, thus again suggesting the importance of timing and the possibility that this country's economic and political history could have taken a very different turn. Indeed, that the Bolshevik Revolution happened in Russia rather than in Germany where industrialization had advanced further and where the proletariat was stronger would appear to be a historical accident from the perspective of Marxist orthodoxy.

We can also discern the idea of path dependency in Rostow's discussion. History sometimes presents opportunities to reset a policy or to launch a new initiative. Decisions taken – or not taken – on these occasions indicate major forks or turning points marking sometimes missed opportunities or if a particular path is taken, the opening of new frontiers and horizons while at the same time foreclosing other possibilities. Certain subsequent policies become more feasible or attractive, while others become less so. Warner Schilling (1973) wrote some time ago about a critical juncture in the history of the hydrogen bomb. His study shows bureaucratic maneuvering among various agencies inside the US government to define the issue, set the agenda, and include or exclude specific actors in the formulation of a recommendation to President Harry Truman about what the USA should do with the hydrogen bomb – common features that we have encountered previously in discussing public policymaking. Schilling's case study indicates that inaction, impasse, or bureaucratic compromises based on the "least common denominator" can be consequential, producing a situation of "deciding without choosing."

Returning to the history of economic development, for a variety of reasons the automobile industry became the leading sector for the US economy after World War II, and this development in turn led to other ancillary phenomena, such as the construction of a national system of highways, the creation of suburbia, and the expansion of petroleum industry – and a reliance on fossil fuel, making it more difficult for us today to wean ourselves from this dependency and switch to alternative sources of energy. Other examples of path dependency come to mind, such as Russia's Bolshevik Revolution on that country's political economy and the spread of communism internationally, World War II's adverse impact on the European countries' economies and their relative decline, and concomitantly this conflict's positive impact on the United States in enabling it to pull further ahead of the European countries.

It is possible ... that British nationalism, transcending caste loyalties, created by a series of intrusions and challenges to a lesser island off a dominant mainland, may have been a major force in creating a relatively flexible social matrix within which the process of building the preconditions for take-off was hastened in Britain... (Rostow [1960] 1971: 35)

Thus, the accident of geographic location can also play a role in economic development. Moreover, the above quotation from Rostow points to the role of nationalism in motivating economic development – a rare observation for economists to make. "Reactive nationalism" – stemming from the indignities and injustices that a country has suffered at the hands of foreigners – is a powerful force energizing its people's commitment and dedication to modernize their country. This phenomenon has characterized the drive to undertake sociopolitical reforms and to industrialize on the part of countries such as Turkey, Japan,

China, India, and Iran – all proud countries that had achieved greatness in their past. Its "century of national humiliation" and the injunction to "never forget national humiliation" motivated and still motivates China's drive to modernize itself (Wang 2014).

Rostow chides Marxists for their caricature of people as economic animals caring only about the profit motive, thus overlooking other incentives that influence their behavior. Intangibles, including emotions such as anger, pride, and perceptions of relative deprivation (Gurr 1970), gratuitous insults, and deliberate slights, are also important sources of national and individual behavior that Marxism's materialist emphasis fails to account for, except perhaps to dismiss them as false consciousness. One would not want to minimize the importance of "chip on the shoulder" as a strong motivation to strive for economic or other kinds of achievement (Chan 2024b). I will return later to argue that states compete and fight for not just power or even security; they also struggle or strive for intangibles such as *gloire*, recognition, and status (e.g., Larson and Shevchenko 2010, 2019; Lebow 2010; Murray 2010, 2019; Pu 2019; Renshon 2016, 2017; Ward 2017; Wolf 2014).

There is another part of Rostow's analysis that is insightful, namely, the intimate relationship between economic development and national security. It is perhaps difficult for some Western Europeans and Americans to imagine that economic development is about more than the provision of plenty to consumers. At the receiving end of historical injustices, people in the Global South do not share this view. Quite literally, economic development for the Chinese and Japanese was about national survival, an imperative lest they suffer the same fate that had befallen on other peoples who had been conquered and subjugated by Western colonists and imperialists and had thus lost their nationhood. It is not an accident that the Chinese and the Japanese, unlike people in many other countries today, continue to speak Chinese and Japanese – rather than English, French, Spanish, or Portuguese.

Economics is not just about meeting consumer needs; it is far more important than that. During the 1960s, South Korea's drive to industrialize also reflected this priority subordinating economics to the need of national security. In this respect, Rostow's analysis of Germany, Japan, and Russia/the USSR's ostensible expansionist policies does not quite capture their respective vulnerability as latecomers in a world where those countries that had arrived earlier had set up rules of the game to the relative disadvantage of the latecomers. It was Germany and Japan's misfortune that when they arrived on the scene, the world had been pretty much picked clean – that the early arrivers had already cornered much of the world as their colonies, overseas markets, and sources of raw resources. As the first communist country, Russia also faced encirclement and was besieged by foreign powers in its civil war between the Reds and Whites. Foreign military intervention also happened to China with the USA assisting the Kuomintang in its civil war against the Communists. What goes around sometimes comes around.

We may disagree with any of Rostow's many historical interpretations, but the analytic insights behind many of his substantive propositions remain invaluable. Finally, predating most international relations scholarship that makes a similar point subsequently, Rostow ([1960] 1971: 116) argues that differences in various states' timing in reaching the stages of their respective economic development plays an important part in the outbreak of major wars. Timing, or rather dyssynchronous timing between Germany, Japan, and Russia/ the USSR's economic development on the one hand and that of Britain, France, and the United States on the other hand, was especially pertinent in elevating the danger of war among these countries. In Rostow's view, the probability of war was a consequence of the policy choices made by the late industrializing countries between pursuing geostrategic expansion versus mass consumption. German, Japanese, and Soviet leaders chose the former policy course.

It was the differential alteration in the power balance, traceable to differences in the timing of the stages of economic growth, that was to provide a terrible temptation to Germany in Eastern Europe and to Japan in China; it was to serve alternately as a source of fear and temptation to Russia, in both regions; and it was to offer chronic danger to France, Britain, and the United States, whose strategic status was radically and permanently altered by both consequences of the spread of industrialization – that is, both by the creation of a single, interacting arena of power across the northern half of the globe and by the emergence of soft spots within it which made the pursuit of Eurasian hegemony appear possible and attractive, at various stages, to Germany, Russia, and Japan. (Rostow [1960] 1971: 116)

The above passage also alludes to another important point. In economic competition and international rivalry, it is a country's *relative* – and not its absolute – performance that matters. How much faster, or earlier, does a country manage to take off economically, develop (the then) cutting-edge technologies, and pioneer leading industries? Scholars belonging to the realist school of international relations are emphatic that a state's *relative gain* over its counterparts is the most important factor in deciding its security (e.g., Grieco 1988a, 1988b; Grieco et al. 1993; Powell 1991). Many economists are also quite emphatic on "first mover" advantages, although some argue that there are also benefits to being "backward" when a country tries to catch up economically based on the backlog of experiences and inventions provided by earlier leaders who were the trailblazers (e.g., Gerschenkron 1962; Veblen 1915). Those who propose the latter view, however, do not deny that their perspective may be limited to a few select cases, especially those that are already endowed with important facilitative conditions to catch up (e.g., Germany, Japan). There appears to be little doubt about whether it is more advantageous to be a front runner or a late upstart. The so-called Matthew Principle of course argues countries that start with advantages gain further advantages whereas those with disadvantages are further handicapped and fall farther behind.

Finally, I pause to take a brief detour here to comment on another part of Rostow's scholarship before moving on to the next section. As an official in the Lyndon Johnson administration, he was generally seen as a policy hawk on the Vietnam War. During those years, there was a great deal of interest among US scholars about the popularity of communist movements in the developing world. Rostow (1965: 232–233) was known for his quip that the communists "are the scavengers of the modernization process." His point is that the modernization process, which of course includes industrialization and economic development, is a traumatic experience for those countries transitioning from their traditional way of life. During this transition period, there are bound to be severe social dislocations, which create conditions for a fertile recruiting ground for communists. He advocated that the US government should assist the transitioning countries to navigate through this period of vulnerability quickly and smoothly. Roger Benjamin and John Kautsky's (1968) research has shown that communist parties have the greatest popularity in countries that are ranked in the middle range of economic development. In other words, the strength of communist parties has a curvilinear relationship with economic development; these parties' appeal to the masses is weak in both the least and the most developed economies, and highest for those in the middle range. This pattern therefore lends some empirical support for Rostow's claim. I will circle back to this line of argument later when I discuss the political ramifications of stalled economic growth and even economic downturns.

Other well-known economists have also pointed to the destabilizing effects of economic growth. For example, Joseph Schumpeter (1939, 1949) has used "creative destruction" to describe this process. Mancur Olson (1963) captures this phenomenon succinctly by entitling one of his leading articles "Rapid Growth as a Destabilizing Force."

Growth Cycles and Major Interstate Wars

As already remarked in the last section, punctuated equilibrium comes to mind when we survey the dynamics of the global economy, which follows cycles of expansion and contraction with alternating periods of rapid growth and relative stagnation, even recession (Modelski and Thompson 1996; Thompson 1990, 1992, 2009; Thompson and Zuk 1982). Joseph Schumpeter (1939) studied the world's ebbs and flows of economic activity which follow a cyclical pattern. He attributed the discovery of this apparent rhythm to the Russian economist Nikolai Kondratieff. This regularity has become known as the Kondratieff cycles, each of them lasting about fifty years (e.g., Modelski 1987a, 1987b; Modelski and Thompson 1996).

Various international relations analysts have called attention to the differential rates of economic growth on the part of major states and to the phenomenon of desynchronization due to their being located at different points of the S-curve (depicting the trajectories of economic growth) at any given time. In addition, the steepness and the height of the S-curve can be different for each country. David Rousseau (2006: 26) argues, "The sequential timing and uneven rates of industrialization imply that domestic changes can have international implications by altering the distribution of power in the system." A recent study by Steve Chan (2024b) has also made the same general point. A state's international standing and its competitiveness are based on the performance of its economy, and this performance is in turn primarily a matter of domestic conditions and policies, including the nature of its cultural dispositions and political institutions. A country's economic dynamism is in turn based on its ability to innovate and invent, to accumulate capital for investment, and to create, nurture, and develop pioneering industries that pull the rest of its economy forward (e.g., Mokyr 1990; Modelski and Thompson 1996; Rasler and Thompson 1985, 1991; Thompson 1990; Thompson and Zakhirova 2019).

There is one strong policy implication from the generalization that states' relative economic performance determines their international standing and competitiveness, and that their relative economic performances are primarily determined by their domestic conditions and policies. This implication is that states would be much better off in getting their own house in order rather than focusing their attention on policies intended to thwart other countries' international ascent. For obvious reasons, officials are in a better position to influence their own country's conditions and policies to promote economic growth than those of other countries, such as to impose trade restrictions or technology embargoes on their adversaries or competitors.

International relations scholars have argued that states' uneven growth rates and their economic desynchronization are the basic cause behind interstate power shifts, which introduce disturbances to the interstate system's existing hierarchy. These changes in turn produce status friction among these states, a topic I will expand on in the next section. Power shifts can produce greater uncertainty and even anxiety and insecurity for leaders concerned about their country's international position. Without necessarily delving into these officials' psychology or decision calculus that incline them to go to war, international relations analysts have argued that power shifts are dangerous to peace and stability. According to power-transition theory (e.g., Gilpin 1981; Organski 1968; Organski and Kugler 1980) and its more recent rendition as Thucydides' Trap by Graham Allison (2015, 2017), these changes in the distribution of power among major states elevate the probability of war between rising and declining countries. Thucydides is of course remembered today for his aphorism that the source of the Peloponnesian War in ancient Greece was Sparta's alarm over Athens' increasing power.

In a nutshell, this view propounds a "rear-end collision" theory of interstate war. It argues that when a newcomer, that is, a new aspirant for recognition as a great power, bursts on the scene, such as Germany, Japan, and Russia/the USSR on earlier occasions and China today, it disrupts the existing hierarchy maintained by the established powers, thus presaging a conflict between these established powers and the upstarts – or so does the conventional story go. The more sudden, faster, and greater the upstarts' rise, the more severe is the disturbance to the existing international system. Their ascendance can thus be seen as introducing a shock to the interstate system, requiring the other great powers to adjust and accommodate the newcomers. Even relatively moderate economic gains made by a newcomer can cause extensive reverberations in a multilateral setting, that is, to cause unexpected consequences with respect to the existing alignment of interests and balance of capabilities, thus engendering uncertainties and anxieties on the part of the leaders of multiple countries among the elite group of great powers (Doran 1991; Doran and Parsons 1980). Russia's rise in the years immediately before World War I is often mentioned as an example in this context, especially with respect to the alarm this development caused in Berlin. Prevailing discourse argues that when states fail to reach a *modus vivendi* in a world shaken by different states experiencing rapid upward and downward mobility, war is more likely to ensue.

War is itself a punctuation that rearranges the interstate hierarchy or pecking order. Historian Paul Kennedy (1987) has studied the rise and decline of great powers in history. Political scientists George Modelski and William Thompson (1996) have also taken up this subject, charting the vicissitudes in the history of the world's leading states. They have plotted cycles in interstate relations. These cycles start with the installation of a new global hegemon presiding over a new international order in the wake of a systemic war. This phase is marked by the concentration of power in the hands of this new dominant state, and the legitimation of the new international order. It is followed subsequently by a phase of power deconcentration, signifying the decline of this state and increasing challenges to its power and legitimacy. The phases of power deconcentration and delegitimation in turn create the conditions for and lead to a rendezvous with another bout of war to start another cycle repeating these phases (Modelski and Thompson 1996; Thompson 2009, 2020, 2022).

Other scholars have also written about the relationship between economic growth and war occurrence. For example, Nazli Choucri and Robert North (1975) point to lateral pressure created by industrialization and population growth as a development contributing to World War I. Bruce Russett has argued that wars tend to occur not at the point of economic trough or nadir, but rather after recovery has already started. He reports that Nikolai Kondratieff had found that the most protracted and extensive wars tend to coincide with periods of economic upswing (cited in Russett 1983: 383). Other scholars, such as William Thompson and Gary Zuk (1982) have studied the relationship between inflation and war, although the results of this study and others are not clearcut or conclusive. There is some tentative evidence suggesting that changes in states' relative power positions tend to coincide with the outbreak of war, especially when this position has deteriorated relative to their rival(s) (Doran and Parsons 1980; Gilpin 1981; Organski and Kugler 1980).

The general dynamic describing these stages shows the properties of lulls and lurches, periods of relative calm and relative turmoil, phases of hegemonic dominance and decline, periods of economic expansion and contraction, and war as the ultimate punctuation shattering the old order and introducing a new one. Each phase or period ends with an acceleration of change leading to the next one, which fluctuates around a new normal until accelerating change produces the one after it. There thus appears to be a rough rhythm or regularity to these ebbs and flows marked by fits and starts. These recurrent patterns feature extended periods of apparent stability (such as the long peace after World War II described by Gaddis 1986, 1989) that are followed by sudden and sharp discontinuities or ruptures brought about by the abrupt collapse or rapid emergence of great powers (such as the USSR and China respectively in the recent past). As already mentioned, systemic war has this effect of reshuffling the interstate hierarchy although, as shown in the USSR's abrupt collapse, it does not always take a war to disclose a world in which the interstate distribution of power has undergone dramatic change (such as World War II in revealing the decline of the "old" European powers and confirming the USA and the USSR as the two new superpowers). The key dynamic driving changes in the international system is the relative power among a handful of great powers, whose standing in the interstate hierarchy is in turn determined primarily by their relative economic performance.

Significantly, the eventual "winners" that emerged to become the new hegemon are often not those engaged in a direct competitive bid for this status. France and Spain had fought repeatedly in the 1600s and 1700s for mastery of Europe. In the end, it was Britain, located at the fringe of the European interstate system, that emerged as the dominant power. In the two world wars, it was the United States, again occupying a peripheral position in the then Euro-centric international system, that became the new dominant power. We also see this tendency in premodern systems of interstate relations, such as Persia's rise as a hegemonic power outside the system of Greek city states, and the Qin dynasty (located at the edge of the Chinese interstate system) during the Warring States period that emerged victorious by conquering the other six states to unify China (Hui 2010; Kaufman et al. 2007; Wohlforth et al. 2007). The main antagonists waging a hegemonic struggle often exhaust themselves to the benefit of a third party. The USA rose to become a regional hegemon in the Western Hemisphere also partly due to the Anglo-French rivalry that distracted these countries. Moreover, London and Paris were inclined to see the USA as a potential ally in their bilateral competition, rather than as a rising power that would eventually displace both of them as the world's leading power (Elman 2004). By implication, today's Sino-American rivalry could redound to the advantage of another rising state, such as possibly India.

Although power-transition theory and its more recent rendition as Thucydides' Trap focus on the relative growth rates of the two leading states in the world – the rising upstart and its established counterpart as the existing global hegemon, there are at any moment several rising states and concomitantly several declining states. Charles Doran and Wes Parsons (1980) point to the ripple effects that the accelerating growth of a relatively minor member of the great-power club, such as Russia before World War I, can set in motion a series of perturbations in the multiple relations among these great powers. John Vasquez (1996, 2009a) has written about when the reality or perception of an ongoing or impending power transition has cascading ramifications for these states and the relevance of statecraft in easing or exacerbating the anxieties, uncertainties, and confusion ensuing from these ramifications. Given their focus on the competition between the two top leading states, power-transition theory and Thucydides' Trap overlook the multilateral relations among several great powers and the importance of coalition formation that determines the outcome of the ensuing military struggle such as World War I.

In the years prior to this conflict, British diplomacy accommodated, even appeased, the United States, conciliated with France and Russia, and formed an alliance with Japan in the Far East, so that London could focus on the threat emanating from Germany which is located nearby. In both world wars, the anti-German coalition was more powerful, and this edge produced victory for them (as well as victory over Japan in World War II). Today, besides China, there are other rising states such as India, Indonesia, Iran, and Saudi Arabia. At the same time, established powers such as the United States, Britain, France, Japan, and Russia have suffered relative decline. Still the collective strength of the established Western countries (including Japan) is much greater than recent upstarts like China and India, notwithstanding some forecasts suggesting that the world would be dominated by Asia's economies by 2050. According to the financial firm Goldman Sach's projection (Lu 2023), the ranking of the world's ten largest economies by then would be in descending order: China, the USA, India, Indonesia, Germany, Japan, Britain, Brazil, France, and Russia.

The histories of recent major wars, however, suggest that it is coalitions rather than individual belligerent states that decide their outcome. The War of Quadruple Alliance (1718–1720, pitting Spain against a coalition made up of Britain, France, Austria, and the Dutch Republic), the Napoleonic Wars, the Crimean War, and the two world wars are such instances. Depending on whether one decides China was a great power in 1950 (I tend to think not), the Korean War might be included in this list. Naturally, these remarks do not deny that there are also bilateral wars fought by two great powers, such as the Russo-Japanese and the Franco-Prussian Wars. The thrust of my observation is that even though China might have closed the power gap separating it from the United States, any coalition one can reasonably imagine for Beijing would not come nearly close to matching the US-led alliance.

Thus, analyses that frame a Sino-American contest in strictly bilateral terms are missing an important dimension. This oversight is often compounded by other problematic judgments. One common mistake is to become obsessed with these two countries' recent economic growth rates or inventory of armament, while not giving enough weight to Washington's more profound structural power in international relations by virtue of its centrality and connectivity in various economic, financial, and information networks, its peerless command of the global commons (sea, air, and space), and its soft power and ideational appeal to the rest of the world as shown by various recent studies (e.g., Allan et al. 2018; Brooks and Wohlforth 2008, 2016; Buzan 2004;

Chan 2023a; Drezner et al. 2021; Farrell and Newman 2019, 2023; Nye 1990, 2002, 2004; Posen 2003). Although Washington's economic power has slipped (relatively) in recent decades, its military, financial, and ideational power is so overwhelming that no other country comes even close to matching it, not to mention overtaking it. This being the case, Beijing is still not quite Washington's peer competitor. It may become so in several decades, but not now or in the immediate future.

Linear extrapolation based on a few recent observations can be highly problematic. It is of course easier to achieve a high rate of economic growth initially when a country's economic size is small. As its economic size increases, it becomes more difficult to maintain the same rate of growth. Simple arithmetic tells us that an increasingly larger gain is required to maintain this rate, when the denominator for calculating the rate of growth becomes bigger. As a country's economy reaches maturity, its growth inevitably slows down. An annual growth rate of 2.5 percent for the USA is considered to be good performance. Growing at a rate between 4.5 percent and 5.5 percent every year, China's economy is likely to continue to narrow the distance separating it from the United States. Although China's economy will grow more slowly than before, it is still growing at a faster rate than the United States which has a larger economy. As already mentioned, it is relative performance that matters according to perspectives such as that of power-transition theory. This relative performance decides whether the gap between a leading, established state and a rising latecomer is narrowing or widening.

It is already evident that China's growth rate cannot be sustained at the same torrid nearly double-digit rate of growth that it had managed to achieve for about thirty years until the last few years. It is only natural and to be expected that its growth will decelerate, albeit still at a level higher than that of the United States. Like other developed countries, such as Norway, Japan, and South Korea, a low birth rate in China means that it will have a shrinking workforce. Moreover, a smaller number of workers would have to support each retiree. Unlike the United States whose population expands due to immigrants, China does not have this source to grow its workforce. Its capital investments have also shown a declining rate of return (Chan 2024b). China has heretofore relied heavily on exports to spur and sustain its growth. This source of growth, however, has become more doubtful for the future as the USA and other Western countries have initiated economic decoupling from China and as other lower-cost manufacturing countries such as Vietnam become more competitive. The so-called dual-circulation model suggests that China's future growth will depend increasingly on its domestic market. Finally, the government in Beijing has become more concerned with the quality of growth rather than its quantity; that is, it no longer emphasizes fast economic expansion at the expense of other desiderata, such as the costs of environmental pollution. For all these reasons, China is unlikely to maintain the same rapid rate of economic growth it had attained previously – a feat that is unique in history for a populous country as large as China. As the German saying goes, trees do not grow to the sky.

Research to date has not settled conclusively whether a faster or a slower power transition between two countries is more conducive to peace and stability. Kenneth Organski (1968: 376) expected originally that war is more likely to occur before the crossover point when a latecomer overtakes an established power in decline. Subsequent studies (e.g., Kugler and Lemke 1996; Organski and Kugler 1980) raised the possibility that it is more likely to occur during the transition period or even after it. This question on timing has strong policy implications for whether timely arrangements can be made to accommodate the newcomer and avert the danger of war. It is also relevant to the issue of empirical verification. A longer transition means a more protracted period during which war has a chance to occur, therefore making it easier to claim that power-transition theory's prediction has been confirmed.

One can argue that on the one hand, a fast transition means a shortened period during which the danger of war is high. Thus, fast transition means a briefer zone of danger for war to break out. It reduces the interval during which the two states in question are vulnerable to war. On the other hand, rapid and abrupt changes compressed into a short period can also be especially jarring. A fast transition elevates the anxieties and uncertainties that officials have to cope with and increases the chances of policy miscalculation. It is more difficult for officials to make timely and adequate adjustments to accommodate the rising newcomer during times of rapid change. However, as just mentioned, a slower transition also means a more protracted period during which war can break out, even though it also gives more time for officials to adjust to the changing international situation. Of course, among the policy options available to the officials of the established but declining state is the choice of preventive war (e.g., Bell and Johnson 2015; Levy 1987, 1997, 2008; Levy and Gochal 2001/2002; Levy and Mulligan 2017; Mueller et al. 2006; Silverstone 2007; Trachtenberg 2007). Germany had waged a preventive war twice against the rising colossus to its east, namely, Russia/the USSR in 1914 and again in 1941 (Copeland 2000; Van Evera 1999). As I have argued elsewhere (e.g., Chan 2023a), the logic of prospect theory and the strong empirical evidence supporting this theory (e.g., Boettcher 2005; He and Feng 2012; Levy 1996; Kahneman and Tversky 1979; McDermott 1998) would suggest that war is more likely to be initiated by a declining but still dominant state than by a rising albeit still weaker latecomer.

At this point, I should like to clarify and expand on several issues brought up in the last paragraph. First, my last remark about the likely initiator of war is pertinent to power-transition theory, because my proposition contradicts what this theory contends, namely, it is a revisionist and cocky upstart that starts a war to displace the incumbent hegemon and upend the existing international order. Second, my reference to Germany waging a preventive war against Russia/the USSR also disagrees with power-transition theory's characterization of both world wars as a German challenge to British primacy. Contrary to this latter view, I argue that both world wars were precipitated by Berlin's preventive motive directed against St. Petersburg/Moscow, and that instead of challenging London, the Germans had wanted to persuade the British to stay on the sideline on both occasions. As I have remarked earlier, the obvious parallel for contemporary Sino-American relations is that should war occur between these countries, it would *not* be due to Beijing's desire to challenge Washington's global dominance; it would rather mean that China has been unable to persuade the USA to refrain from interjecting itself in the Chinese Civil War, specifically, on the question concerning Taiwan's status. The occurrence of such a conflict would indicate that China's diplomacy to convince Washington to refrain from this interference has failed, just as Berlin had failed to persuade London to stay neutral in what turned out to be the two world wars. Fighting the United States would be the last resort rather than the first preference for Beijing. Third, and as just alluded to, I do not see the two world wars as a titanic struggle between *just* the two most powerful countries at the pinnacle of the interstate hierarchy. By 1914 and certainly by 1938, the United States had already become the world's preeminent power, and Germany never came close to matching US power – and hence there was not any power transition between (just) the world's two top dogs prior to both world wars as power-transition theory claims. In fact, this transition – the replacement of Britain by the United States as the world's dominant power – had occurred peacefully and earlier during the last decades of the nineteenth century. Fourth, it follows that the phenomenon of systemic wars that concern power-transition theorists and other scholars interested in studying the phenomenon of major wars are not typically bilateral contests between the two leading countries but are rather multilateral affairs in line with my earlier argument that these are coalitional conflicts. Finally, power-transition theory and other similar formulations claim that wars are more likely when there is a power parity or an impending power parity between states – and thus their attention to power *transition*. This claim contradicts the traditional realist argument about a balance of power enhancing the prospects of interstate peace and stability. I will return to this last point again in the next section.

Much of the current literature on power transition may be questionable because of problems concerning the validity of its measures (that is, how analysts go about measuring national power, see Beckley 2018; Rauch 2017). Although aggregate economic size matters, it is not the most valid measure of a country's power. Its people's productivity is more relevant. The average US per capita income in recent years has been more than six times higher than China's in nominal terms, and more than three times higher if adjusted for purchasing power parity. Put in a different way, the average American worker is more than six times, or more than three times, as productive as his or her Chinese counterpart depending on whether one uses the currency exchange rate or price adjusted for purchasing power to compute their relative productivity. Michael Beckley (2018: 28) shows that although indicators measuring a country's bulk suggest that China was stronger than Japan in 1930, the actual balance of power favored Japan. Indeed, even in the mid-1800s China still had the largest economy and army on earth – even though it was already falling seriously behind the world's premier powers. Beckley argues persuasively that although Britain's economy was only half of India's in 1850, its gross domestic product per capita was four times higher – thus enabling it to colonize India.

A reliance on aggregate measures of size can therefore be highly misleading. Accordingly, "many of the cases identified as power transitions may not have involved an actual transition in power, and, conversely, many genuine power transitions may not have ... been identified as such" (Beckley 2018: 42).

A final point about the relationship between economic performance and the outbreak of war pertains to the sociopolitical consequences of stalled economic growth or even its reversal (meaning when a country's economy actually shrinks such as in a recession or more ominously during a serious and protracted depression as in the late 1920s and early 1930s). As the reader can infer from the preceding discussion, the discourse of international relations analysts has been focused on the question of war probability due to the emergence of fast-growing latecomers. They do not pay nearly as much attention to the reverse situation, namely, what happens when a country's economy experiences severe strain or distress, especially after a period of rapid growth causing a revolution of rising expectations on the part of its citizens. Ted Gurr (1970) has written about relative deprivation – the *discrepancy* between a people's expectations and their actual life circumstances. Social turmoil and political instability do not occur when people expect little from their lives and their lives are actually miserable, that is, when there is little discrepancy between expectation and reality. The danger of turmoil and instability rises when people are given hope for a better life, but reality falls short of their aspiration. In other words, the danger of turmoil and instability becomes elevated when people's hopes are dashed. Of course, this hope happens when the economy is actually growing even though people's aspirations can outstrip this growth – hence the danger of sociopolitical instability and turmoil due to the revolution of rising expectations.

In electoral competitions, the rhetorical question "Are you better off than four years ago" captures neatly the idea of relative deprivation. Many Americans feel that they are worse off not only compared to four years ago, but also compared to previous generations. They are not alone in their disaffection. Voters in practically all Western democracies with developed economies have felt this way (e.g., Norris 1999, 2011; Norris and Inglehart 2019; Pharr and Putnam 2000). Their disaffection has caused a surge of support for fringe, right-wing parties. In the case of the United States, white, blue-collar workers without a college degree have provided the main support base for

Donald Trump's MAGA (Make America Great Again) movement. This phenomenon shows that established democracies with mature economies can also be subject to the psychological effects and political consequences of relative deprivation. Furthermore, there has been the development of a political movement in reaction to the traditional view of the USA as a "melting pot" and the liberal push to emphasize diversity and inclusiveness. More Americans with conservative political views and fundamentalist, religious beliefs now see diversity as a national liability rather than strength, and they argue that the USA was conceived and is destined to be a white Christian nation.

Various pundits and commentators have written that the most dangerous time for a dictatorship is when it starts to make reforms which give people hope that their lives can be better. Thus, Alexis de Tocqueville ([1865] 1955) remarked, "The regime that a revolution destroys is almost always better than the one that immediately preceded it, and experience teaches that the most dangerous time for a bad government is usually when it begins to reform" (https://en.wikipedia .org/wiki/Tocqueville_effect). The domestic consequences of slower or stalled economic growth after a period of rapid economic improvement raising people's expectations can be as concerning as its international consequences. This situation characterizes especially the challenge facing China's leaders, even though this discussion has also just now pointed to the trauma and destabilizing effects of relative deprivation felt by the citizens of Western matured economies, including the United States.

When their record of policy performance is highly unpopular, politicians often resort to diversion by shielding themselves behind their patriotic credentials and targeting foreign scapegoats to appease domestic discontent. Whipping up nationalist fervor is thus a favorite way for them to legitimatize their rule when the economy suffers decline and citizens experience hardship. The behavior of the Argentine generals in launching the Falklands/Malvinas War becomes more understandable in this context. Quite aside from this linkage, however, officials may be also incentivized to consider waging a preventive war, such as in Germany's case, when they realize that their country is poised to experience relative decline in view of an ascending adversary with faster economic growth. German leaders believed that war in 1914 might be still winnable, but this window of opportunity would be closing soon. German Chancellor Bethmann Hollweg acknowledged in 1918, "Yes, my God, in a certain sense it [World War I] was a preventive war." He explained in 1914 "war is still possible without defeat, but not in two years!" (quoted in Van Evera 1999: 77). He added, "... our military men were fully convinced that now [July 1914] they could *still* come out of a war victorious; but in a few years, i.e., 1916, after the completion of the Russian railroads, [this] would no longer be so" (quoted in Lebow 1981: 229; italic in original).

As I will explain further shortly, we should expect a rising China to be more willing to "play nice" than a declining China. Prospect theory tells us that when people are in the domain of loss, they are more likely to take risks to reverse this setback. For this and other reasons given above, an exclusive concern with another country's faster economic growth could create a blind spot that overlooks the danger that declining or stalled growth can also encourage foreign belligerence (Beckley 2023). Finally, as Thomas Christensen (2001) argues persuasively, a China experiencing stymied economic growth or economic setback (in contrast to a China that is rapidly growing economically) can also be unsettling. He states succinctly that China can pose problems for the United States without catching up. In the past, a decrepit China during the Qing dynasty, a faltering Ottoman Empire during the late 1880s, and an Austro-Hungarian Empire in precipitous decline and in danger of disintegrating before World War I were as much a challenge to international peace and stability as rising powers.

Finally, it is useful to recall and compare the recent experiences of China and Russia. Of course, Russia has experienced a sharp decline in its capabilities and status since the heydays of the USSR, notwithstanding its more recent recovery to some extent from the depth of its fall. However, Russia's loss of power, including the disintegration of the USSR and the demise of the Warsaw Pact that Moscow used to lead, had not improved its relations with the West. Neither Russia's weakness nor its large and unilateral concessions has had this effect. Charles Kupchan (2010: 397) has remarked, "From Moscow's perspective, Russia for successive years made a series of concessions to the West, including accommodating NATO expansion, reacting with restraint to democratic revolutions in its 'near abroad,' and facilitating strategic access for the United States in Central Asia and Afghanistan." These concessions include the Kremlin's willingness to have a reunited Germany become a NATO member. They did not, however, stop NATO and the EU's (European Union) eastward expansion. The

USA and its allies continue to demand more concessions, and they continue to promote various color revolutions and regime change in Russia's near abroad. Russia's invasion of Ukraine was an outcome of this Western pressure and encroachment rather than the cause of the deterioration of its relations with the West (Mearsheimer et al. 2014). Just imagine how any US president would have reacted if Russia or China was complicit in orchestrating a regime change in Mexico and that Mexico had wanted to join the Warsaw Pact. The main point of these remarks, however, is that power shifts or capability changes in themselves cannot explain the vicissitudes of Russia or China's relations with the West in general and with the United States in particular. Even though one of them is a declining state and the other a rising one, these relations have deteriorated in both cases. Some other variables need to be introduced to explain this similar outcome.

What Do States Fight For?

I have skirted an important issue until now. Specifically, what do major states fight for? Some scholars such as Kenneth Organski and Jacek Kugler (1980) claim that they struggle to be the top dog in the interstate hierarchy or for something vaguely called "international order." Others such as structural realists like Kenneth Waltz (1979) suggest that states seek security or try to ensure their survival. Still others, the so-called offensive realists like John Mearsheimer (2001), argue that states try to maximize their power and expand as much as they possibly can until they are stopped by other states. In contrast, defensive realists claim that states go to war to preserve a balance of power. Striving to achieve or maintain a position as the top dog sounds like pursuing status. As for international order, it is not something that can be imposed unilaterally even by a superpower, and it also appears to be something intangible that in the final analysis can only be accorded by others' recognition that the pertinent rules are legitimate. In any case, these supposed rules are always evolving, being negotiated, or renegotiated constantly (e.g., Goh 2013, 2019).

In other words, the idea that the rules of international order can be established by the most powerful country in the interstate hierarchy once and for all appears rather fanciful (Chan et al. 2021). As for the pursuit of security or survival, what happens when a state such as the United States attains such overwhelming capabilities that these objectives are no longer in question? It seems hard to claim with a straight face that given its awesome capabilities, the physical survival of the United States is in any doubt. What then motivates a unipolar power without any peer competitor in sight (I argue that China is still only a regional power that cannot project its capabilities very far from its borders and that it does not represent a peer competitor to the United States now or in the immediate future)? Put perhaps in more modest terms, how much more resources would a superpower be willing to invest for that small, extra increment of safety or security after it has attained practical invulnerability? As for the pursuit of power for its own sake or the quest for global dominance that offensive realism is inclined to propose as a motivation for states, hubris is the word that comes to mind in describing these objectives. Naturally, such motivation can have its source not only in the ambitions of individual leaders but also in the mass psyche influencing their domestic politics.

The established states want to hold on to their existing status, whereas rising states clamor for recognition of their newly attained achievements and "a seat at the table." Germany's Chancellor Bernhard von Bülow told the *Reichstag* in 1897, "We do not want to put anyone into the shade, but we demand a place for ourselves in the sun" (Holmes 2010). Rising states such as Wilhelmine Germany ask for admission to the elite club of great powers. Their frustration mounts when they perceive the established states continue to deny them the status recognition that they believe their country deserves. It may be difficult for contemporary readers to comprehend, but when the victorious allies met at the Versailles Conference after World War I, they refused to accept the principle of equality of races and states. This egregious insult and other practices – such as Washington's blatantly discriminatory and racist policy to ban immigrants from Asia – were especially humiliating to the Japanese (Ward 2017). As already mentioned in the last section, states do not just fight for territory or resources; they also go to war over grievances stemming from status denial, and their perceptions of flagrant and deliberate injustices and indignities inflicted on them. A people's collective memory of these mistreatments, such as those from China's "century of humiliation" at the hands of Western and Japanese imperialists, is a powerful motivation – a chip on their shoulder, if you will – for them to strive for national rejuvenation as already mentioned (Wang 2014). Chinese school children were told about a sign that was once posted at a public park operated by foreigners in Shanghai that banned "dogs and Chinese" from entry (Bickers and Wasserstrom 2009).

One can sometimes detect in Western discourse hints that other countries, especially China, should "get over" their mistreatments in the past – such as Chinese memories of a "century of national humiliation," and for them and the Koreans to stop harping on their grievances against Japanese atrocities committed in a bygone era. Such hints are in themselves seen as an insult. One does not often hear from the same commentators or pundits telling Jewish people to "get over" their experience with the holocaust or Americans about Pearl Harbor or 9/11. How would the French react if they were told to forget about Alsace and Lorraine? In short, there is not enough consideration in current literature about the importance of emotions in influencing national mobilization of efforts such as for economic development and the pursuit of statecraft.

Economic performance can be characterized by fits and starts, and stagnation and even reversal and decline are possible. As noted earlier, China still had the world's largest economy in the mid-1800s. But it fell on hard times. It was besieged by economic decay, political chaos, and subjugation by foreign powers in subsequent years. Foreigners literally carved China into their respective zones of influence. In areas of the so-called foreign concessions foreign laws and not Chinese laws held sway, foreign police were in charge, and foreigners were exempted from paying Chinese taxes given their so-called extraterritorial rights that the Chinese government was compelled to concede to the Europeans, Japanese, and Americans. Foreigners also operated China's customs house, and they were given unfettered access to different parts of China to preach and trade. Indeed, foreign military forces were stationed on Chinese soil and foreign gunboats patrolled up and down China's major waterways, as those old enough to have seen the 1966 movie *Sand Pebbles* starring Steve McQueen would recall.

Presumably, Americans would not take kindly if Chinese gunboats had similar unfettered access to sail up and down the Mississippi River. And the British people would not accept the argument that in the name of free trade China had the right to sell cocaine to them despite their government's objection – which was of course the cause for the Opium War that Britain had initiated against China in order to sell this commodity to Chinese addicts. The legacies of these indignities and injustices, including Hong Kong becoming a British colony as a result of the Opium War, continue to be felt by the Chinese today – but long forgotten by the Western powers. When the Chinese people hear nowadays allegations of Chinese threat, they are understandably offended, even infuriated. because there has never been a single hostile Chinese soldier setting foot on European, Japanese, or US soil. The same situation does not apply to these latter countries' historical presence in China.

There is of course an extensive history of China waging wars (for an analysis of Chinese strategic discourse on resort to arms, see Johnston 1995), including wars of aggression and conquest. In contrast to other countries that had climbed to the front ranks of great powers such as Britain, France, Russia/the USSR, Japan, and the United States, China's recent rise has not been associated with wars of conquest or territorial expansion. Although China does have sovereignty disputes and border disagreements such as in the East and South China Seas and its boundary with India (for studies of Chinese settlement of its border disputes, see Fravel 2005, 2007–2008, 2008), its recent rise (or reemergence as a great power, if you will) has been due exclusively to its meteoric economic performance – that is, due to the growth of its domestic economy in contrast to the frequent resort to arms and coercion associated with the rise of predecessors such as Britain, France, Japan, and the United States.

Graham Allison (2017: 90) writes that during the late 1800s and early 1900s:

The US [had] declared war on Spain, expelling it from the Western Hemisphere and acquiring Puerto Rico, Guam, and the Philippines; threatened Germany and Britain with war unless they agreed to settle disputes on American terms; supported an insurrection in Colombia to create a new country, Panama, in order to build a canal; and declared itself the policeman of the Western Hemisphere, asserting the right to intervene whenever and wherever it judged necessary – a right it exercised nine times in the seven years of TR's [Theodore Roosevelt's] presidency alone.

In a similar vein, John Mearsheimer (2001: 238) quotes Henry Cabot Lodge saying that during the years of its ascendance, the USA had compiled "a record of conquest, colonization, and territorial expansion unequaled by any people in the nineteenth century." Germany's territorial conquests would appear rather small when compared to that of the United States.

There is a large body of research on the so-called status inconsistency theory (or status discrepancy theory). Johan Galtung (1964) wrote about it some time ago. Instead of focusing on the relative capabilities (or power) of major states, he stressed the gap between a country's capabilities or achievements on the one hand and the recognition or respect it receives from other states on the other hand. Some countries receive more status recognition than their actual capabilities or achievements. Britain and France's permanent seats on the United Nations Security Council offer an example. Other countries, such as Japan, Germany, and India, are not accorded the same recognition or prestige even though by any number of objective criteria, such as their demographic and economic size, they are more deserving than Britain and France. They receive a lower ascribed status than their actual achieved status (as indicated by their capabilities and achievements). Galtung pointed to this latter phenomenon of under-recognition as a source of dissatisfaction on the part of latecomers in economic development. Since his writing there have been other studies that attend to this phenomenon of status inconsistence (or discrepancy) as a psychological reason for the occurrence of international instability or conflict (e.g., East 1972; Gochman 1980; Ray 1974; Renshon 2016, 2017; Wallace 1973; Ward 2017).

As mentioned earlier, there is also a growing literature suggesting that people care about their country's international status, and they harbor strong resentments against perceived disrespect shown to their country (e.g., Larson and Shevchenko 2010, 2019; Lebow 2010; Murray 2010, 2019; Pu 2019; Renshon 2016, 2017; Ward 2017; Wolf 2014). They react strongly to any perceived attempts by other countries to block or thwart their country's aspiration for the international recognition that in their view it deserves. The desire for status recognition, prestige, or *gloire* are important motivations for states to go to war – even more than their pursuit of security. Lebow (2010: 18) documents that the quest for status has been the primary or secondary reason in sixty-two of ninety-four wars involving great powers since 1648. This line of research is more compelling than prevailing explanations of war occurrence based only on the distribution of power among states without explicating the reason why changes in this distribution should motivate leaders to go to war. Status-inconsistency theory takes explicitly into account the hypothesized motivation for interstate conflicts, namely, the rising states' struggle for recognition and the established states' refusal to extend such recognition. As John Vasquez (2009a: 133, italic in original) has stated succinctly, "War and violence occur because of *grievances* and not just power."

Rationalist explanations of war argue that states fight because they expect to make gains from fighting – or more specifically, when leaders believe that their country can perform better on the battlefield than their adversary gives them credit for, so that they can demonstrate that these adversaries must make adjustments to accommodate whatever they are demanding, adjustments that these adversaries have refused to accord them in the absence of war (Fearon 1995). Put in a different way, war makes sense only when leaders believe that their country's capabilities or achievements warrant adjustments by others to accommodate their demand. The strong implication of this statement is of course that states do not go to war when they are already extended more recognition than they deserve given their current actual capabilities or achievements. In such a situation, leaders cannot expect to improve their bargaining position – as they will not be able to get more of what they want because they are already over-compensated. Crucially, it is the *discrepancy* or *gap* between a state's capabilities and achievements on the one hand and the benefits and status recognition that they receive from other states on the other hand that holds the key to conflicts among countries. Capabilities – or power – in itself does not explain why wars happen. Wars occur because there is an inconsistency between a state's capabilities on the one hand, and the benefits or entitlements that these capabilities warrant. This view therefore argues that the war phenomenon cannot be attributed just to the policies of pushy latecomers. One needs also to ask why the established powers refuse to accommodate the latecomers. Why do these established powers decline to trim their sense of self-importance or to downsize their self-designated role in international affairs according to their declining capabilities?

Robert Powell makes a cogent argument that the balance or distribution of power is not in itself the cause of war as prevailing discourse in the West suggests. He states:

If the distribution of benefits mirrors the distribution of power, no state can credibly threaten to use force to change the status quo and the risk of war is smallest. If, however, there is a sufficiently large disparity between the distribution of power and benefits, the status quo may be threatened regardless of what the underlying distribution of power is. (Powell 1999: 199)

Thus, for wars to happen the leaders of at least one belligerent state must believe that their country's power entitles it to greater tangible and intangible compensation (e.g., land, prestige) than it is currently receiving. Put differently, the rationalist perspective argues that if a country's relative power is aligned with its current share of benefits or entitlements, it could not credibly threaten to go to war because fighting will not improve the amount of benefits or entitlement it is already receiving. As the above quote from Powell indicates, when the international distribution of power corresponds with the international distribution of benefits, the danger of war is the smallest – regardless of whether the balance of power is shifting in favor of one country or another. As Vasquez's remark cited earlier also argues, it is a sense of grievance, or a feeling of relative deprivation emphasized by Gurr, that holds the key to explaining a rising state's frustration and disappointment. And as I mentioned briefly above, it takes two factors to explain the occurrence of war. On the one hand, it is one belligerent state's feeling that it has been under-compensated or under-recognized given its actual accomplishments, and that it can improve its share of benefits and entitlements by going to war. On the other hand, it is the established states' refusal or reluctance to accommodate the under-compensated state's demands, that is, the established states' decision to withhold this compensation or recognition due to either their unwillingness or inability to make such adjustment adequately or promptly due to their cognitive rigidity, psychological difficulty, or institutional impediments to coming to terms with tangible or intangible loss (whether money, territory, prestige, or status) as explained by prospect theory, or for political reasons due to this declining state's domestic politics and entrenched bureaucratic interests. This sluggishness or delay should not be surprising – after all, punctuated equilibrium tells us to expect such forces of conservatism to hold back change, but also sharp ruptures when changes do occur. The accumulation of grievances and the associated increasingly insistent demand for adjustment create rising pressure and increasing tension that are eventually "released" to cause a major disruption in the form of war. This is of course the dynamic described by punctuated equilibrium and observed in natural phenomena such as earthquakes, avalanches, and the eruption of volcanoes.

Finally, in line with the argument that stalled economic growth and even absolute economic decline can be a source of trouble for international peace and stability, Powell's (1999) study makes an important point. A rising state is likely to be inclined to postpone its demand for other states to fully recognize its status commensurate with its achievements, when it is still on its upward trajectory so as not to upset the established powers. However, when its growth is stalled or even reversed, it is no longer interested in delaying this gratification. It is more likely to demand full and immediate recognition by other states of the status that it believes it is entitled to. For this and other reasons explained by Thomas Christensen (2001) and Michael Beckley (2023), a China beset by economic troubles can also be a problem for the United States and the world.

6 Political Entrepreneurship, Narrative Construction, and Pitching the Enemy Image

Sino-American relations has clearly taken a turn for the worse in recent years (e.g., Lampton 2019). What can account for this deterioration, and what is to be done? We hear American critics of Washington's China policy saying that its engagement with China has not worked, and a reset is necessary. This argument fits our earlier discussion about public policymaking. Setting the policy agenda and framing the policy discourse are a critical part of this policymaking process. Defining or redefining a problem and mobilizing a new policy image are important because as someone has said, "you cannot beat something with nothing."

This chapter turns to a discussion of political entrepreneurship. Political entrepreneurs are change agents. They are the participants in the "garbage can" model of policymaking introduced earlier. They play a critical role in the policymaking process by bringing problems and solutions together. They also are the ones who develop new issue images for problems, shop, and sometimes even create, new policy venues to promote their favored solutions. They propagate a new definition of problem and call public and elite attention to it, they popularize particular narratives to frame policy debate, and they mobilize media coverage and recruit constituents to join a movement for change. Their role is indispensable in creating support and momentum for a policy punctuation. The following discussion starts with the question of what ails Sino-American relations which has clearly suffered a serious deterioration in recent years. Of course, a problem must be said to exist before a solution can be recommended to remedy it. As the "garbage can" model of policymaking suggests, just as problems can be looking for solutions, solutions can also be on the lookout for problems. Sometimes, one needs to redefine a situation to suggest a problem exists. Panama's former president Omar Torrijos was quoted earlier to say, "To resolve a problem, the first thing you have to do is *make* it a problem." I discuss specifically the role played by academic researchers and scholars wittingly or unwittingly in the construction of popular narratives about the threat posed by a rising China to international peace and stability.

So, What Is the Problem?

It is only natural for advocates of a new policy to argue that the old one has become outdated or that it has failed to achieve its objectives. This expectation is reflected in the current prevailing discourse in the USA, contending that a new approach to dealing with Beijing is necessary and overdue. What then is the old policy that should be discarded and how has it failed? Current and former US officials have typically described the old policy as engagement, and it is said to have failed because it has not transformed China and Chinese policy (e.g., Campbell and Ratner 2018; Campbell and Sullivan 2020; Campbell and Rapp-Roper 2020). What does a policy of engagement mean? Writers using this term are not always clear about what they mean by it, but presumably engagement would at least start with the recognition that China exists, and that it is important to have dialogue with it. This means that a policy of engagement would at least differ from Washington's policy in the 1950s and 1960s when it refused to recognize China or to have any dealings with it (Thurston 2021). US officials argued then that the Chiang Kai-shek government on Taiwan was the legitimate representative of China and thus, for example, was entitled to China's seat in the United Nations, and that the government in Beijing was a proxy or even a puppet of the USSR, and as an alien regime, it could not therefore represent the Chinese people. In fact, given its alien character (especially the Beijing government's embrace of the alien ideology of communism), the communist government in Beijing could not last and must therefore be a "passing phenomenon" – according to popular US discourse in the 1950s and 1960s.

One would also presume that in addition to opening communication channels for exchanges of information and ideas, a policy of engagement could or would involve various forms of intercourse such as exchanges in goods, people, investment, and even coordination and collaboration in undertaking international projects such as arms control, fighting terrorism, and combating global warming. The opposite of engagement is presumably isolation, containment, and boycott. When people argue that engaging China has been a mistake, the natural reaction is to ask whether these people are calling for isolation, containment, and boycott of China. The advocates for a new policy toward China would probably deny that they are proposing any such change to return to the US policy toward China in the 1950s and 1960s. There is, however, little doubt that they are proposing a new policy of "getting tough" on China, although they are not always clear about what this means. It is reasonably clear though that those suggesting that a policy of engagement has failed are contrasting their call for a new policy with the previous one – implying that the previous one has been based on naive and unrealistic illusions about China, such as Washington's ability to "manage" or transform China (e.g., Kagan 2005).

Implicitly at least, those who are calling for a more hard-line policy toward China distinguish the new policy course they propose with the old one which is judged to be somehow deficient because it was soft, uncritical, or wide-eyed. In short, it has not been realistic. As I will discuss later in this chapter, realism and its fundamental tenet of balance of power have different strands and meanings. One of them connotes or suggests an insistence on seeing the world as it is rather than how one wishes it to be. Realist thinking is supposed to stand for clear-headed and tough-minded recognition of the correlation of forces, and a realistic definition of national interests and an honest appraisal of the available resources to obtain the desired objectives. This job is to be done without sentimentalism, legalism, idealism, or illusions detached from "the facts on the ground" for if it stands for anything, realism stands for being realistic.

Before moving on further, it is important to point out that in the preceding paragraphs I have deliberately referred to the "old" rather than "existing" policy that proponents of change in US policy toward China have been advocating. My reason is that this policy has already been undergoing change before the Obama administration and its "pivot to Asia." Therefore, recent calls for the USA to "get tough" on China tend to reflect and follow changes that have already been happening or under way. When these calls were made or published, the then existing US policy toward China has already "gotten tough." Many of the events upsetting Sino-American relations predated these calls, such as the US bombing of China's embassy in Belgrade, the issuance of a visa for Taiwan's President Lee Teng-hui to visit the United States, the decision to sell F-16 jet fighters to Taiwan, and the

184   *Political Entrepreneurs and Narrative Construction*

collision of a US spy aircraft and a Chinese jet fighter off the Chinese island Hainan.

When detractors of an engagement policy toward China say that it has failed, what do they mean by this failure? It is often said euphemistically that it has not "transformed" China, How so? Does transformation mean converting China into a Western-style democracy, persuading the Chinese Communist Party to give up power, making Chinese society and economy more open, persuading the regime to accord greater respect to human rights, or getting Beijing to give up its sovereignty claim over Taiwan? If so, some of these objectives would have indeed represented a tall order based on naivety and unrealistic expectations. But did the architects of engaging China – such as Richard Nixon and Henry Kissinger – harbor these illusions? Were they and US presidents who followed their footsteps and continued to engage China, such as Gerald Ford, Jimmy Carter, George H. W. Bush, and Bill Clinton, woolly and confused liberals who had entertained such false hopes? I believe not. Instead, criticisms of unrealistic expectations motivating US engagement policy toward China have been aimed at, one might say, a "straw man."

There are two immediately evident problems with the critics' line of reasoning. First, its logic would suggest that Beijing could also argue that its rapprochement or engagement with the USA has been a failure because it has not converted the United States into becoming a communist country, persuading it to reject capitalism, or discouraging it from promoting color revolutions and regime changes abroad. Second, it is incumbent on the proponents of a policy of "getting tough" on China to demonstrate that the policy they advocate would actually yield the desired results. For example, would more vociferous US condemnation of China's record on human rights, or sanctions of Chinese officials for suppressing protesters in Hong Kong and dissidents in Xinjiang produce better results? Would a "get tough" policy advance the cause of human rights and political freedom in China? If not or if anything it is likely to produce the opposite results, these proponents for more pressure on China are being disingenuous. Their advocacy of protecting human rights and political dissidents would not appear to be their sincere intention or genuine agenda. It suggests subterfuge. Moreover, as indicated above, it is not at all that clear that those US presidents and officials who are being implicitly criticized for adopting the engagement policy that has allegedly failed had in fact these goals uppermost on their mind when they undertook the said policy – that is, that they were in fact guilty of entertaining those false hopes being attributed to them.

There is a history of US politicians as candidates seeking to become the occupant of the Oval Office to criticize the incumbent office holder for misguided policies toward China (e.g., Kelemen 2012). For example, Ronald Reagan criticized Jimmy Carter for "abandoning Taiwan" in his presidential campaign, and Bill Clinton accused his predecessor George H. W. Bush for "coddling the butchers of Beijing." On the campaign trail in 2000, George W. Bush claimed that Clinton had misconstrued US relations with China as a "strategic partnership," and vowed to redefine it as one of "competitor." He also stated that he would do "whatever" to support Taiwan only to reverse course after he was elected. Mitt Romney also declared his intention to call China a "currency manipulator" to sell cheap goods to Americans if he became the president. However, for both Bill Clinton and George W. Bush, their policy toward China after assuming the presidency turned out to be more moderate than their campaign rhetoric. As with Donald Trump, their campaign rhetoric suggests that criticizing China helps to win votes. Of course, after criticizing Trump on the campaign trail, Joe Biden has maintained basically the same policy toward China without, however, the same "bombasticity."

These examples also suggest three other points. First, flip flops are not infrequent for politicians and officials. They can say one thing as a candidate for office and do the exact opposite later after being elected. Of course, politicians and officials can also be sincere and honest in expressing publicly their views and intentions. Second, politicians' campaign rhetoric and their statements while in office both represent attempts to frame political discourse and mobilize public support. There are credible commitments, and then there are also "hot air and "empty talk" (Fearon 1995). Third, there is an important and intimate connection between domestic politics and political popularity on the one hand, and the calculation and conduct of foreign policy on the other hand. What is said and done may be in the interest of the individual politician or official, or her political party or institution, but it may not be in the best interest of the country. This generalization applies to both democracies and nondemocracies.

Contrary to the assertions of the "get tough" proponents, US policy toward China has been a specular success as I have argued elsewhere

(Chan 2023c). For example, Beijing has given up its previous support for armed insurgencies abroad, and it now accepts and indeed participates actively in various international agreements on arms control – something that it had condemned vociferously previously. China has also opened its economy to private enterprises and foreign investors since the time when Nixon visited Beijing, and it is now deeply embedded in and integrated with the international economy compared to its economic isolation in 1972. It is now a strong supporter of international institutions, including the United Nations, even though it had criticized and opposed them during the Maoist years. In fact, China is today the largest contributor to United Nations peacekeeping missions. There is no doubt that Chinese society is more open and pluralistic today than in the 1950s, 1960s, and 1970s. These are huge changes, especially the fact that China's economic reform policies have raised the living standards of the largest number of people in the shortest amount of time and by the greatest improvement ever in human history. If human rights include the alleviation of poverty, this feat and other changes just mentioned should make China more congenial to the United States. Washington should be celebrating and congratulating itself for having contributed to these achievements – instead of wringing its hands and bemoaning that its engagement policy has failed. Statements by American hard-liners are mystifying for any objective observer who is even only casually familiar with China's recent history (Chan 2023c; Chan and Hu 2025a).

In addition to those changes mentioned in the preceding paragraph that should make China more congenial to US values and interests, Beijing has collaborated with Washington in opposing the Soviet Union, easing the US exit from Vietnam, waging war on international terrorism, and containing the spread of nuclear weapons by North Korea and Iran. In view of these considerations, what has changed to cause Washington to focus its ire on China in recent years? The collapse of the USSR had made China more dispensable as a strategic ally. Similarly, the end of US involvement in the Iraq War and its victory over Al Qaeda meant less need for Chinese cooperation. At the same time, with its increasing power, China has emerged as the one country that could mount a serious challenge to US hegemony.

What has changed therefore is a power shift to the relative detriment of the United States, and not anything in particular that China has said or done (Chan 2023c). Beijing has not become more aggressive or undertaken any action more egregious than Washington's own conduct. The power shift narrowing the gap separating China and the United States has motivated Washington to adopt a policy shift and, as I have argued elsewhere (Chan 2024a), this policy shift has in turn influenced academics so that there is a problem shift in their scholarship, one that, as explained in the next section, has motivated them to move away from their traditional emphasis on balance-of-power thinking to arguments advanced by power-transition theory and Thucydides' Trap claiming that the emergence of a rising power tends to upend the international order and presage an increased danger of war.

The interpretation just presented to explain the US policy shift toward China points to traditional realist reasoning – even though Washington has often cloaked its pronouncements in liberal terms such as its support for human rights and democracy. In many past situations involving a conflict between the promotion of human rights and democracy and other US strategic interests, such as with respect to the actions or policies of conservative, even reactionary, governments and military juntas in Chile (under Augusto Pinochet), Argentina (under Leopoldo Galtieri), Nicaragua (under Anastasio Somoza), Iran (under the Shah), Egypt (under Hosni Mubarak), South Korea (under Park Chung-hee), Taiwan (under Chang Kai-shek), and South Vietnam (under Ngo Dinh Diem), Washington has abandoned its lofty ideals in favor of its strategic interests. Arman Grigoryan (2020) calls attention to Washington's discrepant treatment of popular movements in Ukraine and Armenia. He argues that whether their government has an anti-Russian orientation was the main reason accounting for this difference in Washington's policy. "Contrary to the popular narrative, the West has supported democracy only when that support has been reinforced by material interests, and rarely, if ever, when it has posed a threat to such interests" (Grigoryan 2020: 158).

Has Beijing's foreign policy become more aggressive or assertive in recent years as it has become more powerful (e.g., Hagstrom and Jerden 2014; Johnston 2013)? Hardly, judged either by its previous conduct or in comparison with the United States itself. Its record of involvement in wars shows that it has participated in fewer such conflicts over time. China's last war occurred in 1979 when it fought Vietnam over their disputed border. The same cannot be said of the United States, which has fought many more wars, undertaken frequent military interventions abroad, and invaded several other countries outright. A partial list would include Grenada, Panama, Afghanistan, Iraq, Libya, Syria, Somalia, and Serbia. Singapore's former Ambassador to the United Nations, Kishore Mahbubani, remarked that even during the relatively peaceful administration of Barack Obama, the USA had dropped 26,000 bombs on seven countries in 2016 alone, whereas China has not fired a single shot across its border since 1979 (quoted in Kang 2020: 140). As Beijing's power grew, it has actually become less coercive in its encounters with other states having a competing sovereignty claim in the South China Sea (Zhang 2019, 2024). In contrast, Monica Toft (2017: no page number) reports that the USA had undertaken 188 military interventions during 1992–2017, compared to 46 during 1948–1991. Thus, whereas China has become less coercive in its state-craft, the USA has trended in the opposite direction in increasing its use of force in relations with the rest of the world. With the USSR out of the way, the incidence of US attacks on other countries has risen after the Cold War, including its invasion of Iraq and Afghanistan without United Nations authorization.

There were other issues that US officials and scholars have brought up to argue the imperative of "getting tough" on China. Beijing's belligerence against Taiwan is usually one of the leading items on their list of indictments. They overlook, however, how the USA itself had dealt with its civil war. Barry Buzan and Robert Cox (2013: 118) point out that:

Parallels could in fact be drawn between the ruthless military anti-secession and rejection of self-determination that underpinned the US civil war, and China's similar current attitudes towards Tibet, Taiwan, and Xinjiang. Abraham Lincoln and the Chinese Communist Party would perhaps have understood each other quite well on this question.

Setting aside the issue of nationalism and national unification, Cuba provides the closest parallel for the United States that Taiwan is to China. Beijing, however, has not thus far launched an invasion of Taiwan as the USA had done at the Bay of Pigs in 1961, or pushed the world to the brink of nuclear war by imposing a naval blockade on Taiwan over US missiles that were once installed on that island as Washington had done vis-à-vis Cuba in the 1962 Missile Crisis. Nor has Beijing undertaken an economic blockade of Taiwan as Washington has done to Cuba – in fact, China has been Taiwan's top trade partner and investment destination. Of course, Beijing has also not been known to order assassination of Taiwan's leaders as Washington had plotted on several occasions against Fidel Castro.

Parenthetically, recent commentaries by US officials, journalists, and academics on possible actions that Beijing may take in a military showdown with Taiwan have included the idea that it will try to "decapitate" Taiwan's leaders – that is, to kill them at the outset of a war. There are also recent references to how Russia had planned to overwhelm Ukraine's defense and conquer it quickly in a matter of weeks or months by waging a military campaign of "shock and awe." The latter description of course came from the US campaign to attack Saddam Hussein's Iraq, which also turned out to be a much more protracted and challenging struggle for Washington as Moscow's war in Ukraine has become. The reference to "shock and awe" also points to the frequent tendency for our views and analyses of other countries' policies and actions to be consciously or unconsciously autobiographical. As I will argue shortly, our comments and characterizations about other countries often reflect more about ourselves than "them."

China has also not undertaken drone attacks against suspected terrorists in other countries such as Pakistan, Syria, and Iraq, or engaged in other forms of extra-judicial killings such as the assassination of Iran's General Qasem Soleimani in Baghdad in January 2020. Nor has Beijing engaged in the extra-judicial "renditions" whereby suspected terrorists are kidnapped and sent to facilities in third countries where they could be imprisoned without trial and interrogated and tortured. While Washington accuses Beijing of various forms of violating human rights, it overlooks its own transgressions such as at the Abu Ghraib prison and at the Guantanamo facilities. Water torture of prisoners was legalized by Washington as an "enhanced interrogation technique."

Washington has also claimed that it supports Taiwan because of this island's democracy and its people's right to self-determination. The US support for Taiwan, however, was strongest when this island was ruled under martial law by the Kuomintang's one-party dictatorship. Washington condemned Russia's annexation of Crimea and several oblasts in Ukraine's Donbass region, arguing that their secession from Ukraine was illegal and that it should be ratified by the entire Ukrainian people and according to Ukraine's constitution. This argument, however, has not been applied to Taiwan's situation.

Similarly, while it used Serbia's "ethnic cleansing" in Bosnia as the justification for leading a NATO attack on Belgrade, it avoids this characterization of Israeli action against the Palestinians living in Gaza and has vetoed the UN Security Council's call for ceasefire on more than one occasion. Pointing to the US wish for a rule-based international order, Wahington criticizes Beijing for not accepting the Permanent Arbitration Court's judgment against Beijing's sovereignty claim over the South China Sea, even though it has not even joined the United Nations Convention on the Law of the Sea, and even though it has similarly rejected the verdict of the International Court of Justice against it for mining Nicaragua's ports. Freedom of navigation appears to only cut one way, and it therefore did not apply the euphemism of "quarantine" when the USA blockaded Cuba.

Americans have alleged election interference by Russia, China, and Iran. These commentators overlook history. Washington has been the most prolific actor in meddling in other countries' elections, starting with the effort by the Central Intelligence Agency to prevent the Italian Communist Party from winning the 1948 election and many other countries' elections in subsequent years (Levin 2020), including that of Chile's Salvador Allende who died in a military coup in which the USA was complicit.

This litany can go on. The USA has accused China of undertaking electronic espionage and internet manipulation. It was the USA, however, that had eavesdropped German Chancellor Angela Merkl's telephone conversations. Edward Snowden's disclosure showed that the US National Security Agency had undertaken massive surveillance programs on Americans with the cooperation of large internet companies and even European governments (Richelson 2013).

As I have written elsewhere (Chan 2023a), Washington has also lodged various complaints against China's trade malpractices. However, Fareed Zakaria pointed to "[a] 2015 report by the financial services giant Credit Suisse [that] provides a useful tally of nontariff barriers against foreign goods put in place by major countries between 1990 and 2013. With a total count of almost 450, the United States is in a league of its own. Next is India, then Russia. China comes in at number five, with one-third as many nontariff barriers imposed as the United States. The picture hasn't changed much in the years since" (Zakaria 2020: 58). Among the newly emergent economies of BRICS (Brazil, Russia, India, China, and South Africa), "China is consistently ranked as the most open and competitive economy" (Zakaria 2020: 57).

The USA has accounted for about 13 percent of the total value of the world's imports, but it has been the target of a disproportionate number of other countries' allegations of protectionist practices in their complaints to the World Trade Organization, accounting for 42 percent of complaints related to all anti-dumping claims submitted to that organization, 34 percent of all complaints about subsidies and countervailing duties, and 44 percent of all complaints about safeguard provisions (Broz et al. 2020: 433).

American officials and commentators have lauded protesters in Hong Kong as pro-democracy demonstrators even though they had attacked bystanders, destroyed properties, and vandalized Hong Kong's Legislative Council. Some of them were rioters and supported Hong Kong's independence. In contrast, US Democrats have labeled those who stormed the Capitol on January 6, 2021, as "insurrectionists" or "seditionists," while Republicans have described their action as participating in "legitimate political discourse" (Cheney 2022).

Finally, US officials, including Mike Pompeo (Secretary of State in Trump's first presidential term) and Antony Blinken (Secretary of State in Biden's administration) have publicly denounced China's treatment of the Uighurs in Xinjiang as "genocide" (Bostock 2021). The Chinese felt such allegations were "over the top" (see *The Economist* 2021), and they saw them as expressions of Washington's hypocrisy and double standard. They remind Americans of the checkered history of the United States such as highlighted by the Black Lives Matter movement and the civil rights campaign, the internment of Americans of Japanese descent during World War II, the deportation of over one million people of Mexican descent in the 1930s, the forced relocation of Native Americans from their ancestral homes to enclaves called "reservations," legalized discrimination against minority groups such as the Chinese Exclusion Act of 1882, brutal campaigns against Native Americans and Filippino nationalists (1898–1902, costing about 250,000 lives), and the enslavement of Black Americans. They also point to Washington's Monroe Doctrine seeking to keep extra-regional influences out of the Western Hemisphere while accusing the Chinese of trying to evict the USA from East Asia. They see hubris and chutzpah. And they react angrily.

In view of the current furor about illegal immigrants, it is ironic that it was not so long ago that Washington was pressing the USSR to let its citizens, especially those of Jewish descent, to emigrate. When Jimmy Carter brought up the issue of human rights, including immigration, Deng Xiaoping reportedly asked him, "How many Chinese nationals do you want? Ten million? Twenty million? Thirty million?" (*The Economist* 2018) In fact, Washington had thanked China for restricting the number of Chinese seeking to settle in the United States. The current heated debate in the USA about border security and illegal immigrants in the 2024 presidential campaign hinged on turning away those from Central America seeking asylum and settlement in the USA as was the case for Haitian refugees during the presidency of George H. W. Bush and Bill Clinton when they practiced a policy of refoulement.

More recently, Donald Trump has declared publicly that the United States wants to purchase Greenland from Denmark, re-assert US sovereignty over the Panama Canal, and annex Canada as the fifty-first state. He also wanted to evict the Palestinians from Gaza and turn it into a real estate development project (Hernandez 2025). Imagine any Chinese official had said that Beijing wanted to buy the island of Borneo, assert control over the Strait of Malacca, incorporate Mongolia into China, and take over Singapore and turn it into a tourist resort. What reactions would Americans have to such a declaration? Which country is more a revisionist power?

At their meeting in Alaska in March 2021, Yang Jiechi, China's top diplomat rebutted Antony Blinken's demand that China should adjust its conduct to conform to international rules, declaring that the USA "does not have the qualification to say that it wants to speak to China from a position of strength" (Rising Power Initiative 2021: no page number). Yang and other Chinese officials have insisted that China would only recognize the United Nations Charter as international law, and not the rules determined unilaterally by a few select Western countries. As already mentioned earlier, Xi Jinping said that China would not put up with sanctimonious preaching. As also mentioned earlier, even though Americans boast that they have the best form of government and others should imitate their political institutions, nearly a third of them thought that Joe Biden was elected due to fraud and an overwhelming number of them have deep distrust and skepticism about the integrity or competency of their elected officials.

This discussion does not condone Chinese policies that can be highly objectionable. One major difference between Washington and Beijing, however, is that Beijing does not preach or lecture to other countries, seek to export its economic model or political system, or try to make the world in its own image. It does not manifest the same missionary zeal to convert the rest of the world as Washington does. The preceding discussion tries to show that advocacy for a tougher US policy toward China reflects political construction and efforts to frame discourse.

The Talmud tells us that "We do not see things as they are; we see them as we are." Andrew Bacevich (2002: 90) remarks, "American statecraft is not, in the first instance, about 'them;' it is about 'us.'" Criticisms of others are often a reflection of oneself. Discourse on foreign policy points to political entrepreneurship and the construction of an enemy image. Just like officials and political pundits, scholars participate in efforts to frame public discourse, manipulate political narrative, and steer the policymaking process to support an agenda or policy they prefer, and in some cases to present post hoc justification of decisions already made.

As discussed in Chapter 2, issue or problem definition is at the heart of political contest. This section asks, "What is the problem?" It is from Washington's perspective that China has increased its power, thereby undercutting the preponderant position that the United States has enjoyed heretofore in international relations. China's rise has been meteoric, at such a rapid pace (at nearly a double-digit annual rate) over such a duration (for about three decades) that the world has never seen before. No other country has performed such a feat before. The rapid expansion of the Chinese economy is impressive when compared to its lethargy prior to Deng Xiaoping's reform policies in the late 1970s. China's economic history therefore shows the dynamic of punctuated equilibrium, a prolonged period of stagnation followed by a sharp and steep rise. It appears to have now settled down to a new normal of growing at a more modest but more sustainable rate.

What then is the solution being proposed by US critics of engagement policy to address China's increasing power? There is usually not sufficient clarity beyond "getting tough" and taking a "harder line" on that country. It is also unclear how this new policy approach would improve over the previous engagement policy in altering the many ways in which China is alleged to have misbehaved. For example, how is the proposed policy of "getting tough" likely to advance the cause of human rights in China or enhance the prospects of democracy in that country? Alternatively, how is such a new policy supposed to restrain China's threat to Taiwan and slow down its defense spending? The causal linkage between the proposed new policy and its expected benefits over the old one is rarely explained – indeed, the possibility that this new policy will actually bring about a worse outcome is not addressed. For instance, could the proposed policy in fact bring about even harsher suppression of human rights, causing greater belligerence against Taiwan, and stimulate Beijing to spend even more on its military? Recalling the US policy toward China during the 1950s and 1960s, it is questionable that a hard-line policy would produce the desired results and the proposed "get tough" policy may even cause further setbacks in these ostensible US objectives.

If the "get tough" policy also includes US economic decoupling from China and the technology embargo against that country – as Washington's recent actions suggest, then it will of course work to economically isolate China rather than integrating it further into the global economy, thus producing the opposite effect of the goal of trade liberalism that Washington had routinely championed in the past. I will turn shortly to balance-of-power arguments in the next section. Suffice it to say here that there are different strands of balance-of-power propositions and their expectations about how states will or ought to behave have often turned out to be incorrect in the past. Moreover, there is tension between the suggestion that a balance of power preserves international peace on the one hand, and that states can or should go to war to preserve this balance.

One can, however, imagine that a "get tough" policy includes greater US presence in the Indo-Pacific region, enhancing Washington's military capabilities and closer collaboration with formal or informal allies there. Its objective would be to improve or maintain the preeminent position that the USA has heretofore enjoyed in this region, and to counteract the recent gains that China has made in its economic and military capabilities. In other words, the argument for a new US policy toward China would be a traditional realist one: to balance against Chinese power, or more precisely, to sustain an *imbalance* of power that has favored the USA up to now (for readers who may disagree about this remark, would they prefer to be in the shoes of a Chinese economic planner or military strategist or an American one?). This is in essence a realist argument, one that, however, is often cloaked in lofty rhetoric about liberal values and principles, such as human rights and democracy. These liberal values and principles have in fact been secondary concerns. As mentioned before, Beijing's authoritarian government, suppression of human rights, communist ideology, and one-party rule had not previously prevented a Sino-American rapprochement and collaboration in the 1970s and 1980s. As stated previously, Beijing's conduct and rhetoric were much more aggressive and assertive previously and the Chinese society and economy were much more closed during the Maoist years than now.

China's sudden and rapid rise to become the world's second largest economy after the United States is problematic for Washington's international position. Even if China were a democracy, this problem would still remain. Recall that during the 1970s and 1980s, there were much anxiety and hand wringing in Washington about the economic competition coming from Japan, a US treaty ally and a fellow democracy. Some readers may recall popular books with titles such as *Japan as Number One* (Vogel 1979), *Trading Places: How We Are Giving Our Future to Japan and How to Reclaim It* (Prestowitz 1990), and even *The Coming War with Japan* (Friedman and LeBard 1991)!

What about Balance of Power?

Scholars strive for objectivity. Those working in the social sciences, however, are embedded in the prevailing social, economic, and political power structures, being inevitably a part of these structures. For students of international relations, they are not just passive observers but also active participants in the power relations that they study as their subject matter. Their perspectives, analyses and conclusions reflect these power relations. Stanley Hoffmann (1977) describes international relations (IR) as an "American social science." Consequently, American views and values dominate this discipline and those who work in it. Michel Foucault (quoted in Pan 2012: 17) insists that "there is no power relation without the correlative constitution of a field of knowledge," nor is there "any knowledge that does not presuppose and constitute at the same time power relations." Similarly, Jim George (quoted in Pan 2012: 17, italic in original) argues that "the process of discursive representation is never a neutral, detached one but is always imbued with the power and authority of the namers and makers of reality – it is always knowledge *as* power." Linus Hagstrom and Bjorn Jerden (2014: 352) write in the same vein, arguing that "... knowledge production, including scholarship, plays an important role in promoting collective understandings in which certain ideas are seen as 'legitimate' and others as 'outlandish.' Knowledge production thus becomes deeply entangled in power politics." Alexander Wendt (1992, 1999) has also written about scholars' ideational constructions. There is nothing neutral or natural about such construction. Anarchy is what states – and scholars – make of it.

If classical realism stands for anything, it argues that a balance of power helps to preserve peace and stability. Leading realists in recent decades, such as Kenneth Waltz (1979) and John Mearsheimer (2001) agree on this basic tenet of realism. Unless under otherwise stipulated conditions, both do not expect to see buck-passing behavior by states (that is, states shifting the burden of defense onto others) or to see states subcontracting their defense to others. They see bandwagoning – states taking the side of the dominant power – as an even more myopic, dangerous, and self-defeating policy. Moreover, Waltz has averred that secondary states should support the weaker side in international contests. Hans Morgenthau ([1948]1978: 173), the leading realist writing soon after World War II, stated flatly that "the balance of power and policies are not only inevitable but are an essential stabilizing factor in a society of sovereign nations." Inis Claude (1962: 28) quoted Morgenthau's assertion that balance of power is "a universal instrument of foreign policy used at all times by all nations who wanted to preserve their independence," and "a natural and inevitable outgrowth of the struggle for power." Henry Kissinger (1975: 195), perhaps the best-known realist scholar-official who was Richard Nixon's National Security Advisor and Secretary of State, claimed that "the balance of power, a concept much maligned in American political writing – rarely used without being preceded by the pejorative 'outdated' – has in fact been the precondition of peace."

As Claude (1962: 11–39) pointed out, Morgenthau and other realists have used the term "balance of power" in alternative ways, sometimes even in a contradictory manner. Realists have used this term to mean a *situation* in which states have an approximately equal amount of power, a *policy* that all states pursue in their external relations, an interstate *system* which exhibits an approximately equal distribution of power among states, a *symbol* of "hard-nosed" approach to managing international relations, and an *advocacy* of a foreign policy intended to preserve power parity with another state. Naturally, if balance of power is an iron law governing states' behavior, there would not be any need for scholars to urge officials to adopt it in foreign policy (hence the inconsistency or contradiction just indicated). More recently, Daniel Nexon (2009) has also written about the distinctions between balance-of-power theories, theories of power balances, and theories of states' balancing policies or their balancing conduct.

There has of course been a large body of empirical studies seeking to determine the effects of situations or systems in which power is distributed roughly equally on the probability or severity of war and other kinds of conflict such as militarized interstate disputes, and also inquiries about the effects that states' ostensible balancing policies or conduct can have on international peace and stability. To cite just two examples from the voluminous literature on how such situations, systems, or policy conduct can affect war and peace, David Singer et al. (1972) and Bruce Bueno de Mesquita (1981) have studied the consequences that "balance of power" can have on uncertainties felt by officials in conducting foreign policy, thereby on the prospects of war and peace. Singer et al. (1972) reported that there is more empirical support for the "peace through parity" model (or balance of power) during the nineteenth century, whereas the "peace through preponderance" model (or an imbalance of power) receives more support for the twentieth century.

By now the reader may be wondering about how relevant this discussion is to the topic of political entrepreneurship in shaping policy discourse, promoting a new problem definition, and mobilizing popular support for a new policy. I will therefore refrain from delving into any further details about various empirical studies on balance of power in its various meanings. I will also not get into the debate on whether realism is a progressive or degenerative research program (e.g., Elman and Elman 1995, 1997; Schroeder 1994, 1995; Vasquez 1997; Vasquez and Elman 2003; Walt 1997; Waltz 1997).

To cut to the chase, recent studies suggesting uneven economic growth to be the leading source of international tension and war generally represent a line of reasoning opposite to the traditional realist claims about balance of power in its various connotations. To be more specific, these studies tend to argue that uneven economic growth introduces disturbances to the existing interstate hierarchy and thus has a destabilizing effect. Some of these studies go further and argue that uneven economic growth rates can elevate the danger of war to the extent that they close the power gap separating the established state(s) and the rising latecomer(s). Robert Gilpin (1981), Kenneth Organski (1968), Organski and Jacek Kugler (1980), and most recently, Graham Allison (2015, 2017) are leading examples of this scholarship. They claim that when the power balance between two countries becomes more equal, there is a greater danger of war occurring between them. This claim stands traditional realism on its head.

So what? The logic of traditional realists espousing balance of power would welcome rather than suggest anxiety and alarm when China catches up to the USA in its capability. This traditional logic proclaims that a balance or parity of power between two countries preserves peace and deters war. More recent scholarship, such as power-transition theory and the formulation that has become known as Thucydides' Trap, argues precisely the opposite, suggesting that war becomes more likely when the power relationship between two countries becomes more balanced (e.g., Chan 2008, 2017b, 2019, 2020a, 2020b, 2021c). Jack Levy and his coauthors have written thoughtfully about the evolving research program on power transition and its attribution of status dissatisfaction to rising states (e.g., Dicicco and Levy 1999; Greve and Levy 2018; Levy and Mulligan 2017; Mulligan and Levy 2019).

The view that power parity presages war and instability predated China's recent rise, and it was already being propounded by Organski in his 1968 book. Therefore, it cannot be argued that China's rise had produced this view. This said, it also seems reasonable to point out that with China's rise, this view that power *disparity* contributes to the maintenance of peace and stability and that the opposite phenomenon of a balance of power or a situation whereby power becomes more balanced augurs the danger of war has gained increasing popularity recently among international relations analysts. It is quite remarkable that the once sacrosanct principle of balance of power has been displaced and dispensed with so rapidly and unceremoniously. Writers and commentators who are self-professed realists rarely show any intellectual discomfiture in arguing that the rise of China has changed the international distribution of power in a way that endangers peace. There is almost a complete disciplinary reorientation without any serious debate. If there is a pushback from adherents to the traditional logic that a more balanced distribution of power enhances prospects for peace in the context of discussing the rise of China, I have not encountered it. That the switch of a fundamental tenet of international relations scholarship to its very opposite has occurred so quickly and completely, and that this cornerstone of international relations writings and an almost article of faith (or an "iron law" in the words of some leading scholars) turned out to be so fragile and so easily abandoned are truly remarkable. This volte-face raises the strong possibility that scholarship is adjusting or playing catch-up to government policy and political correctness.

There is another important change in recent scholarship on Sino-American relations compared to the earlier works on realism. Realists such as Kenneth Waltz and John Mearsheimer have posited the sameness of the basic units operating in the international system – namely, all states are alike. In his classic study on international relations, Waltz (1979) considers three variables that determine the nature of all social systems. Is this system anarchic or hierarchical? Are its units differentiated or undifferentiated? And do the units have equal or unequal power? Because the international system is anarchic and its units are undifferentiated, two of Walz's three variables are constants, therefore leaving the third variable – the interstate distribution of capabilities (or power) as *the* key determinant of war and peace, which has been the focus of this discussion. Waltz's influential work argues that all states have the same motivation to seek security and prioritize their survival in conducting foreign policy.

In his view, systemic pressure from an anarchic world forces all states to behave in the same manner. Socialization further fosters conformity or the sameness of states, States that defy the realist injunction to balance against power do not survive, and their extinction contributes to the "iron law" of balancing power. Waltz (1979: 121) asserts emphatically, "balance-of-power politics prevail whenever two, and only two, requirements are met: that the [interstate] order be anarchic and it be populated by units wishing to survive."

Although his theory is sometimes described as defensive realism to distinguish it from Mearsheimer's offensive realism, Waltz (1979: 118) in fact recognizes that states can harbor offensive ambitions, when remarking states "at a minimum, seek their own preservation and, at maximum, drive for universal domination." Nevertheless, the emphasis of Waltz's theoretical formulation is decidedly on his postulation that states are alike in their pursuit of security or survival.

Mearsheimer's (2001: 2) position on this matter of states' basic character or motivation is also quite clear:

> The overriding goal of each state is to maximize its share of world power, which means gaining power at the expense of other states. But great powers do not merely strive to be the strongest of all the great powers, although that is a welcome outcome. Their ultimate aim is to be the hegemon – that is, the only great power in the system.... There are no status quo powers in the international system, save for the occasional hegemon that wants to maintain its dominating position over potential rivals ... the desire for more power does not go away, unless a state achieves the ultimate goal of hegemony.

In Mearsheimer's offensive realism, all states seek to maximize power. They continue to expand until they encounter effective resistance to their ambition. In his words, "Even when a great power achieves a distinct military advantage over its rivals, it continues looking for chances to gain more power. The pursuit of power only stops when hegemony is achieved," and "States do not become status quo powers until they completely dominate the system" (Mearsheimer 2001: 34, 35).

The upshot of both Mearsheimer and Waltz's theories is their emphasis on states' sameness. So what? Those who are alarmed by China's rise introduce a distinction that contradicts this emphasis. Specifically, for example, power-transition theory posits that there are two kinds of states: the revisionist ones (such as China) who seek to change the international order, and the status quo ones (such as the United States) who want to defend this order. They make this distinction without usually being clear about the evidence necessary to establish and distinguish states' revisionist or status quo tendencies, and the benchmarks for assessing these tendencies. Indeed, in the pertinent literature revisionism is sometimes implied to represent a challenge to the existing international order (without, however, defining or specifying the nature and components of this order) and sometimes as a challenge to the existing distribution of interstate power. This analytic move to suggest two different kinds of states – usually based on assertion rather than evidence – is naturally at variance with the view that all states are alike in their character and motivation. In the works of some scholars, the attribution of revisionist or status quo intentions to states serves as the *deus ex machina* to explain war and peace. Power concentrated in the hands of some states (the ones that are allegedly committed to the "status quo") helps to keep peace and stability, but power gains made by the revisionist sort have the opposite effect of endangering peace and stability.

I hasten to add that distinctions separating the so-called satisfied from dissatisfied states (Carr 1946), sated from unsated states (Schuman (1948), imperialist from status quo states (Morgenthau [1948] 1978), revolutionary from status quo states (Kissinger 1957), and revisionist from status quo states (Wolfers 1962) were introduced long before China's recent rise. Therefore, I am not arguing that this terminology was somehow invented in order to communicate the danger that China's ascent poses to world peace and stability. This said, it also seems to me that there has been a recent surge in the deployment of the concept or idea of "revisionism" in scholarship to indicate this danger from rising states in general, and a concomitant abandonment of the postulation that all states are motivated by the same concerns and interests, as espoused by Waltz and Mearsheimer. Revisionism is a term always attached to rising states, and in some analysts' view established states are *by definition* satisfied states, and they cannot therefore be revisionist. For example, Ronald Tammen et al. (2000: 9) assert "By definition, the dominant power is satisfied …[and therefore] is the defender of the status quo. After all, it creates and maintains the global or regional hierarchy from which it accrues substantial benefits."

This view strips much empirical content from the idea of revisionism, and it rules out the possibility as a matter of definition that the already established states, including the United States as the global hegemon, would want to bend the existing rules of international order or invent new ones to further advance their interests. It also overlooks the possibility that the dominant state's incentive to defend the existing order may change; that is, it may not be committed forever to the rules it has created, especially when it finds itself in decline (meaning that the rules no longer serve its interests). Conversely, it ignores the possibility that although a latecomer's capabilities to challenge this order may have increased, this state has also acquired a larger stake in this order that has enabled its ascent, and it is therefore likely to become more supportive of it. The prevailing Western narrative shuttles its logic, focusing on a rising state's increased capabilities to upend the international order without attending to its diminished incentive to do so, while at the same time overlooking the incentive of an established state in decline to revise the existing rules to halt or reverse its decline. Moreover, by casting rising powers as troublemakers bent on challenging "the" international order, this portrayal in effect characterizes them to be not just opponents to the established state(s) but rather the entire international community. Of course, such a sleight of hand also conflates the interests of the hegemon with the interests of the international community as a whole. These are in my view examples of ideational construction that present, consciously or otherwise, the perspective of established states and propagate a narrative in furtherance of their interests.

Alexander Cooley et al. (2019) present an important exception to the criticism just made. Their discussion points to a common confusion caused by the use of the term "revisionism" to refer to both attempts to change a power balance in one's favor and efforts to upend the existing international order. These are obviously different things. To define any attempt to improve a state's power position as revisionist would be tantamount to saying that all rising states (i.e., states that are making relative gains in their capabilities and moving up the interstate hierarchy) are revisionist regardless of whether they intend to alter the rules of international order or challenge the existing hegemon. Cooley et al. (2019) recognize the possibility that a country may be satisfied with its power position but wants to alter the international order. The United States, in their view, is such a state. Conversely, some states may be "distributive revisionists" seeking to improve their share of benefits from the international system, while others are more ambitious "radical revisionists" trying to alter the system itself (Ward 2017). The current prevailing practice of assigning states to binary categories of revisionist or status quo types is also problematic for another reason. Randall Schweller (1994, 2015) calls attention to this problem when he suggests that revisionist states may have limited or unlimited objectives. Hence, it makes sense to treat revisionism as a scalar variable rather than a dichotomous classification.

It is pertinent at this point to bring into this discussion Stephen Walt's (1997) theory of balance of threat, which he intended to improve upon Waltz's (1979) balance-of-power theory but which Waltz rejected because of Walt's reductionism, that is, his introduction of actors' perceptions into his theory and thereby changing the nature of Waltz's theory as a structural theory and one that is framed at the interstate level (and not at the unit level of states). Walt's theory of balance of threat obviously assigns a critical role to the perceptions of officials. Being a subjective variable, it becomes difficult to disconfirm any proposition based on it – even when these officials' perceptions are not grounded in reality. After all, which official or for that matter, which person acts contrary to her subjective understanding of reality? A person poised to jump off the Golden Gate Bridge may be described as acting rationally – according to her *perception* of her situation. Thus, this subjective variable (i.e., perceived threat) introduces a large fudge factor such that, for example, any policy adopted by a state toward China, or any other state, can be justified on the ground of the relevant officials' alleged perceptions about whether China poses a threat, or not, to their country. Officials from two different states can accordingly pursue different policies toward China, one based on their perception of a threat coming from China and the other based on the lack of such perceived threat, and both cases would be supported by balance-of-threat theory. It becomes practically impossible to falsify this theory. One can ask specifically, what evidence would be necessary to disconfirm its proposition that states react to perceived threats to them, or in other words, is its proposition falsifiable? This proposition appears almost tautologically true.

At the risk of being repetitive and not to put too fine a point on it, this view represents academic revisionism. Naturally, science progresses via a series of empirical observations, tests, and revisions, and there is nothing wrong with changing postulations and altering conclusions – unless they reflect changing political currents or government policies rather than any newly available evidence, and when these changes are made in an ad hoc manner to suit an analyst's preferred conclusions. The introduction of the distinction between revisionist and status quo states obviously alters another basic tenet of traditional realism. David Rosseau (2006: 19, italic in original) states clearly that "For classical realists, current or potential power asymmetries are *sufficient* to produce threats." Similarly, Michael Doyle (1997: 168) remarks, "The balance of power doctrine makes the special claim that power – capacity – is the valid and complete measure of threat and that we need to balance against capacity, whatever the intentions that the states are currently expressing."

The label "revisionist state" is brandished about usually without any systematic attempt to document this characterization, which reflects a post hoc designation referring often to former defeated enemies (Chan

2021a; Chan et al. 2021; He et al. 2021). In the pertinent literature, there is rarely any serious discussion about what exactly did Wilhelmine Germany, imperial Japan, Czarist Russia, and contemporary China and Iran do to warrant this label. Which conduct or policy on their part would distinguish these states from Britain, France, or the United States when these latter states were rising powers? In contrast to Nazi Germany and communist USSR, it is more difficult to imagine how international order would have been altered fundamentally if, say, Wilhelmine Germany or imperial Japan had prevailed in World War I and II respectively. Writing about China, Susan Shirk (2007: 4), a political scientist and former Deputy Assistant Secretary of State in Bill Clinton's administration, declares "History teaches us that rising powers are likely to provoke war." It is unclear whether she would include the Unites States in her designation of rising states – or for that matter, Britain and France. Weren't these countries a rising state at one time?

Readers knowledgeable about power-transition theory and other similar explanations of war will recall that these formulations attribute the outbreak of armed hostilities to the revisionist agenda of rising powers – to these countries' cockiness, impatience, and brazen efforts to overthrow the existing international order. These formulations do not typically ask how the established powers became powerful in the first place. Did Britain, France, or the United States behave as status quo countries when they were rising powers? Or did they violate the then prevailing rules of international order? Indeed, what were/are these rules? Those scholars who assign responsibility for starting war to the rising states do not usually specify which rules they had in mind when asserting the alleged revisionist states' violations of international order, or whether the supposed rules were/are just, fair, or obsolete. Kenneth Organski (1968) and his coauthor Jacek Kugler (1980) are prominent exceptions to this generalization. They admit forthrightly that the rules were/are rigged by the established powers to give them disproportionate benefits.

That the designation of some states as "revisionist" and others as committed to the "status quo" continues to be based on assertion rather than analysis cannot be attributed to a lack of evidence or an absence of empirical studies on this topic (e.g., Chan 2015; Chan et al. 2019, 2021; Johnston 2003, 2019; Kastner and Saunders 2012; Sample 2018). A variety of data across countries and over time are available to assess the extent of a country's commitment to the international order, albeit none of them are perfect. Such data include the number of wars waged by a country, its incidence of involvement in militarized interstate disputes, the frequency of its membership in international organizations, its accession to or withdrawal from international accords, the degree of concordance of its voting record in international organizations with the majority of their members, and finally the favorite measure of quantitative international relations analysts, the amount of its defense spending relative to that of other peer countries. One can also consult verbal statements made by leaders to discern whether they want to change or overthrow the international order, such as Donald Trump's declarations introduced earlier.

By any number of objective indicators, the United States appears to be more revisionist than China (Chan 2003b, 2004, 2015; Chan et al. 2021). Judged by its votes in the United Nations General Assembly and its frequency of veto exercised on the Security Council, Washington is far more likely to find itself isolated and out of step with other member states in recent years. This phenomenon contrasts with the early days of the United Nations when Washington and its allies dominated this organization. The USSR and its allies were in the minority, and Moscow was often criticized for its frequent resort to its veto power to block the organization's majority wishes. Since then, the USA has increasingly found itself in a minority and has taken a similar opposition role. Compared to China, it has also rejected or withdrawn from more international accords or agreements, or refused to sign or ratify them. Donald Trump has pulled the United States from various international agreements and organizations, such as the World Health Organization, the Trans-Pacific Partnership, the Iran nuclear deal, and the Paris Climate agreement. While urging other countries to join these accords and multilateral diplomacy, Washington often pulls back from similar commitments – dating back to its refusal to join the League of Nations. Of course, the United States has been involved in far more wars, military attacks, and militarized interstate disputes than China, and it outspends China on its military by several fold. For example, in 2019 US military spending was more than the next eleven highest countries *combined*. Its military spending was 2.8 times greater than China's, accounting for 3.4 percent of its gross domestic product compared to China's 1.9 percent (Stockholm International Peace Research Institute 2020). Finally, Washington has publicly espoused an agenda to promote regime change abroad and has supported color revolutions in other countries to overthrow their government. In words and deeds, if this is not revisionism – meaning an intention to alter the existing world order – what would revisionism entail?

Yet, Western analysts continue to apply labels of "revisionism" and "status quo" to countries without any regard for systematic evidence (e.g., Chan 2003b, 2004, 2015, Chan et al. 2019, 2021). Thus, a country that has declared its commitment to the Westphalian principles of respecting other states' sovereignty and noninterference in their internal affairs, such as China, is characterized "revisionist." Conversely, a country with an avowed and unabashed agenda to promote regime change abroad and one that openly propagates novel doctrines such as the right to wage preventive war, namely the United States, is considered a status quo state. Here again, terms are deployed to indicate the exact opposite of their customary meaning, and key concepts are used to suggest a writer's approval or disapproval of a country's policies rather than this country's actual conduct. This is another instance of ideational construction to generate a political narrative. There are of course important exceptions to this generalization, such as works by Jennifer Lind (2017), Rosemary Foot and Andrew Walter (2011), Iain Johnston (2003, 2019), Randall Schweller (2015) and Stephen Walt (2005).

Finally, the usual discourse in the USA and other Western countries is one-sided in that it holds revisionist countries responsible for international instability or tension because these countries are supposedly clamoring for a "seat at the table," demanding others extend to them the recognition that they feel they deserve. The usual discourse does not ask why the established states decline to accord them this recognition. Or in other words, why do the established states fail to accommodate the rising states? Presumably, the reason for tension stems not only from the alleged revisionist states' "pushiness" in demanding adjustments in others' policies, but also from the reluctance of these other countries to make timely and adequate adjustments. Wars can also happen because the established states refuse to make changes that are warranted because of their relative decline. For any number of psychological, institutional, or political reasons, states experiencing downward mobility may face difficulties in making such adjustments. They want to hold on to the vestiges of their past prestige and privileges, and they decline to trim their sense of self-importance in view of their relative decline. It takes both factors, the rising states pushing for recognition and the refusal by the established states in decline to downsize their agenda and to deflate their ego, to explain interstate conflict. The typical narrative on why wars happen is distorted to present only one side of the story. This bias reflects social construction and political entrepreneurship intended at least in part to mobilize support for acceptance of the established states' perspectives and policy agendas. The word "ambition" is often used to describe alleged revisionist states in ascendance, but it and the word "hubris" are rarely applied to established but declining states wishing to hold on to their power and status.

The conventional and prevailing narrative in the West is also one-sided in another respect. It assigns the role of aggressor to rising states and their leaders' arrogance, rashness, and cockiness. It is of course possible for rising latecomers to have these attributes and to start a war. But it is puzzling why they would want to do so rather than waiting for the ongoing trend to continue to favor them and improve their relative position. To paraphrase Paul Kennedy (1987), why didn't Germany just wait so that mastery of Europe would fall in its laps without having to fight a war? Why start a premature war (the supposed revisionist upstarts have failed in every instance they have launched a military bid for hegemony, leading to their devastating defeat in all these wars)?

My answer would be that conventional accounts given by proponents of power-transition theory have made an error in depicting the two world wars as a German bid to displace Britain as the global hegemon. Rather, these two epic struggles were started by Germany against Russia/the USSR (Chan 2020a). They were preventive wars by a country poised to enter into a period of relative decline vis-à-vis a rising colossus to its east. As already remarked, the two world wars happened not because Berlin had wanted to fight the British, but rather because its diplomacy had failed to persuade the British to stay neutral in these wars.

Adolf Hitler had said, "Everything I undertake is directed against the Russians; if the West is too stupid and blind to grasp this, then I shall be compelled to come to an agreement with the Russians, beat the West, and then after their defeat turn against the Soviet Union with all my forces" (quoted in Copeland 2000: 135). On another occasion, he declared:

Originally I wanted to work together with Britain. But Britain has rejected me again and again. It is true, there is nothing worse than a family quarrel, and racially the English are in a way our relatives ... It's a pity that we have to be locked in this death struggle, while our real enemies in the East can sit back and wait until Europe is exhausted. That is why I do not wish to destroy Britain and never shall. (quoted in Higgins 1966: 55)

Thus, proponents of power-transition theory and others who present the two world wars as Germany's offensive bid to seize world leadership from a declining Britain are mistaken. The real target of Germany's aggression was Russia/the USSR, and these were preventive wars to snuff out a rising competitor that would present a future threat to Germany as German leaders saw it (Copeland 2000; Van Evera 1984, 1999; see also Levy 2008, 2011; Levy and Gochal 2001/2002; Levy and Mulligan 2017). They were not started by a cocky, overconfident upstart to seek global hegemony. They reflected instead anxiety, even alarm, that Germany's best days were already behind it, with apprehensions about its potentially declining international position in the future. Prior to World War I, German leaders saw their country isolated and their only ally, Austria-Hungary, suffering a precipitous and inevitable decline. Their strategic situation would get even worse in the coming days. "They saw themselves encircled, blocked, threatened with demotion or even disappearance. German chancellor Bethmann Hollweg wondered 'if there is any purpose in planting new trees' on his estate near Berlin, as 'in a few years the Russians would be here anyway'" (*The Guardian* 2014: no page number).

The dominant narrative that the two world wars was a hegemonic struggle initiated by Germany against Britain strikes me as another example of historical revisionism and political construction. Although Berlin was aggressive, it was more interested in dominating Europe and thwarting Russia's rise than bidding for global hegemony. It never came close to matching the power of United States, a country that had already displaced Britain as the world's most powerful country before World War I. Ironically, in the one indisputable case in modern history pointing to the overtaking of an established global hegemon by a rising latecomer – that of the United States taking over Britain's hegemonic position – this leadership transition was peaceful.

There can of course be valid and legitimate reasons for advancing different historical interpretations. In my view, however, the serious distortions one finds in popular and even scholarly renditions of the two world wars and other historical events raise serious questions about distortion. They reflect more than a small extent of social and political construction, seeking to force historical realities to conform to a preferred, "politically correct" account of how history had unfolded. With respect to power-transition theory's interpretation of history, Ned Lebow and Benjamin Valentino (2009: 40) have remarked:

> Should war come between the United States and China in the future it will not be a result of a power transition. The greater risk is that conflict will result from the misperception that such a transition is imminent, and the miscalculation by decision-makers in the United States (or China) that China will soon be in a position to do what no state has done before – unilaterally dictate the rules of the international system. Power transition theory would be made self-fulfilling – generating its own corroboration where history has failed to oblige.

Kenneth Waltz (2000: 36, italic in original) has also commented candidly, "When Americans speak of preserving the balance of power in East Asia through their military presence, the Chinese understandably take this to mean that they intend to maintain the strategic hegemony they now enjoy in the *absence* of such a balance." In other words, when Americans argue for maintaining a balance of power in East Asia, they really have in mind sustaining an *imbalance* of power in favor of the United States. Words and phrases such as revisionism and balance of power do not always mean what they say (Chan et al. 2021). They are deployed in ways that often depart from their customary meaning, sometimes referring to the exact opposite of this customary meaning. Analytic flip flops, innuendos, and contortions are not infrequent in the statements of officials or analyses presented by scholars. Moreover, scholars often adjust their analyses to reflect changes in their government's official policy. As I have observed elsewhere (Chan 2024a) and will discuss further later in this chapter, problem shifts, policy shifts, and power shifts often tend to follow and echo one another.

The flip flop from traditional realist views on states' sameness to the idea that there are two types of states, revisionist and status quo types, can be a sign of scholarly entrepreneurship. As with realism's basic tenet that balance of power conduces peace and stability, a complete reversal is possible and can occur rather quickly. The fragility of disciplinary consensus on its core propositions and assumptions has been quite astonishing. Scholarly fashions come and go, often seemingly adjusting to the turns and twists of a government's official policies. Adam Przeworski and Henry Teune (1970) expressed their hope that someday students of comparative politics would be able to replace the names of countries with those of variables in their studies. It appears that this day is still some time away for students of international relations.

Before closing this section, I should like to make three points. First, although realism is still the dominant theoretical paradigm in the study of international relations, it has not performed well in advancing the frontier of our knowledge. Often scholars have to engage in various analytic contortions in order to shoehorn the available evidence to fit their expectation. The rather arbitrary designation of revisionism to states comes to mind as an example. Perceptions of threat, as in Walt's theory of threat, is another example that is practically non-falsifiable. It would be one thing if a theory misses its target in this or that instance. As my earlier reference to Gary Goertz suggests, it would be setting the bar too high to argue that even one disconfirming case would invalidate a theory. It would, however, be another matter if a theory misses repeatedly the "big things," that is, momentous events such as the fall of the Berlin Wall, the demise of the Soviet Union, the outbreak of world war, and the peaceful leadership transition between Britain and the United States – both the occurrence of events that were unexpected and the nonoccurrence of the expected. Regarding the latter phenomenon, China had overtaken Russia, Japan, Germany, and Britain, and war had not happened between them.

As just mentioned, the peaceful collapse of the Soviet Union is another example. Realism would not expect a state to accept its disintegration without putting up a fight. Realism would also not expect the peaceful end of the Cold War, or for that matter, most major states joining the US side (that is, supporting the stronger rather weaker side) during the Cold War. This bandwagon behavior would appear puzzling for many self-professed realists, but it would be an even more disturbing anomaly if a state manages to become predominant because, as Jack Levy has noted, all realists would in his view agree that the rise of such a unipolar power should be resisted by all states and therefore should not happen (e.g., Levy 2003, 2004). Realists would of course also not expect major states to subcontract their defense to another state, such as Germany and Japan have done in relying on the United States for their security.

These and other countries have eschewed arming themselves with nuclear weapons even though they clearly have the wherewithal to develop and acquire them. It is even more enigmatic from the realist point of view when a country already in possession of these weapons agrees to give them up in exchange for security guarantees from other countries – as Ukraine did and is now suffering the consequences of its decision (that is, becoming the victim of Russian invasion).

Second, not all conflicts are necessarily due to the security dilemma (Jervis 1978). This concept refers to the regrettable consequences that ensue when two defensively minded states attempt to protect themselves and yet their behavior is misinterpreted by their counterpart as a sign of offensive intention, causing it to in turn take actions intended to protect itself. The resulting sequence of actions and reactions can cause a mirror image of hostility or suspicion to persist and escalate. The security dilemma, however, has been overused. It has been applied to explain some wars of choice. In these latter cases, officials start a war intentionally with their eyes wide open, and therefore these situations cannot be attributed to misunderstanding or misinterpretation. Germany's initiation of the two world wars are such instances (Lieber 2007). It is also difficult to explain the US invasion of Iraq as the result of unfortunate misinformation or misperception as the reasons given for this invasion were that Saddam Hussein had weapons of mass destruction and ties to Al Qaeda. Both claims turned out to be false – fabrications used to justify its invasion.

Third and relatedly, it is possible that leaders can understand quite well their counterparts' fears, concerns, and red lines. I tend to believe that this situation describes the relationship between China and the United Sates, although I do not have any direct evidence to support this conjecture. However, Iain Johnston (2011: 28) has written that "... there is evidence that the very top levels of both sides actually have a better understanding of each other's interests and red lines than is implied in public debates." My view thus concurs with his statement. Sometimes leaders on both sides of Sino-American relations are able to push the other country's "buttons" and pull back just before getting too close to the danger zone of confrontation, precisely because they know well what really irritates the other side as well as its bottom line. Their actions also sometimes reflect domestic political considerations. In either case, tension between these two countries cannot always be explained as the result of misunderstanding or a failure of communication. Naturally, saying so does not rule out accidents or lapses, or the possibility that events may get out of the officials' control.

The Production and Propagation of Enemy Images and Political Narratives

I have argued earlier that China's increasing capabilities is the "problem" from the US perspective. China's rise has eroded the preeminent position that Washington has enjoyed thus far, even though the USA continues to be the most powerful country in the world. There is, however, an important linkage that my presentation has omitted thus far, and it should now be introduced in the discussion to qualify my earlier assertion. Specifically, another country's power or capabilities can be interpreted in different ways. This phenomenon can be seen as inconsequential or even a positive development to the extent that the rising country in question is an ally. Alternatively, it may be perceived as an ominous development causing anxiety and even alarm for the relevant officials. The point I am trying to drive at is of course about how a country's capabilities are translated into threat perception in the eyes of other countries' officials – or not.

Threat perception is a social construct (Rousseau 2006). People tend to perceive, sort, and assign others into an in- or out-group. "Social identities are bundles of shared values, beliefs, attitudes, norms, and roles that are used to draw a boundary between the 'in group' and the 'out group'" (Rousseau 2006: 12). People treat others differently on the basis of these identities, even when the features that separate the in- and out-groups are trivial, temporary, and artificially imposed, such as when people are assigned arbitrarily to different teams in experiments on human behavior. Shared identities between the people of two countries tend to dampen fear or concern, when a counterpart country makes important relative gains. Conversely, when this counterpart is seen to belong to another group, its increasing capabilities are likely to be seen as threatening. In other words, when the other side is seen to be different from "us," we are likely to perceive its increasing capabilities as threatening.

The versions of realism espoused by Waltz and Mearsheimer discussed in the last section would argue that the identity of the counterpart country is irrelevant in one's threat assessment of that country. Experimental results show, however, that the identification of this other country as "us" or "them" makes an important difference in this assessment. "Similar states are seen as less threatening and similarity decreases the salience of relative gains" (Rousseau 2006:116). As discussed earlier, threat perception – the belief that the other country harbors aggressive intentions – is, however, the key distinction that separates Walt's theory of balance of threat from Waltz's theory of balance of power. Walt refers to this variable to explain, for example, why major states joined the USA in opposing the USSR during the Cold War, even though the USA was clearly stronger than the USSR. Waltz's theory would have expected these states to instead join the USSR to oppose the USA. The current discussion should make clear that Walt's balance-of-threat theory is not wrong, but it presents practically a truism – and the key empirical question involved is how leaders decide whether another state poses a threat.

American college students saw China to be more dissimilar from the United States compared to other countries such as Britain, Japan, Russia, Brazil, and Cuba – at a time (spring 2001) when Sino-American relations were not as rocky and tense as it has become in more recent days. David Rousseau (2006: 106, 149) reports that only 4 percent of these students saw China to be similar to the United States, and the American public "seems to be skeptical of the liberal-constructivist claim that democratization and marketization of China will improve bilateral relations." The latter comment suggests that the general public had already come to a conclusion that the US officials supposedly came only belatedly to realize in more recent years. This phenomenon suggests that either the general public was more far-sighted than the officials, or the officials were more naive than the general public – or that the officials were aware of what the general public had professed in 2001 but failed to express their views publicly as strongly and clearly as they have done more recently.

My earlier discussion has referenced recent comments by US officials and scholars pointing to various Chinese transgressions such as sup-pressing political dissidents in Hong Kong and Xinjiang, denying Chinese citizens' human rights, intimidating China's neighbors includ-ing Taiwan, and engaging in malpractices such as industrial espionage and election meddling. I have also questioned whether these alleged offenses committed by Beijing were really the primary reason for the worsening relations between Beijing and Washington in recent years. This said, these charges are important in framing popular discourse and heightening the salience of differences between the two countries in the public's mind. That is, words like democracy, human rights, unfair trade practices, and coercion and intimidation of neighbors have an important impact in priming the audience so that they see more and sharper distinctions between "us" and "them" – even though objectively, as I have argued, China has not acted more egregiously than the USA. It is, however, perceptions that matter, and political entrepreneurship in this case involves the accentuation of the differences between the United States and China.

These differences were further propounded and propagated by the popular press, comments by pundits, and the ubiquitous internet. Western media and blogsphere were responsible for creating an echo chamber, amplifying popular memes and producing a "discursive tidal wave" (Johnston 2013: 47) such as the image of a newly assertive China that promotes a simplistic and distorted view of reality. These memes and narratives became widely circulated after 2018 when the US government designated China as a revisionist state in its national security documents. The image of an assertive, even aggressive, China started to gain prominence among media pundits and even scholars. They crowded out opposing views or alternative interpretations (Breuer and Johnston 2019).

Rapid transformation of the image one holds about another country, even a complete reversal of this image, has happened before. The views of leading US figures and even popular perceptions of Wilhelmine Germany were at one time highly favorable. Woodrow Wilson, who was to later become the president of the United States was one of them. Kaiser's Germany was seen as a constitutional monarchy, a nation practicing the rule of law, and an efficient bureaucratic state par excellence. But as World War I approached, these views were quickly replaced by images of marauding Teutonic knights bent on military conquest of their peaceful neighbors (Oren 2003). American image of Japan also went through a quick transformation from one that existed during and immediately before World War II to that in the wake of the Korean War: from a conniving aggressive state on a rampage to one representing a loyal US ally and a powerful bulwark against communism in East Asia. US support of and image about Iran had also experienced such drastic change in a short time after the overthrow of the Shah's government by the supporters of Ayatullah Khomeini – even though little had changed in these respective governments' credentials as a democracy or their treatment of human rights. What had changed was their relations with Washington and official US policies toward these countries. As suggested in the last section, the analyses and conclusions of scholars tend to reflect these latter changes, adjusting to what is seen to be politically correct at any given moment. Major theoretical tenets and seeming disciplinary consensus can turn out to be quite fragile. They can be jettisoned and replaced by opposite analytic positions with remarkable ease and speed. Policy shifts by governments and problem shifts by academic researchers can be closely connected notwithstanding the vaunted idea of scholarly objectivity and independence.

7 | Conclusion

From Sino-American Relations to the Evolving Global Picture

In this concluding chapter, I summarize the key ideas and propositions presented in the preceding discussion, and then turn to a brief review of Sino-American relations from the perspective of punctuated equilibrium and recent events in US domestic politics that appear to presage a new era in its foreign policy. Donald Trump, who campaigned on a platform of Make America Great Again, won the 2024 presidential election. The results of this election showed that Americans were seriously divided in their political and cultural outlook. Public acrimonies and deep partisanship continue to dominate American politics. Trump's statements on the campaign trail have raised more than a few eyebrows. For example, he has said that if a NATO ally did not pay enough for its own defense, his administration would not protect it and would instead "encourage [Russia] to do whatever the hell they want" (www.youtube.com/watch?v=HloWfFfXj7I). His post-election statements, such as those introduced earlier, continue to be controversial, not only at home but abroad as well. The adage that "all politics is local," usually attributed to Tip O'Neill, a former Speaker of the US House of Representatives, suggests the primacy of domestic politics in politicians' agenda. Foreign policy will have to take a back seat.

Gary Goertz (2003: 172) is certainly right when he remarks that problems come and go, and we therefore do not have eternal problems. As the global hegemon, the United States is in a uniquely powerful position to define problems and mobilizing collective action to tackle them. However, what Washington considers to be a problem may not be perceived as such by other countries. Goertz (2003: 173) describes this phenomenon as "hegemonic problem creation," a term with *double entendre*, to contrast it with the traditional view that hegemons are helpful and necessary for solving collective action problems such as according to the hegemonic stability theory (e.g., Kindleberger 1973). "Problem definition is a social construction, at the same time it is an exercise of power" (Goertz 2003: 174).

That the histories of public policies tend to be characterized by long periods of stasis or stagnation only to be followed by sudden bursts of large and dramatic change represents the central idea of punctuated equilibrium and this book's main theme. Significant changes are rare; but when they happen, they tend to be big, fast, and sudden. Certainly, Sino-American relations have undergone twists and turns and peaks and valleys. The history of these relations also presents the characteristics of both lulls and lurches, marked by watershed events such as China's entry into the Korean War and Nixon's visit to Beijing. In retrospect, these turning points plunged their relations to a new nadir or lifted them to a new height – in either case, setting these countries' relations on a new course and a new "normal" around which these relations would drift or fluctuate only in a minor way until the next phase or era. As such, one can demarcate these relations to belong to different "epochs." As I have remarked earlier, it is also possible for Sino-American relations to experience a steady process of change without any dramatic landmark event marking a clear turning point. It appears that China and the United States have already entered a period of more contentious relationship in the early 2000s, and it is not clear whether they have found a new equilibrium yet.

The forces of positive and negative feedback play a large part in influencing public policies. Positive feedback loops amplify the demand and pressure for change, and they accelerate the momentum for this change. "Going with the winner" psychology provides one example of such bandwagon effect, contributing to a self-fulling prophecy. The history of rollcall votes on recognizing the Beijing government to represent China in the United Nations shows these forces in operation, and this process gives expression to the saying that an inevitable outcome or ineluctable event whose moment has finally come. Media "feeding frenzy" that grabs public and legislative attention offers another illustration. In international relations, we sometimes see a similar dynamic when states' actions create a conflict spiral such as in Lewis Richardson's (1960) classic model of armament begetting counter-armament. The events leading to the outbreak of World War I has also sometimes been analogized to a run-away locomotive due to the leaders of European countries becoming overwhelmed by the rush of events and losing control of their policy machinery such as the Kaiser's inability to alter the Schlieffen plan on the eve of hostilities (Tuchman 1962).

In contrast to positive feedback, the forces of negative feedback tend to dampen the pressure for change or to put a brake to the momentum to bring it about. These forces have therefore a stabilizing effect, tending to reinforce the status quo or to restore a situation to its prior state after a perturbation. In the 1980s, 1990s, and even early 2000s, disturbances to Sino-American relations, such as China's bloody crackdown of protestors at Tiananmen Square in 1989, the US bombing of China's embassy in Belgrade in 1991, George W. Bush's decision to sell F-16 fighter aircraft to Taiwan in 1995, the issuance of a visa by Washington for Taiwan's President Lee Teng-hui to visit the USA in 1995, and the collision of a Chinese fighter jet and a US intelligence aircraft off China's Hainan Island in 2001, were managed by both sides in such a way to avoid escalation and to return their relations to normalcy. As I have argued, deep and extensive commercial and financial ties served as a ballast to stabilize Beijing and Washington's bilateral relations. Domestic interests and voices on both sides of the Pacific urged caution and moderation on these previous occasions. In more recent years, these interests and voices have become much more subdued or muted.

Moreover, the economic decoupling and technological embargo initiated by the USA against China have removed these forces of negative feedback that have heretofore held back escalating tension and contained mutual acrimony. Domestic forces in both countries appear to have become more pronounced to push for a policy of getting tough on the other side. The US business community, for example, has not been inclined recently to lobby for a softer approach to China as it had done previously, and both US political parties have also come to a consensus to pursue a hard-line policy toward China even though they rarely agree on other issues. Recent congressional initiatives, such as to ban Tik Tok from operating in the USA unless it divests itself of ownership by China-based company ByteDance (Tik Tok's global headquarters are based in Los Angeles and Singapore), sends a dangerous signal that can put the two countries' relations on a steep course of deterioration. It can potentially invite Beijing's retaliation against US-owned or -domiciled multinational corporations such as Apple, Microsoft, Nike, and Tesla.

The forces of positive and negative feedback can be reinforced or held in check by political action. The threat of retaliation or punishment would have surely restrained the allies and partners of Napoleon,

Hitler, or Stalin from thoughts of defection. Moscow's repression of the Hungarian uprising in 1956 and the Prague Spring in 1968 would also have this chilling effect. Similarly, small countries in the Western Hemisphere and even relatively large countries in other regions would have to think twice before antagonizing the USA after they have observed Washington's actions toward Grenada, Panama, Libya, Serbia, and Iraq. With respect to Napoleon's France, Hitler's Germany, and the USSR, we know that when an opportunity was presented for the victims of their coercion to defect, the result was immediate and dramatic. A country's own policies and practices could abet or hinder the forces of either positive or negative feedback. Washington's frequent and even increasing resort to commercial sanctions and financial embargoes has the effect of incentivizing countries that are concerned about becoming the targets of such economic coercion in the future to take anticipatory precaution by diversifying their trade away from the USA and divesting their dollar-denominated assets.

A focusing event is often present in calling attention to the existence of a problem that requires urgent attention. Such an event, when publicized by the media and political entrepreneurs, presents a choice opportunity to alter existing policy. I have mentioned nuclear accidents and the discovery of a hole in the earth's ozone as examples in the anti-nuclear movement and the environmental movement. Some developments in interstate relations show the role of a trigger or precipitant in bringing about a punctuation, such as the unraveling of Napoleon's wartime coalition in the wake of his military debacle in Russia, the outbreak of World War I that followed the assassinations at Sarajevo, and Mao and Nixon's respective decisions that placed Sino-American relations on a new footing for the following decades. We can point in retrospect to these events or decisions indicating historic turning points, whether they themselves caused these sharp discontinuities or ruptures from a previous situation, or they played an important role in introducing the preconditions or setting the stage for the major changes to follow. The defeat of Napoleon's *Grande Armée* in Russia and the assassination of Archduke Ferdinand and his wife in the summer of 1914 had the effect of introducing or creating a choice opportunity, whereas Mao's decision to intervene in the Korean War and Nixon's decision to travel to Beijing represented in themselves the policy choices that these leaders had made.

On other occasions, we cannot discern clearly even in retrospect any trigger or precipitant that could have played a decisive role in bringing about a historical transformation. The collapse and dissolution of the USSR, the ongoing deterioration in Sino-American relations, and China's representation in the United Nations appear to be the culmination of a protracted process and cannot be attributed to any single catalyst. Their occurrence appears to be the cumulative result of multiple contributing factors. Moreover, even after a situation has taken an important turn, we are often still unsure whether it has settled down to a new equilibrium. It is hard to tell, for example, whether Russia and China's relations with the West, especially the United States, have stabilized at a new level. Honesty also dictates that we acknowledge our uncertainty when it comes to deciding cause-effect relationships. For example, is the current Russo-Ukrainian War a punctuation and a turning point marking the onset of a fundamentally different relationship between Russia and the West, or was it itself the culmination of a series of prior decisions and developments? It can be both.

As noted already on several previous occasions, although the perspective of punctuated equilibrium may be enlightening in studying many issue areas, and although it offers an accurate description of the policymaking process, it is unable to help us make predictions about exactly when and where major changes will occur. This acknowledgment, however, would also apply to many areas of the physical and biological sciences, where experts are also unable to make precise predictions even though they have a rather good grasp of the basic dynamics and processes involved in producing earthquakes and cancers, for example. To paraphrase Stephen Gould, who with his co-author, Niles Eldredge, introduced and popularized the idea of punctuated equilibrium, reality is too complex for us to be dogmatic or, one might add, overconfident. Intellectual humility is a virtue.

Although we cannot pinpoint the timing of a punctuation, it is reasonable to hypothesize that the longer change has been held at bay, the greater the accumulated pressure to induce a punctuation and when it comes, it is likely to appear with greater suddenness and force. The forces that produce a long overdue change, however, can be so strong as to cause overshooting or overreaction. Thus, Baumgartner et al. (2009: 607) remark:

... the violent earthquake results from the friction and the associated buildup of pressure, not any momentary increase on the forces pushing to overcome the friction. At any given time, the response to the pressure is out of synch with the level of pressure applied: friction causes the linkage between inputs and outputs of the system to be disproportionate – underresponse because of friction, then overresponse in response to built-up pressures.

Acknowledging my own limitations, although I have introduced in my discussion several ongoing processes, I have not delved into them to make predictions about how specifically they will unfold and whether any specific outcome will occur, and if so, when and how. Thus, for example, although I have mentioned an ongoing movement abetted by some countries such as China and Russia to dethrone the dollar in international commerce and finance, I have not undertaken any deep analysis of this process. Similarly, although I have mentioned that there is the possibility of an anti-US coalition emerging around China, I have also not said much beyond arguing that such a coalition may either not occur at all or if it does, it will happen quickly. One of the predictions of punctuated equilibrium is of course that punctuations are rare but when they happen, they are big and fast. I have not done an extensive analysis of the dollar's future status and the prospects for an anti-US coalition to form because it will require a separate book and much deeper understanding of the ongoing dynamics in these cases. My guess is that even those working in the international finance community and officials involved in the Shanghai Cooperation Organization and BRICS associations also are not in a position to make definitive predictions about these possible developments.

The future evolution of the SCO and the BRICS group can be informative about how non-Western countries are placing, or hedging, their bets. Do these institutions continue to expand their membership, or is their expansion showing signs of stalling? It is important to stress, however, membership in these institutions does not necessarily mean a commitment to an anti-Western coalition. It can instead simply signify hedging behavior or diversification of relations. Such conduct can be meaningful in revealing how leaders of the pertinent countries are judging the direction in which international relations are moving. There are other possible indicators of states' alignment or realignment behavior, ranging from public opinions in different countries (which, at least before Trump 2.0, showed more favorable views of the United States and unfavorable views of China, reversing the phenomena just a few years ago when Trump 1.0's policies have caused US popularity to plummet) to the intensity in their trade relations and their positions on United Nations rollcall votes. A recent study by Moyer et al. (2021) seeks to establish relative US and Chinese influence in different countries, and if such studies can be extended longitudinally, they can track changes over time. They can provide us with an idea about the persistence or fragility of US influence, the speed of any change, the reversibility of this change, and variations across different countries and issue areas.

Among the important insights provided by the "garbage can" model of policymaking is the idea of serendipity or fortuitous timing. It is inherently difficult to predict when and how independent streams of problems, solutions, participants, and choice opportunities would converge to produce a major policy change – or fail to have such an effect. This phenomenon suggests that it is difficult for anyone to have complete control of the policy agenda, although clearly the rules of the game and the differences in their influence suggest that some political actors are in a stronger position to exercise this control than others.

What we have learned from the first generation of scholars on policymaking – luminaries such as Lindblom, Simon, and Wildavsky – continue to be valid. People's cognitive limitations, their inclination to accept "satisficing" as a decision heuristic, and their tendency to "muddle through" suggest that inertia and continuity prevail most of the time. This conservative tendency is also assisted by the usual organizational proclivities, bureaucratic politics, and interpersonal dynamics such as groupthink (Janis 1982). Thanks to the pathbreaking works of Kingdon and Baumgartner and Jones, we have gained additional insights on policymaking processes. We now understand that stasis and change can be the opposite sides of the same coin. Policies can stagnate or fluctuate within a narrow band for a long time until cumulative pressure culminates in a major transformation. When the accumulated pressure is finally released, it can cause overreaction.

Several ideas have made repeated appearance in my analysis: time, momentum, cumulative pressure, conjunction, shocks, or focusing events introducing or creating choice opportunities, and limitations in policymakers' resources – including their time, attention, and political conviction, capital, and courage. There is, moreover, the idea of equifinality, suggesting that there are multiple paths that can lead to the same outcome. Thus, although I have focused on the danger of Taiwan becoming the fuse that ignites a Sino-American armed conflict, other possibilities exist such as an incident on the Korean peninsula or in the South China Sea. Possible incidents in the latter areas are less likely in my mind to trigger a Sino-American clash, but the danger is still there. Before August 1914, no one had anticipated that there would be a successful assassination plot carried out in Sarajevo to set the European countries on a collision course.

Time is important and relevant for gestation and maturation to occur. An idea before its time is difficult to gain widespread support or acceptance. As time goes by, pressure for change accumulates. An idea gains popularity and gathers momentum, providing the necessary conditions that lay the groundwork for punctuation to occur. Timing is also important. Windows of opportunity may open only briefly, and choice opportunities are fleeting. Smart policymakers and political entrepreneurs benefit from timely moves to capitalize on these moments. It is always more effective and expedient to ride with the wave than to go against the tide. Germany's chancellor, Otto von Bismark, had remarked, "The statesman's task is to hear God's footsteps marching through history, and to try and catch on to His coattails as He marches past" (www.goodreads.com/quotes/217967-the-statesman-s-task-is-to-hear-god-s-footsteps-marching-through).

With respect to Sino-American relations, it appears that we may be in a zone of greatest danger in the next twenty to twenty-five years. During this period, China is/will be strong enough to cause US concerns and even anxieties, but not so strong that it can convincingly deter Washington from getting into an armed conflict against it. Many in Washington who are advocating a policy of strategic clarity to support Taiwan obviously believe that should there be a showdown, the USA still holds the military edge now. They have also evidently not thought much beyond the next twenty-five years. China's economic growth is expected to slow down from its torrid pace in the 1980s, 1990s, and even the early 2000s. But it is still likely to outpace the US rate of growth. Most analysts anticipate that in nominal terms China's economy will be larger than the US economy by 2050 if not a bit earlier. By then, there should be a more stable balance between the two countries. As remarked earlier, although many who advocate a hard-line US policy toward China consider themselves to be realists, they do not usually share the realist tenet that a balance of power contributes to peace and stability. Rather, to the extent that they share the premise of power-transition theory (Organski 1968; Organski and Kugler 1980) and Thucydides' Trap (Allison 2015, 2017), they believe that interstate power shifts that bring about greater parity or balance of power among states augur war and instability – at least when US power is being balanced. If the traditional realists are right, the risk of war will diminish greatly after the next two and half decades because by then the balance of power would discourage both sides from contemplating the use of force.

But even now, the consequences of a war between great powers armed with nuclear weapons are too horrible to contemplate – one reason why in every previous episode involving such risk in cases studied in Chapter 4 Washington had decided not to intervene militarily. Indeed, the idea of one nuclear-armed great power defeating another even in a conflict limited to conventional forces is fraught with danger. This said, China does not have to defeat the USA in a crisis involving Taiwan; it has just to show that the consequences of a conflict will exceed the costs that the USA is willing to bear. It will have the "home court" advantage, whereas US capabilities will be attenuated by the loss-of-power gradient due to Taiwan's distance from its home base (Boulding 1962). As mentioned earlier, simulations undertaken by US analysts have shown repeatedly that China prevails in these gaming exercises pertaining to a military showdown over Taiwan. Indeed, discussions of an asymmetry in the military capabilities of the two sides are dangerously incomplete because they overlook the asymmetry in their respective stake in a dispute and thus also the asymmetry in their respective resolve. Interstate disputes are as much a contest of power as they are a contest of will. As Thomas Schelling (1966) remarked some time ago, international confrontation involves diplomatic and military brinksmanship that leaves something to chance. It is an exercise of competitive risk-taking. Differences in relative stake and resolve point to which side is more willing to run greater risks, and which side is more willing to endure heavier costs and persevere greater hardship.

Momentum creates its own dynamic of positive reinforcing feedback. It can stem from people's feeling or perception that something's time has come – which political entrepreneurs seek to foster or dampen depending on whether they are in favor of or against the change in question. An important part of momentum is people's psychology of "going with the winner," which can and often does create a snowball or bandwagon effect in political contests with people flocking to the perceived winner or front runner. Perceptions create their own reality, and the dynamic of "going with the winner" can create a self-fulfilling prophecy in national elections, movements in the stock market, and international developments such as the continued dominance of the USA or possibly its precipitous decline. The phenomenon of "going with the winner" can accelerate momentum and produce oversized winning coalitions.

Taking timely advantage of opportunities is easier said than done. Whether strategic opportunism is feasible depends in part on what else one already has on one's plate. Domestic partisan politics, election campaigns, personal or family scandals, and any number of other possible issues such as the physical age of top officials in charge of foreign policy can limit or impede their attempt to seize the moment. As emphasized on several occasions, the window of opportunity must be open simultaneously for multiple actors to achieve a policy punctuation, especially in international relations (Nincic 2011). The stars are, however, usually not aligned for this to happen.

Whether pressures build up over time to lay the groundwork for a subsequent punctuation depends of course on whether policymakers make appropriate and timely adjustments to head off ruptures, even disasters, that can otherwise occur. Baumgartner and Jones point to institutional frictions as a cause of delayed or inadequate response to a looming policy problem even when officials are aware of its existence. They have other more immediate and pressing priorities such as winning elections. Thus, that the Social Security program is headed for insolvency has not prevented US politicians from kicking the proverbial can down the road. Short-term considerations often trump the necessity of making hard choices that may be unpopular. Electoral cycles and term limitations incline politicians in democracies to limit their attention to the near term. Short attention span and a short time horizon are a common phenomenon. Randall Schweller (2008) also tells the story of domestic discord causing Britain and France's lethargic and inadequate balancing against the emergent threat coming from Germany in the 1930s. Thus, political constraints, in addition to people's cognitive rigidity, their focus on the near term, and their psychological commitment to the status quo, can contribute to an inability to address problems before they threaten to explode, sometimes literally as in the case of World War I.

An important point from my discussion is that domestic challenges and opponents are often the primary focus of officials and politicians' attention. Tip O'Neill's quip that "all politics is local" suggests that politics does *not* stop at the water's edge. Domestic politics and foreign policy are inevitably and intimately intertwined, and usually the former takes precedence over the latter. Robert Putnam's (1988) two-level games show the importance of their interactions which are a two-way street – meaning that just as domestic politics, such as a president's policy space, can affect her ability and incentive to conclude a foreign policy deal, foreign policy can also affect this official's domestic popularity and effectiveness. The situation facing Israeli Prime Minister Benjamin Netanyahu in the wake of Hamas' attack in October 2023 illustrates vividly this situation, as do the dynamic interactions between Russia and Ukraine in their ongoing war and the domestic standing of both Vladimir Putin and Volodymyr Zelensky.

The suggestion about linkages between domestic politics and foreign policy is not an abstract proposition. Republicans have explicitly linked the funding of US assistance to Ukraine in its war against Russia to the passage of a legislation on US border security. That aid to Ukraine can thus be held up as a hostage in domestic politics compromises Washington's reputation for reliability abroad, especially because officials and politicians from both US political parties have proclaimed how important it was to provide this aid to Ukraine to stop Russian aggression. When these statements fail to be backed up by action, Washington's credibility suffers.

Election politics can also seriously impair this credibility. When Senate negotiators were rumored to have reached a bipartisan package deal linking legislation to aid Ukraine to US border security in early 2024, Donald Trump urged Republican legislators to abort this bipartisan deal. He appeared less interested in fixing the immigration and border issues than to use them to campaign against Biden and Harris in the 2024 presidential election (Knight 2024). Republican Speaker of the House of Representative Mike Johnson declared that the Senate deal would be "dead on arrival" in the House (Brooks 2024). In the meantime, House Republicans passed the resolution to impeach Secretary of Homeland Security Alejandro Majorkas by a margin of a single vote (Alemany 2024).

On previous occasions, US officials and politicians had also declared loudly and repeatedly how important Vietnam and Afghanistan were to US national security in part to "sell" interventions in these countries to a skeptical public. These exaggerated declarations were intended to overcome the public's resistance to US overseas involvements (sometimes reflecting the American people's traditional isolationist sentiments, Kupchan 2020), but they had the effect of creating a rhetorical trap, making subsequent policy reversals more difficult to undertake and when the decision was made to extricate the USA from the morass, its reputation suffered greater damage because officials and politicians had staked their country's reputation to these misadventures, having declared earlier that US involvement was a test of its will and that vital national interests were at stake.

To the extent that politicians often try to demonize or scapegoat foreigners in their competition to demonstrate their patriotic credentials to their domestic audience (Colaresi 2005), these words can box them in. Their words can also cause adverse reverberations in the target country, such as the effects that US anti-Asian (immigration) legislation had in Japan in abetting its nationalists and militarists prior to World War II (Ward 2017). Reciprocation of enemy images in turn exacerbated these countries' relations. Domestic politics and discourse in one country can thus have an impact on those of another country, such as in this case in enhancing the credibility and popularity of Japan's nationalists and militarists, by creating a positive feedback loop of mutual recrimination linking the respective countries' domestic and international politics. This book has argued that threat perception involves social construction – one that, however, has often been dominated, even hijacked by, political demagogues and partisan entrepreneurs to arouse emotions and mobilize support for their agenda. Ironically, in this process the hard-liners of opposing countries are often one another's best allies, creating an echo chamber by their rhetoric and creating and sustaining mirror images of hostility that has a tendency to become entrenched.

As argued previously, people's cognitive rigidity and their conscious or unconscious reluctance to alter their accustomed ways of thinking and acting are an important reason why we observe stasis or stagnation in public policymaking. Bureaucratic protocols, entrenched interests, gatekeepers that preserve policy monopolies, the tendency for satisficing and muddling through to permeate the policymaking process, and simply the fact that people live busy lives with many distractions and pressing deadlines work to perpetuate the status quo and stall necessary changes.

As these words were being written, news media reported that three US soldiers were killed in a drone attack on a military outpost in northern Jordan near Syria. This attack produced the predictable calls from conservative politicians such as Lindsey Graham (US Senator from South Carolina), Donald Trump, and Nikki Haley (the latter two were candidates at that time competing for the Republican Party's nomination in the 2024 presidential election, although Haley subsequently dropped out of this race) to retaliate by striking targets inside Iran, which was suspected to be the sponsor for this and other groups behind attacks on US bases in the Middle East. Biden's failure to respond to this provocation would compromise his domestic political standing, making him appear weak to the electorate. But retaliation can escalate and spread a conflict that his administration was trying to prevent in the ongoing war between Israel and Hamas. Indeed, the deployment of US personnel in exposed and vulnerable positions abroad turns the initiative to US adversaries who can try to provoke Washington to react and overreact. They can expect domestic hawks inside the USA to call for decisive military action. Thus, hardliners on both sides are partners in abetting an escalatory dynamic. The president, in this case Joe Biden, was boxed in by his domestic opposition. If he failed to respond to foreign provocations, he would be criticized for being weak and irresolute. If he had responded militarily, he could be accused of overreacting and entangling the USA in another foreign mess. Biden's domestic detractors thus sought to put him in a no-win situation. In this example again, domestic politics trumps (no pun intended) foreign policy.

Self-entrapment often results from such episodes. Moreover, as already remarked, rhetorical exaggeration and the demonization of foreign adversaries have the effect of boxing in officials and politicians, causing a mistaken policy to continue for longer and the political fallout from an eventual reversal to be more serious. We see here again the dynamics of policy persistence and subsequently punctuation in its reversal. Daniel Ellsberg (1972) had aptly described the incentives to maintain Washington's Vietnam policy as "the stalemate machine" before this policy was finally abandoned. When the overdue reversal eventually occurred, the political damage to US reputation was greater.

As suggested by punctuated equilibrium, the cumulative pressure that had held back change also tends to cause overreaction and overshooting – as displayed by the so-called Vietnam allergy or Somali syndrome named after the debacle causing American casualties as shown in the movie *Blackhawk Down*.

Various case histories show that democracies, especially those characterized by many veto players and policy bottlenecks, are more likely to experience institutional frictions, retarding or diluting efforts to address impending problems. As just mentioned, to the extent that these frictions stall or prevent the necessary reforms, they tend to cause a sharper and more dramatic punctuation later on. Democracies, however, compensate for this shortcoming by their higher quality and more timely information from multiple sources and channels. In contrast, the information reaching autocratic or authoritarian leaders may be highly distorted because of the subordinate officials' desire to ingratiate themselves and the general pressure to ensure policy conformity and political loyalty in these governments. There are few mechanisms for self-correction in authoritarian systems to check policy excesses and to provide timely warnings that things are going badly. In the absence of institutional guardrails and timely information, bad policies can go on for a considerable period of time before they are reversed. China's disastrous Great Leap Forward campaign and its so-called Cultural Revolution are prime exhibits of this tendency. Tardy policy reversal means that a country has already suffered serious damage from an ill-conceived policy.

This book has also emphasized the conjunctive logic, which rejects the ability of monocausal explanations – such as the recent popularity of Thucydides' Trap focusing on power shifts between China and the United States as the sole explanation of a possible war between them – to satisfactorily account for most social science phenomena. It instead argues that complex phenomena such as war and peace are usually the outcome of a combination or confluence of factors. The focus of the "garbage can" model is on the matching or mismatching of problems, solutions, participants, and choice opportunities. In addition to suggesting that monocausal explanation tends to distort rather than clarify matters, the conjunctive logic points to the difficulty of predicting the exact timing and nature of policy outputs. Sometimes, the merging of the four independent streams just mentioned produces a new policy. But even when circumstances are ripe for punctuation, a trigger or focusing event may be required to jolt participants to take actions or to set in motion events to create a choice opportunity. There is no denying, however, that the "garbage can" model presents a messy reality and one that is hard to predict and is often at the whims of accidents and serendipity beyond anyone's control. But as with people's lives depicted in the 2009 movie starring Meryl Streep and Alec Baldwin entitled *It's Complicated*, the world out there is indeed complicated.

In the physical and biological sciences, specialists have come to understand many phenomena that they study better than social scientists such as those of us in the field of international relations with an interest in topics pertaining to the causes of war and peace. Still, even earth scientists and medical researchers are still grappling with the challenges of predicting earthquakes, avalanches, and volcano eruptions, and struggling to develop better explanations of cancer and more effective ways to treat it.

The idea about conjunction also points to the dynamics of contagion and the extent to which developments in different places may be nested or clustered. As these words were being written, Israel and Hamas have been in an intense fight in Gaza with mounting casualties, especially on the Palestinian side suggesting a looming humanitarian tragedy. This bilateral conflict has shown some signs of becoming multilateral. Yemen's Houthis have joined the fray by firing missiles at ships in the Red Sea, and the USA and Britain have retaliated by striking at Houthi targets. Moreover, there have been fire exchanges between Israel and the Hezbollah forces located in southern Lebanon. Pro-Iranian groups have also shelled US bases in Iraq and Syria, which in turn caused the USA to return fire. As already remarked, US soldiers have already suffered fatalities, and Iran and the USA may be on a collision course. In short, the struggle between Israel and Hamas has caused several ongoing or incipient conflicts to merge or in other words, this conflict is in some danger of becoming metastasized.

On even a larger scale beyond the Middle East, there is the ongoing war in Ukraine and tension across the Taiwan Strait. Should this confluence of conflicts come to pass, Paul Kennedy's (1987) warning about the USA facing the risk of imperial overstretch will become a more palpable concern. As a regional power, China's attention is focused primarily on its immediate neighborhood. In contrast, the USA has – or sees – its interests engaged in many different parts of the world. Can Washington juggle several regional conflicts at the same time? The case studies taken up in this book include an analysis of the prospects of US intervention in a crisis involving Taiwan. Although the conclusion of this analysis, which includes past episodes of US intervention and nonintervention involving the possibility of a direct clash with either Moscow or Beijing, suggests that Washington is perhaps more reluctant to fight a war with China over Taiwan than some recent scholarly studies and official pronouncements have suggested, this danger is still there. As I have argued earlier, in conflicts such as World War I, unexpected and unpredictable events can become a catalyst to set off a powder keg.

Daniel Treisman (2004) has written about rational appeasement. Philip III and Philip IV of Spain were determined to crush all their opponents, sometimes subjecting this monarchy to simultaneous wars on multiple fronts. Spain fought to protect its reputation to stand firm against all challengers. Don Baltasar de Zúñiga, who served as the senior minister to Philip III, argued that reputation is worth fighting for, declaring that "a monarchy that has lost its *reputación*, even if it has lost no territory, is a sky without light, a sun without rays, a body without soul" (quoted in Treisman 2004: 366). This policy, however, weakened Spain financially and militarily and thus had the counterproductive effect of inviting more challenges to Madrid. It bankrupted Spain and set it on a process of inexorable decline.

In contrast, prior to World War I Britain accommodated the USA, conciliated with France and Russia, and even formed an alliance with Japan (Friedberg 1988; Vasquez 1996, 2009a), so that it could better concentrate its limited resources on Germany, a threat that was closer to Britain's home islands. When faced with limited resources, Britain's policy of selective appeasement turned out to be more prudent and effective than Spain's policy of taking on all challengers or competitors, a policy that had the effect of causing its precipitous decline. Instead of deterring would-be opponents, Madrid's policy depleted its resources, making it weaker to resist further challenges and thus had the opposite of its intended effect by encouraging more challenges whose conjunction weakened it further in a vicious cycle. In other words, attempts to preserve Spain's reputation and demonstrate its resolve to defeat any and all opponents backfired on it; multiple wars ruined Spain, encouraging rather than deterring its enemies, even those who could or would have stayed on the sideline to join the fray. Here is another example of a positive feedback loop producing a snowball and bandwagon effect, in this case an adverse chain of events from Madrid's perspective due to mimicking and imitation by Spain's enemies to its detriment.

As the reader who has come to this point of the book will understand, the example about imperial Spain highlights the danger of self-defeating policy and the idea of gathering momentum that can put even a powerful country on a path of steep decline as the USSR experienced leading to its eventual demise and disintegration. The Soviet empire clearly suffered from an exhaustion of its resources, falling seriously short on meeting basic consumer demands and thus causing its citizens to lose confidence in the ruling communist regime, because of the Kremlin's mistake of imperial overstretch that Paul Kennedy (1987) has warned the USA about. Thucydides' account of the Peloponnesian War is now familiar to those who are acquainted with Graham Allison's (2015, 2017) invocation of this ancient Greek general and historian's remark, suggesting that the rise of Athens and the fear that this development had caused in Sparta was the root cause of this conflict (hence, the name "Thucydides' Trap" in Allison's warning of a possible war between China and the United States as a result of the former's possible overtaking of the latter's power). Some readers may have noticed the irony of this rendition that equates China with Athens (the supposed model and predecessor for contemporary Western democracies) and presents Sparta (a martial state ruled by an oligarchy in constant fear of slave rebellion) as an analogue for today's United States.

It is possible and even likely that many people have not heard about other injunctions and insights from Thucydides' masterpiece, *The History of the Peloponnesian War* (e.g., Bagby 1994; Kirshner 2012, 2019a, 2019b). He did not attribute any more moral superiority to his own polity Athens than the other Greek city states. In Thucydides' words, Athens had established a "tyrannical empire;" and he reminded his fellow Athenians of their leader Pericles' warning, "Nor can [you, the Athenian people] now give [the empire] over for already [your] government is in the nature of a tyranny, which is both unjust for you to take up and unsafe to lay down" (quoted in Platias and Trigkas 2021: 11). Pericles cautioned them "not to extend your empire at the same time as you are fighting the war [in Sicily] and not to add self-imposed dangers, for I am more afraid of our own mistakes than the strategy of our opponents" (quoted in Kagan 1969: 192) – hence, my earlier remark about self-injurious actions inflicted by a country on itself, my reference to Paul Kennedy's injunction about the imperative of not taking on more foreign missions and responsibilities than the available resources a country has to meet them, and the example showing hubris, arrogance, and myopia on the part of Spain's monarchs causing them to overreach by taking on all comers that eventually led to their country's ruin. Susan Shirk (2023) has recently written a book about China committing this error of overreaching.

In addition to its crowded agenda on foreign policy, Washington faces a busy domestic political calendar with looming deadlines for funding the federal budget, legislations on immigration and border security, and of course the onset of the election season. This incomplete list alerts us to the possible consequences of crowded agendas, pressing deadlines, distracted attention, and bitter partisanship – and the toll that they can exact on the physical stamina and energy of an elderly official. Baumgartner and Jones have pointed out that time and attention tend to be chronically in short supply, especially at the highest echelons of policymaking. As mentioned already on several occasions, tardy responses to necessary policy changes cause pressure to build up so that when these changes do occur, they tend to be more disruptive and are more likely to produce overreaction.

A final argument advanced by this book is about the idea that an issue whose time has come, or the belief that a problem whose solution is overdue. Such an idea or belief can pick up support quickly or, to adopt the phrase used by Baumgartner and Jones ([1993] 2009] to "catch fire" (and in some other situations such as media coverage to cause "a feeding frenzy")). I have introduced historical examples such as the quick unraveling of Napoleon and Hitler's wartime coalitions, and the rapid collapse of communist regimes in Eastern Europe and the disintegration of the USSR in the final days of the Cold War. Accelerating momentum is an important source promoting change, and it is also pertinent to the sudden and massive ruptures in foreign policies and international relations. My case study of rollcall votes on the question of China's representation in the United Nations gives one such example. China's entry into the Korean War and Nixon's visit to Beijing also set in motion rapid and profound changes in these countries' relations for many years afterward. These historical turning points accelerated changes not only in these countries' diplomatic interactions but also other spheres such as in their economic and cultural exchanges.

Gathering momentum – or perceptions of it – can be one of the causes for change. Just ask anyone who was on the scene when the Vietcong captured Saigon and when Kabul fell to the Taliban. The widely shared understanding that the USA was withdrawing from these conflicts accelerated the final denouement, catching many officials and journalists by surprise about how quickly the unraveling happened. Of course, the same spectacle had also played out in the rapid collapse of communist regimes in Eastern Europe in quick succession of each other, which also surprised politicians, pundits, and scholars. More important than the actual forces characterizing the dynamics of a situation, popular perceptions (which may or may not reflect accurately an unfolding process) and shared expectations that something whose time has come have a powerful influence on outcomes. Moreover, human psychology to "go with the winner" has this self-fulfilling property such as by creating momentum for the winning candidate in an election. Because of this and other reasons given in this book, although there are long periods of seeming normalcy or even stagnation, history can sometimes "turn on a dime" and show sudden and massive disruptions that catch people off guard. It can therefore take on the characteristics of lulls and lurches with all their policy and other implications.

References

Alemany, Jacqueline. 2024. "U.S. House Impeaches Secretary of Homeland Security." *The Washington Post*, February 13. www.texastribune.org/2024/02/13/us-house-alejandro-mayorkas-impeachment/

Alexandrova, Petya, Marcello Carammia, and Arco Timmermans. 2012. "Policy Punctuations and Issue Diversity on the European Council Agenda." *Policy Studies Journal* 40(1): 69–88.

Allan, Bentley, Srdjan Vucetic, and Ted Hopf. 2018. "The Distribution of Identity and the Future of International Order: China's Hegemonic Prospects." *International Organization* 72(4): 839–869.

Allison, Graham T. 1971. *Essence of Decision: Explaining the Cuban Missile Crisis.* New York: HarperCollins.

2015. "The Thucydides Trap: Are the U.S. and China Headed for War?" *The Atlantic,* September 24. www.theatlantic.com/international/archive/2015/09/united-states-china-war-thucydides-trap/406756/

2017. *Destined for War: Can America and China Escape Thucydides's Trap?* Boston: Houghton Mifflin Harcourt.

Axelrod, Robert. 1984. *The Evolution of Cooperation.* New York: Basic Books.

Bacevich, Andrew J. 2002. *American Empire: The Realities and Consequences of U.S. Diplomacy.* Cambridge, MA: Harvard University Press.

Bagby, Laurie M. 1994. "The Use and Misuse of Thucydides in International Relations." *International Organization* 48(1): 131–153.

Bailey, Sydney D. 1971. "China and the United Nations." *The World Today* 27(9): 365–372.

Barker, Thomas Jones. 2015. *Bonhams Magazine* 42 (2015): 34. www.bonhams.com/magazine/18632/

Bartels, Larry M. 1987. "Candidate Choice and the Dynamics of the Presidential Nominating Process." *American Journal of Political Science* 31(1): 1–30.

Baumgartner, Frank R. 2006. "Punctuated Equilibrium Theory and Environmental Policy." In Robert Repetto, ed., *Punctuated Equilibrium and the Dynamics of U.S. Environmental Policy.* New Haven, CT: Yale University Press, 24–46.

Baumgartner, Frank R., Christian Breunig, Christoffer Green-Pederson, Bryan D. Jones, Peter B. Mortensen, Michiel Nuytemans, and Stefaan Walgrave. 2009. "Punctuated Equilibrium in Comparative Perspective." *American Journal of Political Science* 53(3): 603–620.

Baumgartner, Frank R., Sylvain Brouard, Christoffer Green-Pedersen, Bryan D. Jones, and Stefaan Walgrave, eds. 2011a. "The Dynamics of Policy Change in Comparative Perspective." *Comparative Political Studies* 44(8): 947–1119.

Baumgartner, Frank R., Marcello Carammia, Derek A. Epp, Ben Noble, Beatriz Rey, and Tevfik Murat Yildirim. 2017. "Budgetary Change in Authoritarian and Democratic Regimes." *Journal of European Public Policy* 24(6): 792–808.

Baumgartner, Frank R., Martial Foucault, and Abel François. 2006. "Punctuated Equilibrium in French Budgeting Processes." *Journal of European Public Policy* 13(7): 1086–1103.

Baumgartner, Frank R., and Bryan D. Jones. 1991. "Agenda Dynamics and Policy Subsystems." *Journal of Politics* 53(4): 1044–1074.

 2002a. *Policy Dynamics*. Chicago: University of Chicago Press.

 2002b. "Positive and Negative Feedback in Politics." In Frank R. Baumgartner and Bryan D. Jones, eds., *Policy Dynamics*. Chicago: University of Chicago Press, 3–28.

 [1993] 2009. *Agendas and Instability in American Politics*. Second edition. Chicago: University of Chicago Press.

 2015. *The Politics of Information: Problem Definition and the Course of Public Policy in America*. Chicago: University of Chicago Press.

Baumgartner, Frank R., Bryan D. Jones, and Michael C. MacLeod. 2000. "The Evolution of Legislative Jurisdictions." *Journal of Politics* 62(2): 321–349.

Baumgartner, Frank R., Bryan D. Jones, and John Wilkerson. 2011b. "Comparative Studies of Policy Dynamics." *Comparative Political Studies* 44(8): 947–972.

Beckley, Michael, 2018. "The Power of Nations: Measuring What Matters." *International Security* 43(2): 7–44.

 2023. "The Perils of Peaking Powers: Economic Slowdowns and Implications for China's Next Decade." *International Security* 48(1): 7–46.

Bell, Sam R., and Jesse C. Johnson. 2015. "Shifting Power, Commitment Problems, and Preventive War." *International Studies Quarterly* 59(1): 124–132.

Benjamin, Roger W., and John H. Kautsky. 1968. "Communism and Economic Development." *American Political Science Review* 62(1): 110–123.

Bernstein, Richard. 2020. "The Scary War Game over Taiwan That the U.S. Loses Again and Again." *RealClearInvestigations,* August 17. www .realclearinvestigations.com/articles/2020/08/17/the_scary_war_game_ over_taiwan_that_the_us_loses_again_and_again_124836.html

Bickers, Robert A., and Jeffrey N. Wasserstrom. 2009. "Shanghai's 'Dogs and Chinese Not Admitted' Sign: Legend, History and Contemporary Symbol." *China Quarterly* 142: 444–466.

Biddle, Stephen, and Ivan Oelrich. 2016. "Future Warfare in the Western Pacific: Chinese Antiaccess/Area Denial, U.S. AirSea Battle, and Command of the Commons in East Asia." *International Security* 41(1): 7–48.

Bikhchandani, Sushil, David Hirshleifer, and Ivo Welch. 1992. "A Theory of Fads, Fashion, Custom, and Cultural Change as Informational Cascades." *Journal of Political Economy* 100: 992–1026.

Birkland, Thomas A. 2004. "'The World Changed Today': Agenda-Setting and Policy Change in the Wake of the September 11 Terrorist Attacks." *Review of Policy Research* 21(2): 179–200.

Blanchard, Ben. 2022. "U.S. Should Recognize Taiwan; Former Top Diplomat Pompeo Says." *Reuters,* March 4. www.reuters.com/world/ asia-pacific/us-should-recognise-taiwan-former-top-diplomat-pompeo- says-2022-03-04/

Bloomfield, Lincoln P. 1966. "China, the United States, and the United Nations." *International Organization* 20(4): 653–676.

Bobrow, Davis B. 1972. "The Relevance Potential of Different Products." In Raymond Tanter and Richard H. Ullman, eds., *Theory and Policy in International Relations*. Princeton, NJ: Princeton University Press, 204–228.

Bobrow, Davis B., Steve Chan, and John A. Kringen. 1979. *Understanding Foreign Policy Decisions: The Chinese Case*. New York: Free Press.

Boettcher, William A. III. 2005. *Presidential Risk Behavior in Foreign Policy: Prudence or Peril?* New York: Palgrave.

Bosco, Joseph, 2023. "Biden Must End 'Strategic Ambiguity' on Taiwan." *The Hill*, December 12. https://thehill.com/opinion/national-security/ 4354235-biden-must-end-strategic-ambiguitambiguity-on-taiwan/

Bostock, Bill. 2021. "Secretary of State Antony Blinken Says He Stands by Mike Pompeo's Designation That China Committed Genocide against the Uighurs." *Yahoo!News*, January 28. https://news.yahoo.com/secre tary-state-antony-blinken-says-110049095.html

Boulding, Kenneth E. 1962. *Conflict and Defense: A General Theory*. New York: Harper.

Boushey, Graeme. 2012. "Punctuated Equilibrium Theory and the Diffusion of Innovations." *Policy Studies Journal* 40(1): 127–146.

Boyer, William W., and Neylan Akra. 1961. "The United States and the Admission of China: The Imminence of Change." *Political Science Quarterly* 76(3): 332–353.

Breuer, Adam, and A. Iain Johnston. 2019. "Memes, Narratives and the Emergent US–China Security Dilemma." *Cambridge Review of International Affairs* 32(4): 429–455.

Breunig, Christian. 2006. "The More Things Change, the More Things Stay the Same: A Comparative Analysis of Budget Punctuations." *Journal of European Public Policy* 13(7): 1069–1085.

Breunig, Christian, and Chris Koski. 2006. "Punctuated Equilibria and Budgets in American States." *Policy Studies Journal* 34(3): 363–380.

2012. "The Tortoise or the Hare: Incrementalism, Punctuations, and Their Consequences." *Policy Studies Journal* 40(1): 45–67.

Brooks, Emily. 2024. "Speaker Johnson: Senate Border Deal 'Dead on Arrival' in House." *The Hill,* January 26. https://thehill.com/home news/house/4431375-speaker-johnson-senate-border-deal-dead-on-arrival-in-house/

Brooks, Stephen G., and William C. Wohlforth. 2008. *World out of Balance: International Relations and the Challenge of American Primacy.* Princeton, NJ: Princeton University Press.

2016. *America Abroad: The United States' Global Role in the 21st Century.* New York: Oxford University Press.

Broz, J. Lawrence, Zhiwen Zhang, and Gaoyang Wang. 2020. "Explaining Foreign Support for China's Global Economic Leadership." *International Organization* 74(3): 417–452.

Bueno de Mesquita, Bruce. 1981. "Risk, Power Distribution, and the Likelihood of War." *International Studies Quarterly* 25(4): 541–568.

Bueno de Mesquita, Bruce, and Alastair Smith. 2012. *The Dictator's Handbook: Why Bad Behavior Is Almost Always Good Politics.* New York: PublicAffairs.

Bueno de Mesquita, Bruce, Alastair Smith, Randolph M. Siverson, and James D. Morrow. 2003. *The Logic of Political Survival.* Cambridge, MA: MIT Press.

Bulut, Alper T., and Tevfik Murat Yildirim. 2019. *Political Stability, Democracy and Agenda Dynamics in Turkey.* Cham, Switzerland: Palgrave Macmillan.

Burnham, Walter D. 1999. "Constitutional Moments and Punctuated Equilibria: A Political Scientist Confronts Bruce Ackerman's We the People." *Yale Law Journal* 108: 2237–2277.

Busenberg, George J. 2004. "Wildfire Management in the United States: The Evolution of a Policy Failure." *Review of Policy Research* 21(2): 145–156.

Bush, Richard C. 2005. *Untying the Knot: Making Peace in the Taiwan Strait*. Washington, DC: Brookings Institution Press.

2013. *Uncharted Strait: The Future China–Taiwan Relations*. Washington, DC: Brookings Institution Press.

Buzan, Barry. 2004. *The United States and the Great Powers: World Politics in the Twenty-First Century*. Cambridge: Polity Press.

Buzan, Barry, and Michael Cox. 2013. "China and the US: Comparable Cases of 'Peaceful Rise'?" *Chinese Journal of International Politics* 6(2): 109–132.

Cabestan, Jean-Pierre. 2024. *Facing China: The Prospect for War and Peace*. Lanham, MD: Rowman & Littlefield.

Cairney, Paul. 2012. "Chapter 9: Punctuated Equilibrium." In *Understanding Public Policy: Theories and Issues*. Basingstoke: Palgrave Macmillan, 175–199.

Campbell, Kurt M., and Mira Rapp-Hooper. 2020. "China Is Done Biding Its Time: The End of Beijing's Foreign Policy Restraint?" *Foreign Affairs*, July 15. www.foreignaffairs.com/articles/china/2020-07-15/china-done-biding-its-time

Campbell, Kurt M., and Ely Ratner. 2018. "The China Reckoning: How Beijing Defied American Expectations." *Foreign Affairs* 97(2): 60–70.

Campbell, Kurt M., and Jake Sullivan. 2020. "Competition without Catastrophe: How America Can Both Challenge and Coexist with China." *Foreign Affairs*, September/October. www.foreignaffairs.com/articles/china/competition-with-china-without-catastrophe?utm_source=academic&utm_medium=email&utm_campaign=CFRAcademicBulletin29Jan2021&utm_term=AcademicBulletin

Carillet, Joel. 2008. "Hidden Treasures: Shanghai Just Like Kansas City?" *Wandering Educators*, September 25. www.wanderingeducators.com/best/traveling/hidden-treasures-shanghai-just-kansas-city.html

Carpenter, Ted G. 2005. *America's Coming War with China: A Collision Course over Taiwan*. New York: Palgrave Macmillan.

Carr, Edward H. 1946. *The Twenty Years' War, 1919–1939: An Introduction to the Study of International Relations*. New York: Harper Row.

Carter, James. 2020. "When the PRC Won the 'China' Seat at the UN." https://thechinaproject.com/2020/10/21/when-the-prc-won-the-china-seat-at-the-un/

Casey, Daniel. 2023. "Punctuated Equilibrium and the Dynamics of Political Participation: The Case of Letter Writing." *Policy Studies* 45(1): 1–20.

Cashore, Benjamin, and Michael Howlett. 2007. "Punctuating Which Equilibrium? Understanding Thermostatic Policy Dynamics in Pacific Northwest Forestry." *American Journal of Political Science* 51(3): 532–551.

Ceccoli, Stephen J. 2003. "Policy Punctuations and Regulatory Drug Review." *Journal of Policy History* 15(2): 157–191.

Chai, Winberg. 1970. "China and the United Nations: Problems of Representation and Alternatives." *Asian Survey* 10(5): 397–409.

Chan, Kwan Nok, and Shiwei Fan. 2021. "Friction and Bureaucratic Control in Authoritarian Regimes." *Regulation & Governance* 15(4): 1406–1418.

Chan, Kwan Nok, and Shuang Zhao. 2016. "Punctuated Equilibrium and the Information Disadvantage of Authoritarianism: Evidence from the People's Republic of China: Punctuated Equilibrium under Authoritarianism." *Policy Studies Journal* 44(2): 134–155.

Chan, Steve. 1978. "Chinese Conflict Calculus and Behavior: Assessment from a Perspective of Conflict Management." *World Politics* 30(3): 391–410.

2003a. "Explaining War Termination: A Boolean Analysis of Causes." *Journal of Peace Research* 40(1): 49–66.

2003b. "Power, Satisfaction, and Popularity: A Poisson Analysis of U.N. Security Council Vetoes." *Cooperation and Conflict* 38(4): 339–359.

2004. "Can't Get No Satisfaction? The Recognition of Revisionist States." *International Relations of the Asia-Pacific* 4(2): 207–238.

2008. *China, the U.S., and the Power-Transition Theory: A Critique.* London: Routledge.

2015. "On States' Status-Quo and Revisionist Orientations: Discerning Power, Popularity and Satisfaction from Security Council Vetoes," *Issues & Studies* 51(3): 1–28.

2016. *China's Troubled Waters: Maritime Disputes in Theoretical Perspective.* Cambridge: Cambridge University Press.

2017a. *Trust and Distrust in Sino-American Relations: Challenge and Opportunity.* Amherst, NY: Cambria Press.

2017b. "The Power-Transition Discourse and China's Rise." In William R. Thompson, ed., *Encyclopedia of Empirical International Relations Theory.* New York: Oxford University Press. http://politics.oxfordre.com/page/recently-published/

2019. "More Than One Trap: Problematic Interpretations and Overlooked Lessons from Thucydides." *Journal of Chinese Political Science.* 24(1): 11–24.

2020a. *Thucydides's Trap? Historical Interpretation, Logic of Inquiry, and the Future of Sino-American Relations.* Ann Arbor: University of Michigan Press.

2020b. "China and Thucydides's Trap." In Kai He and Huiyun Feng, eds., *China's Challenges and International Order Transition: Beyond* the *"Thucydides Trap."* Ann Arbor: University of Michigan Press, 52–71.

2021a. "Challenging the Liberal Order: The US Hegemon as a Revisionist Power." *International Affairs* 97(5): 1335–1352.

2021b. "In the Eye of the Storm: Taiwan, China, and the U.S. in Challenging Times." In Cal M. Clark, Karl Ho, and Alexander C. Tan, eds., *Taiwan's Political Economy.* New York: Nova Science Publishers, 61–78.

2021c. "Why Thucydides' Trap Misinforms Sino-American Relations." *Vestnik RUDN, International Relations* 21(2): 234–242.

2022. "Precedent, Path Dependency, and Reasoning by Analogy: The Strategic Implications of the Ukraine War on Sino-American Relations and Relations across the Taiwan Strait." *Asian Survey* 62(5–6): 945–968.

2023a *Rumbles of Thunder: Power Shifts and the Danger of Sino-American War.* New York: Columbia University Press.

2023b. "Chinese Strategic Thinking and the Idea of Shocks: Old Literature, New Application?" In Thomas Volgy and William R. Thompson, eds., *Shocks and Political Change: A Comparative Perspective on Foreign Policy Analysis.* New York: Springer, 211–226.

2023c. "Bewildered and Befuddled: The West's Convoluted Narrative on China's Rise," *Asian Survey* 63(5): 691–715.

2024a. "America's Reaction to China's Rise: Power Shift, Problem Shift, and Policy Shift." In Maxmilian Mayer, Emilian Kavalski, Marina Rudyak, and Xin Zhang, eds., *Routledge Handbook on Global China.* New York: Routledge, 67–77.

2024b. *Culture, Economic Growth, and Interstate Power Shift: Implications for Competition between China and the United States.* Cambridge: Cambridge University Press.

2024c. *Taiwan and the Danger of a Sino-American War.* Cambridge Elements Series on Indo-Pacific Security. Cambridge: Cambridge University Press.

2025. *Fuses, Chains, and Backlashes: China, the United States, and the Dynamics of Conflict Contagion and Escalation.* Oxford University Press.

Chan, Steve, Huiyun Feng, Kai He, and Weixing Hu. 2021. *Contesting Revisionism: China, the United States, and the Transformation of International Order.* Oxford: Oxford University Press.

Chan, Steve, and Weixing Hu. 2024. "Taiwan as a Flash Point: Possible Lessons from the War in Ukraine." In William Thompson and Thomas Volgy, eds., *Reconsidering East Asia Peace: Confluences, Regional Characteristics and Societal Transformations.* New York: Routledge, 153–181.

2025a. "Rising Powers and the Liberal World Order: The Case of China." *International Affairs*.

2025b. *Geography and International Conflict: Ukraine, Taiwan, Indo-Pacific, and Sino- American Relations: Geopolitics and International Relations*. New York: Routledge.

Chan, Steve, Richard W.X. Hu, and Kai He. 2019. "Discerning States' Revisionist and Status-Quo Orientations: Comparing China and the U.S." *European Journal of International Relations* 27(2): 613–640.

Chen, Jian. 1994. *China's Road to the Korean War: The Making of the Sino-American Confrontation*. New York: Columbia University Press.

Cheney, Kyle. 2022. "What the GOP Meant When It Called Jan. 6 'Legitimate Political Discourse.'" *Politico*, February 15. www.politico.com/news/2022/02/15/gop-meaning-jan-6-legitimate-political-discourse-00008777

Cho, Ki Woong, and Kyujin Jung. 2019. "Illuminating the Sewol Ferry Disaster Using the Institutional Model of Punctuated Equilibrium Theory." *Social Science Journal* 56(2): 288–303.

Chong, Dennis. 1991. *Collective Action and the Civil Rights Movement*. Chicago: University of Chicago Press.

Choucri, Nazli, and Robert C. North. 1975. *Nations in Conflict: National Growth and International Violence*. San Francisco: Freeman.

Christensen, Thomas J. 2001. "Posing Problems without Catching Up: China's Rise and Challenges to U.S. Security Policy." *International Security* 25(4): 5–40.

Christensen, Thomas J., and Jack Snyder. 1990. "Chain Gangs and Passed Bucks: Predicting Alliance Patterns in Multipolarity." *International Organization* 44(2): 137–168.

Cioffi-Revilla, Claudio A. 1981. "Fuzzy Sets and Models of International Relations." *American Journal of Political Science* 25(1): 129–159.

1998a. *Politics and Uncertainty: Theory, Models, and Applications*. Cambridge: Cambridge University Press.

1998b. "The Political Uncertainty of Interstate Rivalries: A Punctuated Equilibrium Model." In Paul Diehl, ed., *The Dynamics of Enduring Rivalries*. Chicago: University of Chicago Press, 64–97.

Claude, Inis L. Jr. 1962. *Power and International Relations*. New York: Random House.

Cohen, Michael D., James G. March, and Johan P. Olsen. 1972. "A Garbage Can Theory of Organizational Choice." *Administrative Science Quarterly* 17(1): 1–25.

Colaresi, Michael. 2005. *Scare Politics: The Politics of International Rivalry*. Syracuse, NY: Syracuse University Press.

Colgan, Jeff D., Robert Keohane, and Thijs Van de Graaf. 2012. "Punctuated Equilibrium in the Energy Regime Complex." *Review of International Organizations* 7(2): 117–143.

Converse, Philip E., and Roy Pierce. 1986. *Political Representation in France*. Cambridge, MA: Harvard University Press.

Cooley, Alexander, Daniel Nexon, and Steven Ward. 2019. "Revising Order or Challenging the Balance of Power? An Alternative Typology of Revisionist and Status-Quo States." *Review of International Studies* 45(4): 689–708.

Copeland, Dale C. 2000. *The Origins of Major War*. Ithaca, NY: Cornell University Press.

Crawford, Timothy W. 2003. *Pivotal Deterrence: Third-Party Statecraft and the Pursuit of Peace*. Ithaca, NY: Cornell University Press.

Crenson, Matthew A. 1987. "The Private Stake in Public Goods: Overcoming the Illogic of Collective Action." *Policy Sciences* 20: 259–276.

Crow, Deserai A. 2010. "Policy Punctuation in Colorado Water Law: The Breakdown of a Monopoly." *Review Policy of Policy Review* 27(2): 147–166.

Daalder, Ivo H., and James M. Lindsay. 2005. *America Unbound: The Bush Revolution in Foreign Policy*. New York: Wiley.

Danilovic, Vesna. 2001a. "The Sources of Threat Credibility in Extended Deterrence." *Journal of Conflict Resolution* 45(3): 341–369.

2001b. "Conceptual and Selection Biases in Deterrence." *Journal of Conflict Resolution* 45(1): 97–125.

Darwin, Charles. 1859. *On the Origin of Species by Means of Natural Selection or the Preservation of Favored Races in the Struggle for Life*. London: Murray.

Davis, Otto A., M. A. H. Dempster, and Aaron Wildavsky. 1966. "A Theory of the Budget Process." *American Political Science Review* 60(3): 529–547.

1974. "Towards a Predictive Theory of Government Expenditure: U.S. Domestic Appropriations." *British Journal of Political Science* 4(4): 419–452.

Deng, Yong. 2022. *China's Strategic Opportunity: Change and Revisionism in Chinese Foreign Policy*. Cambridge: Cambridge University Press.

Dicicco, Jonathan M. and Jack S. Levy. 1999. "Power Shifts and Problem Shifts: The Evolution of the Power Transition Research Program." *Journal of Conflict Resolution* 43(6): 675–704.

Diehl, Paul F., ed. 1998. *The Dynamics of Enduring Rivalries*, Urbana: University of Illinois Press.

Diehl, Paul F., and Gary Goertz. 2000. *War and Peace in International Rivalry*. Ann Arbor: University of Michigan Press.

Diehl, Paul F., and Charlotte Ku. 2010. *The Dynamics of International Law*. Cambridge: Cambridge University Press.

Diez Acosta, Tomas. 2002. *October 1962: The "Missile" Crisis as Seen from Cuba*. New York: Pathfinder Press.

Doran, Charles F. 1977. *Myth, Oil, and Politics: Introduction to the Political Economy of Petroleum*. New York: Free Press.

   1991. *Systems in Crisis: New Imperatives of High Politics at Century's End*. Cambridge: Cambridge University Press.

Doran, Charles F., and Wes Parsons. 1980. 'War and the Cycle of Relative Power." *American Political Science Review* 74(4): 947–965.

Doshi, Rush. 2021. *The Long Game: China's Grand Strategy to Displace American Order*. Oxford: Oxford University Press.

Downs, Anthony. 1972. "Up and Down with Ecology: 'The Issue Attention Cycle'." *Public Interest* 28(Summer): 38–50.

Doyle, Michael W. 1997. *Ways of War and Peace: Realism, Liberalism, and Socialism*. New York: Norton.

Dress, Brad. 2024. "China Will be Ready for Potential Taiwan Invasion by 2027: US Admiral Warns." *The Hill*, March 21. https://thehill.com/policy/defense/4547637-china-potential-taiwan-invasion-2027-us-admiral-warns/

Drezner, Daniel W., Henry Farrell, and Abraham L. Newman. 2021. *The Uses and Abuses of Weaponized Interdependence*. Washington, DC: Brookings Institution Press.

Durant, Robert F., and Paul F. Diehl. 1989. "Agendas, Alternatives, and Public Policy: Lessons from the U.S. Foreign Policy Arena." *Journal of Public Policy* 9(2): 179–205.

Dziengel, Lake. 2010. "Advocacy Coalitions and Punctuated Equilibrium in the Same-Sex Marriage Debate: Learning from Pro-LGBT Policy Changes in Minneapolis and Minnesota." *Journal of Gay & Lesbian Social Services* 22(1–2): 165–182.

East, Maurice A. 1972. "Status Discrepancy and Violence in the International System." In James N. Rosenau, Vincent Davis, and Maurice A. East, eds., *The Analysis of International Politics*. New York: Free Press, 299–319.

The Economist. 2018. "Surging Numbers of Chinese People Going Abroad Should be Welcomed." May 17. www.economist.com/china/2018/05/17/surging-numbers-of-chinese-people-going-abroad-should-be-welcomed

The Economist. 2021. "'Genocide' Is the Wrong Word for the Horrors of Xinjiang: To Confront Evil, the First Step Is to Describe It Accurately." February 13. www.economist.com/leaders/2021/02/13/genocide-is-the-wrong-word-for-the-horrors-of-xinjiang

Eldredge, Niles, and Stephen J. Gould. 1972. "Punctuated Equilibria: An Alternative to Phyletic Gradualism." In T. J. M. Schopf, ed., *Models in Paleobiology*. San Francisco: Freeman Cooper, 82–115.

Ellsberg, Daniel. 1972. *Papers on the War*. New York: Simon & Schuster.

Elman, Colin. 2004. "Extending Offensive Realism: The Louisiana Purchase and America's Rise to Regional Hegemony." *American Political Science Review* 98(4): 563–576.

Elman, Colin, and Miriam F. Elman. 1995. "Correspondence: History vs. Neo-Realism: A Second Look." *International Security* 20(1): 182–193.

1997. "Lakatos and Neorealism: A Reply to Vasquez." *American Political Science Review* 91(4): 923–926.

Erickson, Andrew S., Evan B. Montgomery, Craig Neuman, Stephen Biddle, and Ivan Oelrich. 2017. "Correspondence: How Good Are China's Antiaccess/Area-Denial Capabilities?" *International Security* 41(4): 202–213.

Fagan, E. J. 2023. "Political Institutions, Punctuated Equilibrium Theory, and Policy Disasters." *Policy Studies Journal* 51(2): 243–263.

Fagan, E. J., Bryan D. Jones, and Christopher Wlezien. 2017. "Representative Systems and Policy Punctuations." *Journal of European Public Policy* 24(6): 809–831.

Farrell, Henry, and Abraham L. Newman. 2019. "Weaponized Interdependence: How Global Economic Networks Shape State Coercion." *International Security* 44(1): 42–79.

2023. *Underground Empire: How America Weaponized the Global Economy*. New York: Holt.

Fearon, James D. 1994. "Signaling versus the Balance of Power and Interests: An Empirical Test of a Crisis Bargaining Model." *Journal of Conflict Resolution* 38(2): 236–269.

1995. "Rationalist Explanations for War," *International Organization* 49(3): 379–414.

2002. "Selection Effects and Deterrence." *International Interactions* 28(1): 5–29.

Feder-Bubis, Paula, and David Chinitz. 2010. "Punctuated Equilibrium and Path Dependency in Coexistence: The Israeli Health System and Theories of Change." *Journal of Health Politics, Policy and Law* 35(4): 595–614.

Feeley, T, Jens 2002. "The Multiple Goals of Science and Technology Policy." In Frank R. Baumgartner and Bryan D. Jones, eds., *Policy Dynamics*. Chicago: University of Chicago Press, 125–154.

Foot, Rosemary and Andrew Walter. 2011. *China, the United States, and Global Order*. Cambridge: Cambridge University Press.

Fravel, M. Taylor. 2005. "Regime Insecurity and International Cooperation: Explaining China's Compromises in Territorial Disputes." *International Security* 30(2): 46–83.

2007–2008. "Power Shifts and Escalation: Explaining China's Use of Force in Territorial Disputes." *International Security* 32(3): 44–83.

2008. *Strong Border, Secure Nation: Cooperation and Order in China's Territorial Disputes*. Princeton, NJ: Princeton University Press.

Friedberg, Aaron L. 1988. *The Weary Titan: The Experience of Relative Decline, 1895–1905*. Princeton, NJ: Princeton University Press.

Friedman, George, and Meredith LeBard. 1991. *The Coming War with Japan*. New York: St. Martin's.

Gaddis, John L. 1986. "The Long Peace: Elements of Stability in the Postwar International System." *International Security* 10(4): 99–142.

1989. *The Long Peace: Inquiries into the History of the Cold War*. Oxford: Oxford University Press.

Galtung, Johan. 1964, "A Structural Theory of Aggression." *Journal of Peace Research* 1(2): 95–119.

Georgetown University Initiative for U.S.–China Dialogue on Global Issues. 2020. "America's Taiwan Policy: Debating Strategic Ambiguity and the Future of Asian Security." October 2. https://uschinadialogue.georgetown.edu/events/america-s-taiwan-policy-debating-strategic-ambiguity-and-the-future-of-asian-security

Gerschenkron, Alexander. 1962. *Economic Backwardness in Historical Perspective: A Book of Essays*. Cambridge, MA: Belknap Press of Harvard University.

Gersick, Connie J. G. 1988. "Time and Transition in Work Teams: Toward a New Model of Group Development." *Academy of Management Journal* 31(1): 9–41.

Gersick. Connie J. G. 1991. "Revolutionary Change Theories: A Multilevel Exploration of the Punctuated Equilibrium Paradigm." *Academy of Management Review* 16(1): 10–36.

Gibbons, Andrew, and Rhonda Evans (2023). "The Executive Lawmaking Agenda: Political Parties, Prime Ministers, and Policy Change in Australia." *Policy Studies Journal* 51(2): 307–325.

Gibbs, Raymond, W. Jr. 1994. *The Poetics of Mind: Figurative Thought, Language, and Understanding*. Cambridge: Cambridge University Press.

Gilpin, Robert. 1981. *War and Change in World Politics*. Cambridge: Cambridge University Press.

1987. *The Political Economy of International Relations*. Princeton, NJ: Princeton University Press.

Givel, Michael S. 2006. "Punctuated Equilibrium in Limbo: The Tobacco Lobby and U.S. State Policymaking from 1990 to 2003." *Policy Studies Journal* 34(3): 405–418.

2008. "Assessing Material and Symbolic Variations in Punctuated Equilibrium and Public Policy Output Patterns." *Review of Policy Research* 25(6): 547–561.

2010. "The Evolution of the Theoretical Foundations of Punctuated Equilibrium Theory in Public Policy." *Review of Policy Research*: 27(2): 187–198.

Givel, Michael S., and Stanton Glantz. 2001. "Tobacco Lobby Political Influence on U.S. State Legislatures in the 1990s." *Tobacco Control* 10(2): 124–134.

Glaser, Bonnie S. 2020. "Dire Straits: Should American Support for Taiwan Be Ambiguous? A Guarantee Isn't Worth the Risk." *Foreign Affairs*, September 24. www.foreignaffairs.com/articles/united-states/2020-09-24/dire-straits

Glaser, Bonnie S., Michael J. Mazarr, Michael J. Glennon, Richard Haas, and David Sacks. 2020. "Dire Straits: Should American Support for Taiwan Be Ambiguous?" Foreign Affairs discussion forum, September 24. www.foreignaffairs.com/articles/united-states/2020-09-24/dire-straits

Glosny, Michael A. 2004. "Strangulation from the Sea? A PRC Submarine Blockade of Taiwan." *International Security* 28(4): 125–160.

Gochman, Charles S. 1980. "Status, Capabilities, and Major Power Conflict." In J. David Singer, ed., *The Correlates of War II: Testing Some Realpolitik Models*. New York: Free Press, 83–123.

Goertz, Gary. 2003. *International Norms and Decision Making: A Punctuated Equilibrium Model*. Lanham, MD: Rowman & Littlefield.

Goh, Evelyn. 2013. *The Struggle for Order: Hegemony, Hierarchy, and Transition in the Cold-War East Asia*. Oxford: Oxford University Press.

2019. "Contesting Hegemonic Order: China in East Asia." *Security Studies* 28(3): 614–644.

Goldstein, Lyle, and William Murray. 2004. "Undersea Dragons: China's Maturing Submarine Force." *International Security* 28(4): 161–196.

Goldstein, L. J., David I. Schneider, and Martha J. Siegel. 1995. *Finite Mathematics and Its Applications*. Englewood Cliffs, NJ: Prentice Hall.

Goldstone, Jack. A. 2002. "Efflorescences and Economic Growth in World History: Rethinking the 'Rise of the West' and the Industrial Revolution." *Journal of World History* 13(2): 323–389.

Gould, Stephen J. 1989. "Punctuated Equilibrium in Fact and Theory." In Albert Somit and Steven A. Peterson, eds., *The Dynamics of Evolution: The Punctuated Equilibrium Debate in the Natural and Social Science*. Ithaca, NY: Cornell University Press, 54–84.

1995. *Dinosaur in a Haystack: Reflections in Natural History*. New York: Harmony Books.

2002. *The Structure of Evolutionary Theory*. Cambridge, MA: Harvard University Press.

Gould, Stephen J., and Niles Eldredge. 1977. "Punctuated Equilibria: The Tempo and Mode of Evolution Reconsidered." *Paleobiology* 3(2): 115–151.

Granovetter, Mark. 1978. "Threshold Models of Collective Behavior." *American Journal of Sociology* 83: 1430–1443.

Green, Brendan R., and Caitlin Talmadge. 2022. "Then What? Assessing the Military Implications of Chinese Control of Taiwan." *International Security* 47(1): 7–45.

Green-Pederson, Christoffer, and Sebastiaan Princen. 2016. "Punctuated Equilibrium Theory." In Nikolaos Zahariadis, ed., *Handbook of Public Policy Agenda Setting*. Cheltenham: Elgar, 69–86.

Greve, Andrew Q., and Jack S. Levy. 2018. "Power Transitions, Status Dissatisfaction, and War: The Sino-Japanese War of 1894–1895." *Security Studies* 27(1): 148–178.

Grieco, Joseph. 1988a. "Anarchy and the Limits of Cooperation." *International Organization* 42(3): 485–507.

1988b. "Realist Theory and the Problem of International Cooperation: Analysis with an Amended Prisoner's Dilemma Model." *Journal of Politics* 50(3): 600–624.

Grieco, Joseph, Robert Powell, and Duncan Snidal. 1993. "The Relative-Gains Problem for International Cooperation." *American Political Science Review* 87(3): 727–743.

Grigoryan, Arman. 2020. "Selective Wilsonianism: Material Interests and the West's Support for Democracy." *International Security* 44(4): 158–200.

The Guardian. 1999a. "Nato Bombed Chinese Deliberately." October 17. www.theguardian.com/world/1999/oct/17/balkans

The Guardian. 1999b. "Truth behind America's Raid on Belgrade." November 28. www.theguardian.com/theobserver/1999/nov/28/focus.news1

The Guadian. 2014. "The Guardian View on the Lessons of the First World War for Today: Editorial." August 3. www.theguardian.com/commentisfree/2014/aug/03/guardian-view-lessons-first-world-war-today

Gurr, Ted R. 1970. *Why Men Rebel*. Princeton, NJ: Princeton University Press.

Haass, Richard, and David Sacks. 2020. "American Support for Taiwan Must be Unambiguous," *Foreign Affairs*, September 20. www.foreignaffairs.com/articles/united-states/american-support-taiwan-must-be-unambiguous

Hagstrom, Linus, and Bjorn Jerden. 2014. "East Asia's Power Shift: The Flaws and Hazards of the Debate and How to Avoid Them." *Asian Perspective* 38(3): 337–362.

Hardin, John W. 2002. "Multiple Topics, Multiple Targets, Multiple Goals, and Multiple Decision-Makers: Congressional Consideration of Comprehensive Health Care Reform." In Frank R. Baumgartner and Bryan D. Jones, eds., *Policy Dynamics*. Chicago: University of Chicago Press, 96–124.

He, Kai and Huiyun Feng. 2012. *Prospect Theory and Foreign Policy Analysis in the Asia Pacific: Rational Leaders and Risky Behavior*. New York: Routledge.

He, Kai, Huiyun Feng, Steve Chan, and Weixing Hu. 2021. "Rethinking Revisionism in World Politics." *Chinese Journal of International Politics* 14(2): 159–186.

Hernandez, Joe. 2025. "Trump Says He Still Wants to Buy Greenland, Suggests Canada Could Become a U.S. State." January 26. *NPR* www.npr.org/2025/01/26/nx-s1-5275375/trump-greenland-canada-israel-gaza.

Higgins, Trumbull. 1966. *Hitler and Russia: The Third Reich in a Two-Front War, 1937–1943*. New York: Macmillan.

Hirschman, Albert O. 1970. *Exit, Voice, and Loyalty: Responses to Decline in Firms, Organizations, and States*. Cambridge, MA: Harvard University Press.

Hoffmann, Stanley. 1977. "An American Social Science." *Daedalus* 106(3): 41–60.

Holmes, James. 2010. "Mahan, a 'Place in the Sun,' and Germany's Quest for Sea Power." *Comparative Strategy* 23(1): 27–61.

Hou, Philip. 2023. "China Won't Invade Taiwan—For Now." *The Diplomat*, December 8. https://thediplomat.com/2023/12/china-wont-invade-taiwan-for-now/

Howlett, Michael, and Andrea Migone. 2011. "Charles Lindblom Is Alive and Well and Living in Punctuated Equilibrium Land." *Policy and Society* 30(1): 53–62.

Hu, Weixing. 2012. "Explaining Change and Stability in Cross-Strait Relations: A Punctuated Equilibrium Model." *Journal of Contemporary China* 21(78): 933–953.

Hui, Victoria Tin-Bor. 2010. *War and State Formation in Ancient China and Early Modern Europe*. Cambridge: Cambridge University Press.

Hulme, Patrick. 2020. "Taiwan, 'Strategic Clarity' and the War Powers: A U.S. Commitment to Taiwan Requires Congressional Buy-In," *Lawfare*, December 4. www.lawfareblog.com/taiwan-strategic-clarity-and-war-powers-us-commitment-taiwan-requires-congressional-buy

Hunt, Valerie F. 2002. "The Multiple and Changing Goals of Immigration Reform: A Comparison of House and Senate Activity, 1947–1993." In Frank R. Baumgartner and Bryan D. Jones, eds., *Policy Dynamics*. Chicago: University of Chicago Press, 73–95.

Huth, Paul K. 1984. What Makes Deterrence Work? Cases from 1900 to 1980." *World Politics* 36(4): 496–526.

  1988a. *Extended Deterrence and the Prevention of War*. New Haven, CT: Yale University Press.

  1988b. "Extended Deterrence and the Outbreak of War." *American Political Science Review* 82(2): 423–443.

  1988c. "Deterrence Failure and Crisis Escalation." *International Studies Quarterly* 32(1): 29–45.

  1998. *Standing Your Ground: Territorial Disputes and International Conflict*. Ann Arbor: University of Michigan Press.

Huth, Paul K., and Todd L. Allee. 2002. "Domestic Political Accountability and the Escalation and Settlement of International Disputes." *Journal of Conflict Resolution* 46(4): 754–790.

Huth, Paul K., Christopher Gelpi, and D. Scott Bennett. 1993. "The Escalation of Great Power Militarized Disputes: Testing Rational Deterrence Theory and Structural Realism." *American Political Science Review* 87(3): 609–623.

Huth, Paul K., and Bruce M. Russett. 1993. "General Deterrence between Enduring Rivals: Testing Three Competing Models." *American Political Science Review* 87(1): 61–73.

Janis, Irving L. 1982. *Groupthink: Psychological Studies of Policy Decisions and Fiascoes*. Boston: Little, Brown.

Jensen, Carsten. 2009. "Policy Punctuations in Mature Welfare States." *Journal of Public Policy* 29(3): 287–303.

Jervis, Robert. 1978. "Cooperation under the Security Dilemma." *World Politics* 30(2): 167–214.

John, Peter. and Shaun Bevan. 2012. "What Are Policy Punctuations? Large Changes in the Legislative Agenda of the UK Government, 1911–2008." *Policy Studies Journal* 40(1): 89–108.

John, Peter, and Helen Margetts. 2003. "Policy Punctuations in the UK: Fluctuations and Equilibria in Central Government Expenditure since 1951." *Public Administration* 81(3): 411–432.

Johnston, A. Iain. 1995. *Cultural Realism: Strategic Culture and Grand Strategy in Chinese History*. Princeton, NJ: Princeton University Press.

  2003. "Is China a Status Quo Power?" *International Security* 7(4): 5–56.

2011. "Stability and Instability in Sino-US Relations: A Response to Yan Xuetong's Superficial Friendship Theory." *Chinese Journal of International Politics* 4(1): 5–29.

2013. "How New and Assertive Is China's New Assertiveness?" *International Security* 37(4): 7–48.

2019. "China in a World of Orders." *International Security* 44(2): 9–60.

Jolicoeur, Mathieu M. 2018. "An Introduction to Punctuated Equilibrium: A Model for Understanding Stability and Dramatic Change in Public Policies." National Collaborating Centre for Healthy Public Policy. www .ncchpp.ca/docs/2018_ProcessPP_Intro_PunctuatedEquilibrium_EN.pdf

Joly, Jeroen, and Friederike Richter. 2019. "Punctuated Equilibrium Theory and Foreign Policy." In Klaus Brummer, Sebastian Harnisch, Kai Oppermann, and Diana Panke, eds., *Foreign Policy as Public Policy? Promises and Pitfalls*. Manchester: Manchester University Press, 41–64.

2023. "The Calm before the Storm: A Punctuated Equilibrium Theory of International Politics." *Policy Studies Journal* 51(2): 265–282.

Jones, Bryan D. 1994. *Reconceiving Decision-making in Democratic Politics: Attention, Choice, and Public Policy*. Chicago: University of Chicago Press

2001. *Politics and the Architecture of Choice: Bounded Rationality and Governance*. Chicago: University of Chicago Press.

Jones, Bryan D., and Frank R. Baumgartner. 2005. *The Politics of Attention*. Chicago: University of Chicago Press.

2012. "From There to Here: Punctuated Equilibrium to the General Punctuation Thesis to a Theory of Government Information Processing," *Policy Studies Journal* 40(1): 1–19.

Jones, Bryan D., Frank R. Baumgartner, Christian Breunig, Christopher Wlezien, Stuart Soroka, Martial Foucault, Abel François, Christoffer Green-Pedersen, Chris Koski, Peter John, Peter B. Mortensen, Frédéric Varone, Stefaan Walgrave. 2009. "A General Empirical Law of Public Budgets: A Comparative Analysis." *American Journal of Political Science* 53(4): 855–873.

Jones, Bryan D., Frank R. Baumgartner, and James L. Jones. 1998. "Policy Punctuations: U.S. Budget Authority, 1947–1995." *Journal of Politics* 60(1): 1–33.

Jones, Bryan D., Frank R. Baumgartner, and Jeffery C. Talbert. 1993. "The Destruction of Issue Monopolies in Congress." *American Political Science Review* 87(3): 657–671.

Jones, Bryan D, and Christian Breunig. 2007. "Noah and Joseph Effects in Government Budgets: Analyzing Long-Term Memory." *Policy Studies Journal*: 35(3): 329–349.

Jones, Bryan D., Derek A. Epp, and Frank R. Baumgartner. 2019. "Democracy, Authoritarianism, and Policy Punctuations." *International Review of Public Policy* 1(1): 7–26.

Jones, Bryan D., Tracy Sulkin, and Heather A. Larsen. 2003. "Policy Punctuations in American Political Institutions." *American Political Science Review* 97(1): 151–169.

Jones, Bryan D., Herschel F. Thomas, and Michelle Wolfe. 2014. "Policy Bubbles." *Policy Studies Journal* 42(1): 146–171.

Jordan, Meagan M. 2003. "Punctuations and Agendas: A New Look at Local Government Budget Expenditures." *Journal of Policy Analysis and Management* 22(3): 345–360.

Kagan, Donald. 1969. *The Outbreak of the Peloponnesian War*. Ithaca, NY: Cornell University Press.

Kagan, Robert. 2005. "The Illusion of 'Managing' China." *The Washington Post*, May 15. www.washingtonpost.com/wpdyn/content/article/2005/05/13/AR2005051301405.

Kahneman, Daniel and Amos Tversky. 1979. "Prospect Theory: An Analysis of Decision under Risk." *Econometrica* 47(2): 263–292.

Kamisar, Ben. 2023. "Almost a Third of Americans Still Believe the 2020 Election Result Was Fraudulent." NBC (National Broadcasting Company) News, June 20. www.nbcnews.com/meet-the-press/meetthe pressblog/almost-third-americans-still-believe-2020-election-result-was-fraudule-rcna90145

Kang, David C. 2020. "Thought Games about China." *Journal of East Asian Studies* 20(2): 135–150.

Kastner, Scott L., and Phillip C. Saunders. 2012. "Is China a Status Quo or Revisionist State? Leadership Travel as an Empirical Indicator of Foreign Policy Priorities." *International Studies Quarterly* 56(1): 163–177.

Kaufman, Chaim. 2004. "Threat Inflation and the Failure of the Marketplace of Ideas: The Selling of the Iraq War." *International Security* 29(1): 5–48.

Kaufman, Stuart, Richard Little, and William C. Wohlforth, eds. 2007. *Balance of Power in World History*. New York: Palgrave Macmillan.

Kelemen, Michele. 2012. "Candidates Criticize China; Presidents Show Caution." NPR (National Public Radio), September 10. www.npr.org/2012/09/10/160880265/candidates-criticize-china-presidents-show-caution

Kemeny, John G., J. Laurie Snell, and Gerald L. Thompson. 1974. *Introduction to Finite Mathematics*. Englewood Cliffs, NJ: Prentice Hall.

Kennedy, Paul M. 1980. *The Rise of the Anglo-German Antagonism: 1860–1914*. London: Allen, Unwin.

1987. *The Rise and Fall of Great Powers*. New York: Vintage Books.

Keohane, Robert O., and Joseph S. Nye. 1977. *Power and Interdependence: World Politics in Transition.* Boston: Little, Brown.

Key, V. O. Jr. 1955. "A Theory of Critical Elections." *Journal of Politics* 17(1): 3–18.

Khong, Yuen Foong. 1992, *Analogies at War: Korea, Munich, Dien Bien Phu, and the Vietnam Decisions of 1965.* Princeton, NJ: Princeton University Press.

Kindleberger, Charles P. 1973. *The World in Depression: 1929–1939.* Berkeley: University of California Press.

Kingdon, John W. 1984. *Agendas, Alternatives, and Public Policy.* Boston: Little, Brown.

Kirshner, Jonathan. 2012. "The Tragedy of Offensive Realism: Classical Realism and the Rise of China." *European Journal of International Relations* 18(1): 53–75.

2019a. "Handle Him with Care: The Importance of Getting Thucydides Right." *Security Studies*, 28(1): 1–24.

2019b. "Offensive Realism, Thucydides Trap, and the Tragedy of Unforced Errors: Classical Realism and US–China Relations." *China International Strategy Review* 1: 51–63.

Kissinger, Henry A. 1957. *A World Restored: Castlereagh, Metternich, and the Problems of Peace, 1812–22.* New York: Houghton, Mifflin.

1975. *White House Years.* Boston: Little, Brown.

Knight, Stef W. 2024. "Trump, House Republicans Plot to Kill Border Deal." Axios, January 29. www.axios.com/2024/01/29/trump-republic ans-border-deal-senate-immigration

Koehler, David H. 1975. "Legislative Coalition Formation: The Meaning of Minimum Winning Size with Uncertain Participation." *American Political Science Review* 19(1): 27–39.

Krasner, Stephen. 1984. "Approaches to the State: Alternative Conceptions and Historical Dynamics." *Comparative Politics* 16(2): 223–246.

Kube, Courtney, and Mosheh Gains. "Air Force General Predicts War with China in 2025, Tells Officers to Prep by Firing 'a Clip' at a Target, and 'Aim for the Head'." NBC New, January 27. www.nbcnews.com/polit ics/national-security/us-air-force-general-predicts-war-china-2025-memo-rcna67967

Kugler, Jacek, and Douglas Lemke, eds. 1996. *Parity and War: Evaluations and Extensions of the War Ledger.* Ann Arbor: University of Michigan Press.

Kuhn, Thomas S. 1970. *The Structure of Scientific Revolutions.* Chicago: University of Chicago Press.

Kupchan, Charles A. 2010. *How Enemies Become Friends: The Sources of Stable Peace.* Princeton, NJ: Princeton University Press.

2020. *Isolationism: A History of America's Efforts to Shield Itself from the World*. Oxford: Oxford University Press.

Lam, Wai Fung, and Kwan Nok Chan. 2015. "How Authoritarianism Intensifies Punctuated Equilibrium: The Dynamics of Policy Attention in Hong Kong." *Governance* 28(4): 549–570.

Lampton, David M. 2019. "Reconsidering U.S.–China Relations: From Improbable Normalization to Precipitous Deterioration." *Asia Policy* 14(2): 43–60.

Landes, David S. 1999. *The Wealth and Poverty of Nations: Why Some Are So Rich and Some Are So Poor*. New York: Norton.

Larsen-Price, Heather A. 2012. "The Right Tool for the Job: The Canalization of Presidential Policy Attention by Policy Instrument." *Policy Studies Journal* 40(1): 147–168.

Larson, Deborah W., and Alexei Shevchenko. 2010. "Status Seekers: Chinese and Russian Responses to U.S. Primacy." *International Security* 34(4): 63–95.

2019. *Quest for Status: Chinese and Russian Foreign Policy*. New Haven, CT: Yale University Press.

Lebow, R. Ned. 1981. *Between Peace and War: The Nature of International Crisis*. Baltimore: Johns Hopkins University Press.

1984. "Window of Opportunity: Do States Jump through Them?" *International Security* 9(1): 147–186.

1985. "Miscalculation in the South Atlantic: The Origins of the Falklands War," In Robert Jervis, R. Ned Lebow, and Janice G. Stein, eds., *Psychology and Deterrence*. Baltimore: Johns Hopkins University Press, 85–124.

2000/2001. "Contingency, Catalyst, and International System." *Political Science Quarterly* 115(4): 591–616.

2003. "A Data Set Named Desire: A Reply to William R. Thompson." *International Studies Quarterly* 47(3): 475–478.

2010. *Why Nations Fight: Past and Future Motivations for War*. Cambridge: Cambridge University Press.

Lebow, R. Ned, and Janice G. Stein. 1990. "Deterrence: The Elusive Dependent Variable." *World Politics* 42(3): 336–369.

Lebow, R. Ned, and Benjamin Valentino. 2009. "Lost in Transition: A Critical Analysis of Power Transition Theory." *International Relations* 23(3): 389–410.

Lerner, I. Michael. 1954. *Genetic Homeostasis*. New York: Wiley.

Leventoglu, Bahar, and Branislav L. Slantchev. 2007. "The Armed Peace: A Punctuated Equilibrium Theory of War." *American Journal of Political Science* 51(4): 755–771.

Levin, Dov H. 2020. *Meddling in the Ballot Box: The Causes and Effects of Partisan Electoral Interventions*. Oxford: Oxford University Press.

Levy, Jack S. 1987. "Declining Power and the Preventive Motivation for War." *World Politics* 40(1): 82–107.

1996. "Loss Aversion, Framing and Bargaining: The Implications of Prospect Theory for International Conflict." *International Political Science Review* 17(2): 177–193.

1997. "Prospect Theory, Rational Choice, and International Relations." *International Studies Quarterly* 41(1): 87–112.

2003. "Balances and Balancing: Concepts, Propositions, and Research Design." In John A. Vasquez and Colin Elman, eds., *Realism and the Balancing of Power: A New Debate*. Upper Saddle River, NJ: Prentice Hall, 128–153.

2004. "What Do Great Powers Balance against and When?" In T. V. Paul, James Wirtz, and Michel Fortmann, eds., *Balance of Power Revisited: Theory and Practice in the 21st Century*. Stanford, CA: Stanford University Press, 29–51.

2008. "Preventive War and Democratic Politics." *International Studies Quarterly* 52(1): 1–24.

2011. "Preventive War: Concept and Propositions." *International Interactions* 37(1): 87–96.

Levy, Jack S., and Joseph R. Gochal. 2001/2002. "Democracy and Preventive War: Israel and the 1956 Sinai Campaign." *Security Studies* 11(2): 1–49.

Levy, Jack S., and William Mulligan. 2017. "Shifting Power, Preventive Logic, and the Response of the Target: Germany, Russia and the First World War." *Journal of Strategic Studies* 40(5): 731–769.

Lieber, Keir A. 2007. "The New History of World War I and What It Means for International Relations Theory." *International Security* 32(2): 155–191.

Lind, Jennifer. 2017. "Asia's Other Revisionist Power: Why U.S. Grand Strategy Unnerves China." *Foreign Affairs* 96(2): 74–82.

Lindblom, Charles. 1959. "The Science of Muddling Through." *Public Administration Review* 19(2): 79–88.

Lindsay, Jon R. 2014/2015. "The Impact of China on Cybersecurity: Fiction and Friction." *International Security* 39(3): 7–47.

Lu, Marcus. 2023. "Ranked: The Top Economies in the World (1980–2075)." Visual Capitalist, July 21. www.visualcapitalist.com/top-economies-in-the-world-1980-2075/

Luard, Evan. 1971. "China and the United Nations." *International Affairs* 47(4): 726–744.

Lundgren, Magnu, Theresa Squatrito, and Jonas Tallberg. 2017. "Stability and Change in International Policy-Making: A Punctuated Equilibrium Approach." *Review of International Organizations* 13(4): 547–572.

MacCormac, Earl R. 1976. *Metaphor and Myth in Science and Religion.* Durham, NC: Duke University.

MacLeod, Michael C. 2002. "The Logic of Positive Feedback: Telecommunications Policy through the Creation, Maintenance, and Destruction of a Regulated Monopoly." In Frank R. Baumgartner and Bryan D. Jones, eds., *Policy Dynamics.* Chicago: University of Chicago Press, 51–72.

MacMillan, Margaret. 2013. *The War That Ended Peace.* New York: Random House.

Manna, Paul. 2006. *School's In: Federalism and the National Education Agenda.* Washington, DC: Georgetown University Press.

Maor, Moshe. 2014. "Policy Bubbles: Policy Overreaction and Positive Feedback: Policy Bubbles." *Governance* 27(3): 469–487.

Mastro, Oriana S. 2021 "The Taiwan Temptation: Why Beijing Might Resort to Force." *Foreign Affairs* 100(4): 58–67.

Mayr, Ernst. 1958. "Change of Genetic Environment and Evolution." In Julian Huxley, A. C. Hardy, and E. B. Ford, eds., *Evolution as A Process.* New York: Collier, 188–213.

  1963. *Animal Species and Evolution.* Harvard, MA: Harvard University Press.

Mazarr, Michael J. 2007. "The Iraq War and Agenda Setting." *Foreign Policy Analysis* 3(1): 1–23.

  2020. "Dire Straits: Should American Support for Taiwan Be Ambiguous? A Guarantee Won't Solve the Problem." *Foreign Affairs,* September 24. www.foreignaffairs.com/articles/united-states/2020-09-24/dire-straits

McDermott, Rose. 1998. *Risk-Taking in International Relations: Prospect Theory in American Foreign Policy.* Ann Arbor: University of Michigan Press.

McDonough, John. 1998. *Interests, Ideas, and Deregulation.* Ann Arbor: University of Michigan Press

McFaul, Michael, Stephen Sestanovich, and John J. Mearsheimer. 2014. "Faulty Powers: Who Started the Ukraine Crisis?" *Foreign Affairs* 93(6): 167–178.

McLendon, Michael K. 2003. "The Politics of Higher Education: Toward an Expanded Research Agenda." *Educational Policy* 17(1): 165–191.

Mearsheimer, John J. 2001. *The Tragedy of Great Power Politics.* New York: Norton.

  2014. "Taiwan's Dire Straits." *National Interest* 130 (March–April): 29–39.

Mearsheimer, John J., and Stephen M. Walt. 2003. "An Unnecessary War." *Foreign Policy*, 134 (January/February): 50–59.

Mercacante, Steve D. 2012. *Why Germany Nearly Won: A New History of the Second World War in Europe*. Santa Barbara, CA: Praeger.

Modelski, George. 1987a. *Long Cycles in World Politics*. Seattle: University of Washington Press.

ed. 1987b. *Exploring Long Cycles*. Boulder, CO: Rienner.

Modelski, George, and William R. Thompson. 1996. *Leading Sectors and World Powers: The Coevolution of Global Economics and Politics*. Columbia: University of South Carolina Press.

Mohan, Surinder. 2022. *Complex Rivalry: The Dynamics of India–Pakistan Conflict*. Ann Arbor: University of Michigan Press.

Mokyr, Joel. 1990. *The Lever of Riches: Technological Creativity and Economic Progress*. Oxford: Oxford University Press.

Montgomery, Evan B. 2014. "Contested Primacy in the Western Pacific: China's Rise and the Future of U.S. Power Projection." *International Security* 38(4): 115–149.

Morgenthau, Hans. [1948] 1978. *Politics among Nations*. Fifth edition. New York: Knopf.

Mortensen, Peter B. 2005. "Policy Punctuations in Danish Local Budgeting." *Public Administration* 83(4): 931–950.

Most, Benjamin A., and Harvey Starr. 1989. *Inquiry, Logic and International Politics*. Columbia: University of South Carolina Press.

Moyer, Jonathan D., Collin J. Meisel, Austin S. Matthews, David K. Bohl, and Mathew J. Burrows. 2021. *China–US Competition: Measuring Global Influence*. Scowcroft Center, Atlantic Council and Frederick Pardee Center for International Futures, University of Denver. www.atlanticcouncil.org/wp-content/uploads/2021/06/China-US-Competition-Report-2021.pdf

Mueller, Karl P., Jason J. Castillo, Forrest E. Morgan, Negeen Pegahi, and Brian Rosen. 2006. *Striking First: Preemptive and Preventive Attack in U.S. National Security Policy*. Santa Monica, CA: RAND.

Mulligan, William, and Jack S. Levy. 2019. "Rethinking Power Politics in an Interdependent World." *Journal of Interdisciplinary History* 49(4): 611–640.

Murray, Michelle. 2010. "Identity, Insecurity, and Great Power Politics: The Tragedy of German Naval Ambition before First World War." *Security Studies* 19(4): 656–688.

2019. *The Struggle for Recognition in International Relations: Status, Revisionism, and Rising Powers*. New York: Oxford University Press.

Nexon, Daniel H. 2009. "The Balance of Power in Balance." *World Politics* 61(2): 330–359.

Niles, Mark C. 2011. "Punctuated Equilibrium: A Model for Administrative Evolution." *John Marshall Law Review* 44: 353–422.

Nincic, Miroslav. 2011. *The Logic of Positive Engagement.* Ithaca, NY: Cornell University Press.

Norris, Pippa, ed. 1999. *Critical Citizens: Global Support for Democratic Government.* Oxford: Oxford University Press.

2011. *Democratic Deficit: Critical Citizens Revisited.* Cambridge: Cambridge University Press.

Norris, Pippa, and Ronald Inglehart. 2019. *Cultural Backlash: Trump, Brexit, and Authoritarian Populism.* Cambridge: Cambridge University Press.

Nye, Joseph S. Jr. 1990. *Bound to Lead: The Changing Nature of American Power.* New York: Basic Books.

Jr. 2002. *The Paradox of American Power.* New York: Oxford University Press.

Jr. 2004. *Soft Power: The Means to Success in World Politics.* New York: PublicAffairs.

O'Hanlon, Michael E. 2000. "Why China Cannot Conquer Taiwan." *International Security* 25(2): 51–86.

O'Hanlon, Michael E., Lyle Goldstein, and William Murray. 2004. "Correspondence: Damn the Torpedoes: Debating Possible U.S. Navy Losses in a Taiwan Scenario." *International Security* 29(2): 202–206.

Olson, Mancur, Jr. 1963. "Rapid Growth as a Destabilizing Force." *Journal of Economic History* 23(4): 529–552.

1965. *The Logic of Collective Action.* Cambridge, MA: Harvard University Press.

1982. *The Rise and Decline of Nations: Economic Growth, Stagflation, and Social Rigidities.* New Haven, CT: Yale University Press.

Or, Nick Hin-Kin. 2019a. *Policy Agendas and Regime Liberalisation: The Case of Hong Kong 1975–2016.* PhD dissertation, University of Southampton. https://eprints.soton.ac.uk/437696/1/thesis_NickOr_final.pdf

2019b. "How Policy Agendas Change When Autocracies Liberalize: The Case of Hong Kong, 1975–2016." *Public Administration* 97(4): 926–941.

Oren, Ido. 2003. *Our Enemies and US: America's Rivalries and the Making of Political Science.* Ithaca, NY: Cornell University Press.

Organski, A. F. K. 1968. *World Politics.* Second edition. New York: Knopf.

Organski, A. F. K., and Jacek Kugler. 1980. *The War Ledger.* Chicago: University of Chicago Press.

Pan, Chengxin. 2012. *Knowledge, Desire and Power in Global Politics: Western Representations of China's Rise.* Cheltenham: Elgar.

Park, Angela Y.S., and Joshua Sapotichne. 2020. "Punctuated Equilibrium and Bureaucratic Autonomy in American City Governments." *Policy Studies Journal* 48(4): 896–925.

Paul, T.V., 2018. *Restraining Great Powers: Soft Balancing from Empires to the Global Era.* New Haven, CT: Yale University Press.

Perl, Anthony, and James A. Dunn, Jr. 2007. "Reframing Auto Fuel Efficiency Policy: Punctuating a North American Policy Equilibrium." *Transport Reviews* 27(1): 1–35.

Pharr, Susan, and Robert D. Putnam. 2000. *Disaffected Democracies: What is Troubling the Trilateral Countries?* Princeton, NJ: Princeton University Press.

Platias, Athanassios, and Vasilis Trigkas. 2021. "Unravelling the Thucydides' Trap: Inadvertent or War of Choice?" *Chinese Journal of International Politics* 14(2): 187–217.

Posen, Barry R. 2003. "Command of the Commons: The Military Foundation of U.S. Hegemony." *International Security* 28(1): 5–46.

Powell, Robert. 1991. "Absolute and Relative Gains in International Relations Theory." *American Political Science Review* 85(4): 1303–1320.

1999. *In the Shadow of Power: States and Strategies in International Politics.* Princeton, NJ: Princeton University Press.

Prestowitz, Clyde V., Jr. 1990. *Trading Places: How We Are Giving Our Future to Japan and How to Reclaim It.* New York: Basic Books.

Prindle, David F. 2012. "Importing Concepts from Biology into Political Science: The Case of Punctuated Equilibrium." *Policy Studies Journal* 40(1): 21–43.

Przeworski, Adam, and Henry Teune. 1970. *The Logic of Comparative Social Inquiry.* New York: Wiley-Interscience.

Pu, Xiaoyu. 2019. *Rebranding China: Contested Status Signaling in the Changing Global Order.* Stanford, CA: Stanford University Press.

Putnam, Robert D. 1988. "Diplomacy and Domestic Politics: The Logic of Two-Level Games." *International Organization* 42(3): 427–460.

1993. *Making Democracy Work: Civic Traditions in Modern Italy.* Princeton, NJ: Princeton University Press.

Qian, Jing, James R. Vreeland, and Jianzhi Zhao. 2023. "The Impact of China's AIIB on the World Bank." *International Organization* 77(1): 217–237.

Quora. www.quora.com/What-is-the-meaning-of-Wellingtons-quote-in-modern-vernacular-of-the-nearest-run-thing-you-ever-saw-in-your-life-when-referring-to-Napoleon-and-the-Battle-of-Waterloo).

Ragin, Charles C. 1987. *The Comparative Method: Moving beyond Qualitative and Quantitative Strategies.* Berkeley: University of California Press.

Rasler, Karen A., and William R. Thompson. 1985. "War and the Economic Growth of Major Powers." *American Journal of Political Science* 29(3): 513–538.

1991. "Technological Innovation, Capability Positional Shift, and Systemic War." *Journal of Conflict Resolution* 35(3): 412–442.

Ratner, Ely. 2021. "Statement by Dr. Ely Ratner, Assistant Secretary of Defense for Indo-Pacific Security Affairs Office of the Secretary of Defense before the 117th Congress Committee on Foreign Relations, United States Senate." December 8. www.foreign.senate.gov/imo/media/doc/120821_Ratner_Testimony1.pdf.

Rauch, Carsten. 2017. "Challenging the Power Consensus: GDP, CINC, and Power Transition." *Security Studies* 26(4): 642–664.

Ray, James L. 1974. "Status Inconsistency and War Involvement among European States, 1816–1970." *Peace Science Society Papers* 23: 69–80.

Renshon, Jonathan. 2016. "Status Deficits and War." *International Organization* 70(3): 513–550.

2017. *Fighting for Status: Hierarchy and Conflict in World Politics*. Princeton, NJ: Princeton University Press.

Repetto, Robert, ed. 2006. *Punctuated Equilibrium and the Dynamics of U.S. Environmental Policy*. New Haven, CT: Yale University Press.

Richardson, Lewis F. 1960. *Arms and Insecurity*. Pittsburgh: Boxwood Press.

Richelson, Jeffrey T. ed. 2013. "The Snowden Affair: Web Resources the Latest Firestorm over the National Security Agency." *National Security Archive Electronic Briefing Book*. Washington, DC: National Security Archive, George Washington University, September 4. https://nsarchive2.gwu.edu/NSAEBB/NSAEBB436/

Riker, William R. 1962. *The Theory of Political Coalitions*. New Haven, CT: Yale University Press.

Rising Power Initiative. 2021. "RPI Policy Alert: Rising Powers React to Contentious U.S.–China Relations: A Roundup." George Washington University, March. www.risingpowersinitiative.org/publication/rising-powers-react-to-contentious-u-s-china-relations-a-roundup/

Robinson, Scott E. 2004. "Punctuated Equilibrium, Bureaucratization, and Budgetary Changes in Schools." *Policy Studies Journal* 32(1): 25–39.

Robinson, Scott E., and Floun'say R. Caver. 2006. "Punctuated Equilibrium and Congressional Budgeting." *Political Research Quarterly* 59(1): 161–166.

Robinson, Scott E., Floun'say R. Caver, Kenneth J. Meier, and Laurence J. O'Toole, Jr. 2007. "Explaining Policy Punctuations: Bureaucratization and Budget Change." *American Journal of Political Science* 51(1): 140–150.

Rooney, Bryan, Grant Johnson, and Miranda Priebe. 2021. *How Does Defense Spending Affect Economic Growth?* Santa Monica, CA: RAND.

Rosenzweig, Paul. 2013. "A Foolish Consistency Is the Hobgoblin of Little Minds: The Metadata Stay." *Lawfare.* www.lawfaremedia.org/article/foolish-consistency-hobgoblin-little-minds-metadata-stay

Ross, Robert. 2000. "The 1995–96 Taiwan Strait Confrontation: Coercion, Credibility, and the Use of Force." *International Security* 25(2): 87–123.

2002. "Navigating the Taiwan Strait: Deterrence, Escalation Dominance, and US–China Relations." *International Security* 27(2): 48–85.

Rostow, Walt W. [1960] 1971. *The Stages of Economic Growth: A Non-Communist Manifesto.* Second edition. Cambridge: Cambridge University Press.

1965. "Guerrilla Warfare in the Underdeveloped Areas." In Walter C. Clemens, Jr., ed., *World Perspectives in International Politics.* Boston: Little, Brown, 231–238.

Rousseau, David L. 2006. *Identifying Threats and Threatening Identities: The Social Construction of Realism and Liberalism.* Stanford, CA: Stanford University Press.

Russett, Bruce M. 1969. "Refining Deterrence Theory: The Japanese Attack on Pearl Harbor." In Dean G. Pruitt and Richard C. Snyder, eds., *Theory and Research on the Causes of War.* Englewood Cliffs, NJ: Prentice Hall, 127–135.

1970. *What Price Vigilance? The Burden of National Defense.* New Haven, CT: Yale University Press.

1983. "Prosperity and Peace: Presidential Address." *International Studies Quarterly* 27(4): 381–387.

Ryu, Jay E. 2009. "Exploring the Factors for Budget Stability and Punctuations: A Preliminary Analysis of State Government Sub-Functional Expenditures." *Policy Studies Journal* 37(3): 457–474.

Salka, William. 2004. "Mission Evolution: The United States Forest Service Response to Crisis." *Review of Policy Research* 21(2): 221–232.

Sample, Susan. 2018. "Power, Wealth, and Satisfaction: When Do Power Transitions Lead to Conflict?" *Journal of Conflict Resolution* 62(9): 1905–1931.

Sartori, Giovanni. 1970. "Concept Misinformation in Comparative Politics." *American Political Science Review* 64(4): 1033–1053.

Schattschneider, E. E. 1960. *The Semi-Sovereign People: A Realist View of Democracy in America.* New York: Holt, Rinehart and Winston.

Schelling, Thomas C. 1966. *Arms and Influence.* New Haven, CT: Yale University Press.

1978. Micromotives and Macrobehavior. New York: Norton.

Schilling, Warner R. 1973. "The H-Bomb Decision: How to Decide without Actually Choosing." In Morton H. Halperin and Arnold Kanter, eds., *Readings in American Foreign Policy: A Bureaucratic Perspective.* Boston: Little, Brown, 240–261.

Schmitt, Gary J., and Michael Mazza. 2020. "The End of 'Strategic Ambiguity' Regarding Taiwan." The American Enterprise Institute, September 17. www.aei.org/op-eds/the-end-of-strategic-ambiguity-regarding-taiwan/

Schneider, Anne L. 2006. "Patterns of Change in the Use of Imprisonment in the American States: An Integration of Path Dependence, Punctuated Equilibrium and Policy Design Approaches." *Political Research Quarterly* 59(3): 457–470.

Schrad, Mark L. 2007. "Constitutional Blemishes: American Alcohol Prohibition and Repeal as Policy Punctuation." *Policy Studies Journal* 35(3): 437–463.

Schroeder, Paul W. 1994. "Historical Reality vs. Neo-realist Theory." *International Security* 19(1): 108–138.

1995. "History and Neorealism: A Second Look." *International Security* 20(1): 193–195.

Schuman, Frederick L. 1948. *International Politics: The Destiny of the Western State System.* New York: McGraw Hill.

Schumpeter, Joseph A. 1939. *Business Cycles: A Theoretical, Historical, and Statistical Analysis of the Capitalist Process.* New York: McGraw Hill.

1949 [1911] (Translated by Redvers Opie). *The Theory of Economic Development: An Inquiry into Profits, Capital, Credit, Interest, and the Business Cycle.* Cambridge, MA: Harvard University Press.

Schweller, Randall L. 1994. "Bandwagoning for Profit: Bringing the Revisionist State In." *International Security* 19(1): 72–107.

1997. "New Realist Research on Alliances: Refining, Not Refuting, Waltz's Balancing Proposition." *American Political Science Review* 91(4): 927–930.

2008. *Unanswered Threats: Political Constraints on the Balance of Power.* Princeton, NJ: Princeton University Press.

2014. *Maxwell's Demon and the Golden Apple: Global Discord in the New Millenium.* Baltimore: Johns Hopkins University.

2015. "Rising Powers and Revisionism in Emerging World Orders." *Russia in Global Affairs.* http://eng.globalaffairs.ru/valday/Rising-Powers-and-Revisionism-in-Emerging-International-Orders-17730

Sciotto, Jim. 2024. *The Return of Great Powers: Russia, China, and the Next World War.* New York: Dutton.

Sebők, Miklós, and Tamás Berki. 2018. "Punctuated Equilibrium in Democracy and Autocracy: An Analysis of Hungarian Budgeting between 1868 and 2013." *European Political Science Review* 10(4): 589–611.

Senese, Paul D., and John A. Vasquez. 2008. *The Steps to War: An Empirical Study*. Princeton, NJ: Princeton University Press.

Shambaugh, David, and Robert Sutter. 2022. "50 Years Later: Nixon's Historic Visit to China." GW Today, March 2. https://gwtoday.gwu.edu/50-years-later-richard-nixons-historic-visit-china

Sharp, Travis. 2019. "Wars, Presidents, and Punctuated Equilibriums in US Defense Spending." *Policy Sciences* 52(3): 367–396.

Shiffman, Jeremy, Tanya Beer, and Yonghong Wu. 2002. "The Emergence of Global Disease Control Priorities." *Health Policy and Planning* 17(3): 225–234.

Shirk, Susan L. 2007. *China: Fragile Superpower*. Oxford: Oxford University Press.

2023. *Overreach: How China Derailed Its Peaceful Rise*. Oxford: Oxford University Press.

Silverstone, Scott A. 2007. *Preventive War and American Democracy*. London: Routledge.

Simon, Herbert A. 1957. *Models of Man*. New York: Wiley.

1977. "The Logic of Heuristic Decision-Making." In Robert S. Cohen and Marx W. Wartofsky, eds., *Models of Discovery*. Boston: D. Reidel, 154–175.

1983. *Reason in Human Affairs*. Stanford, CA: Stanford University Press.

Singapore Now. 2011. "No American Intervention If Taiwan Is Invaded." www.youtube.com/watch?v=q_gr3dtBaic

Singer, J. David, Stuart Bremer, and John Stuckey. 1972. "Capability Distribution, Uncertainty, and Major Power War, 1820–1965." In Bruce M. Russett, ed., *Peace, War, and Numbers*. Beverly Hills, CA: Sage, 19–48.

Slantchev, Branislav L. 2010. "Feigning Weakness." *International Organization* 64(3): 357–388.

Stockholm International Peace Research Institute. 2020. "2020 Fact Sheet (for 2019)" SIPRI Military Expenditure Database. https://en.wikipedia.org/wiki/List_of_countries_by_military_expenditures#As_a_share_of_GDP

Stolper, Thomas E. 1985. *China, Taiwan and the Offshore Islands*. New York: Routledge.

Talbert, Jeffery C., Bryan D. Jones, and Frank R. Baumgartner. 1995. "Nonlegislative Hearings and Policy Change in Congress." *American Journal of Political Science* 39(2): 383–405.

Tammen, Ronald L., Jacek Kugler, Douglas Lemke, Allan Stam III, Mark Abdollahian, Carole Alsharabati, Brian Efird, and A. F. K. Organski. 2000. *Power Transitions: Strategies for the 21st Century*. New York: Chatham House.

Tanaka, Miya. 2023. "Ex-U.S. Indo-Pacific Commander Sticks to 2027 Window on Taiwan Attack." Kyoto News, January 23. https://english.kyodonews.net/news/2023/01/018a26a02962-ex-us-indo-pacific-commander-sticks-to-2027-window-on-taiwan-attack.html

Tang, Shiping. 2013. *The Social Evolution of International Politics*. Oxford: Oxford University Press.

      2020. *On Social Evolution: Phenomenon and Social Paradigm*. New York: Routledge.

Thompson, William R. 1983. "Uneven Economic Growth, Systemic Challenges, and Global Wars." *International Studies Quarterly* 27(3): 341–355.

      1990. "Long Waves, Technological Innovation, and Relative Decline." *International Organization* 44(2): 201–233.

      1992. "Dehio, Long Cycles, and the Geohistorical Context of Structural Transition." *World Politics* 45(1): 127–153.

      2003. "A Streetcar Named Sarajevo: Catalysts, Multiple Causation Chains, and Rivalry Structures." *International Studies Quarterly* 47(3): 453–474.

      ed. 2009. *Systemic Transitions: Past, Present, and Future*. New York: Palgrave Macmillan,

      2020. *Power Concentration in World Politics: The Political Economy of Systemic Leadership, Growth, and Conflict*. Cham, Switzerland: Springer.

      2022. *American Global Pre-Eminence: The Development and Erosion of Systemic Leadership*. Oxford: Oxford University Press.

Thompson, William R., and Leila Zakhirova. 2019. *Racing to the Top: How Energy Fuels Systemic Leadership in World Politics*. Oxford: Oxford University Press.

Thompson, William R., and L. Gary Zuk. 1982. "War, Inflation, and the Kondratieff Long Wave." *Journal of Conflict Resolution* 26(4): 621–644.

Thomson, James C. 1973. "How Could Vietnam Happen? An Autopsy." In Morton H. Halperin and Arnold Kanter, eds., *Readings in American Foreign Policy: A Bureaucratic Perspective*. Boston: Little, Brown, 98–110.

Thurston, Anne F. 2021. *Engaging China: Fifty Years of Sino-American Relations*. New York: Columbia University Press.

Time Magazine. 2022. "Biden: US Would Defend Taiwan from 'Unprecedented Attack.'" September 18. https://time.com/6214511/biden-defend-taiwan-china-us/

Toal, Gerard. 2017. *Near Abroad: Putin, the West, and the Contest over Ukraine and the Caucasus*. Oxford: Oxford University Press.

de Tocqueville, Alexis. [1856] 1955. *The Old Regime and the French Revolution*. New York: Anchor Books.

Toft, Monica D. 2017. "Why Is America Addicted to Foreign Interventions?" *The National Interest*. https://nationalinterest.org/feature/why-america-addicted-foreign-interventions-23582?nopaging=1

Trachtenberg, Marc. 2007. "Preventive War and U.S. Foreign Policy." *Security Studies* 16(1): 1–31.

Treisman, David. 2004. "Rational Appeasement." *International Organization* 58(2): 344–373.

True, James L. 1999. "Attention, Inertia, and Equity in the Social Security Program." *Journal of Public Administration Research and Theory* 9(4): 571–596.

2002. "The Changing Focus of National Security Policy." In Frank R. Baumgartner and Bryan D. Jones, eds., *Policy Dynamics*. Chicago: University of Chicago Press, 155–183.

True, James L., Bryan D. Jones, and Frank R. Baumgartner. 2007. "Punctuated-Equilibrium Theory: Explaining Stability and Change in Public Policymaking." In Paul A. Sabatier, ed., *Theories of Policy Process*. Boulder, CO: Westview, 155–187.

True, James L., and Glenn Utter. 2002. "Saying 'Yes', 'No', and 'Load Me Up' to Guns in America." *American Journal of Public Administration* 32(2): 216–241.

Tuchman, Barbara W. 1962. *The Guns of August*. New York: Dell.

Tyler, Patrick. 1999. *A Great Wall, Six Presidents and China: An Investigative History*. New York: Perseus.

Van den Dool, Annemieke, and Jialin Li. 2023. "What Do We Know about the Punctuated Equilibrium Theory in China? A Systematic Review and Research Priorities." *Policy Studies Journal* 51(2): 283–305.

Van Evera, Stephen. 1984. "The Cult of Offensive and the Origins of the First World War." *International Security* 9(1): 58–107.

1999. *Causes of War: Power and the Roots of Conflict*. Ithaca, NY: Cornell University Press.

Vasquez, John A. 1993. *The War Puzzle*. Cambridge: Cambridge University Press.

1996. "When Are Power Transitions Dangerous? An Appraisal and Reformulation of Power Transition Theory." In Jacek Kugler and

Douglas Lemke, eds., *Parity and War: Evaluations and Extensions of the War Ledger*. Ann Arbor: University of Michigan Press, 35–56.

1997. "The Realist Paradigm and Degenerative Versus Progressive Research Programs: An Appraisal of Neotraditional Research on Waltz's Balancing Proposition." *American Political Science Review* 91(4): 899–912.

2009a. "Whether and How Global Leadership Transitions Will Result in War: Some Long-Term Predictions from Steps-to-War Explanation." In William R. Thompson, ed., *Systemic Transitions: Past, Present, and Future*. New York: Palgrave Macmillan, 131–160.

2009b. *The War Puzzle Revisited*. Cambridge: Cambridge University Press.

Vasquez, John A., and Colin Elman, eds. 2003. *Realism and the Balance of Power: A Debate*. Upper Saddle River, NY: Prentice Hall.

Vasquez, John A., and Marie T. Henehan. 2011. *Territory, War, and Peace*. New York: Routledge.

Veblen, Thorstein. 1915. *Imperial Germany and the Industrial Revolution*. New York: Macmillan.

Vogel, Ezra F. 1979. *Japan as Number One: Lessons for America*. Cambridge, MA: Harvard University Press.

Wachman, Alan M. 2007. *Why Taiwan: Geostrategic Rationales for China's Territorial Integrity*. Stanford, CA: Stanford University Press.

Walgrave, Stefaan, and Rens Vliegenthart, 2010. "Why Are Policy Agendas Punctuated? Friction and Cascading in Parliament and Mass Media in Belgium." *Journal of European Public Policy* 17(8): 1147–1170.

Wallace, Michael D. 1973. *War and Rank among States*. Lexington, KY: Heath.

Walt, Stephen M. 1987. *The Origins of Alliances*. Ithaca, NY: Cornell University Press.

1997. "The Progressive Power of Realism." *American Political Science Review* 91(4): 931–935.

2005. *Taming American Power: The Global Response to U.S. Primacy*. New York: Norton.

Waltz, Kenneth N. 1979. *Theory of International Politics*. Reading, MA: Addison-Wesley.

1997. "Evaluating Theories." *American Political Science Review* 91(4): 913–917.

2000. "Structural Realism after the Cold War." *International Security* 25(1): 5–41.

Wang, Zheng. 2014. *Never Forget National Humiliation: Historical Memory in Chinese Politics and Foreign Policy*. New York: Columbia University Press,

Ward, Steven. 2017. *Status and the Challenge of Rising Powers*. Cambridge: Cambridge University Press.

Wendt, Alexander. 1992. "Anarchy Is What States Make of It: The Social Construction of Power Politics." *International Organization* 46(2): 391–425.

1999. *Social Theory of International Politics*. Cambridge: Cambridge University Press.

Whiting, Allen S. 1960. *China Crosses the Yalu: The Decision to Enter the Korean War*. Stanford, CA: Stanford University Press.

1975. *The Chinese Calculus of Deterrence: India and Indochina*. Ann Arbor: University of Michigan Press.

Wikipedia 2024. "Shanghai Cooperation Organization" https://en.wikipedia.org/wiki/Shanghai_Cooperation_Organisation

2024. "Stylized Fact." https://en.wikipedia.org/wiki/Stylized_fact

Wildavsky, Aaron. 1964. *The Politics of the Budgetary Process*. Boston: Little, Brown.

1975. *Budgeting: A Comparative Theory of Budgetary Process*. Boston: Little, Brown.

1992. *The New Politics of the Budgetary Process*. Boston: Little, Brown.

Wingrove, Josh. 2022. "Biden Says US Would Defend Taiwan in 'Unprecedented Attack.'" Bloomberg, September 18. www.bloomberg.com/news/articles/2022-09-18/biden-says-us-would-defend-taiwan-from-unprecedented-attack

Wohlforth, William C., ed. 2003. *Cold War Endgame: Oral History, Analysis, Debates*. State College: Pennsylvania State University Press.

Wohlforth, William C., Richard Little, Stuart J. Kaufman, David Kang, Charles A. Jones, Victoria Tin-Bor Hui, Arthur Eckstein, Daaniel Deudney, and William L. Brenner. 2007. "Testing Balance-of-Power Theory in World History." *European Journal of International Relations*, 13(2): 155–185.

Wolf, Reinhard. 2014. "Rising Powers, Status Ambitions, and the Need to Reassure: What China Could Learn from Imperial Germany's Failures." *Chinese Journal of International Politics* 7(2): 185–219.

Wolfe, Michelle. 2012. "Putting on the Brakes or Pressing on the Gas? Media Attention and the Speed of Policymaking." *Policy Studies Journal* 40(1): 109–126.

Wolfers, Arnold. 1962. *Discord and Collaboration: Essays on International Politics*. Baltimore: Johns Hopkins University Press.

Wood, Robert S. 2006a. "The Dynamics of Incrementalism: Subsystems, Politics, and Public Lands." *Policy Studies Journal* 34(1): 1–16.

2006b. "Tobacco's Tipping Point: The Master Settlement Agreement as a Focusing Event." *Policy Studies Journal* 34(3): 419–436.

Worsham, Jeff, and Chaun Stores. 2012. "Pet Sounds: Subsystems, Regimes, Policy Punctuations, and the Neglect of African American Farmers, 1935–2006." *Policy Studies Journal* 40(1): 169–190.

Xi, Jinping. 2021. "China Welcomes Helpful Suggestions but Won't Accept Sanctimonious Preaching." *Xinhua*, July 1. www.xinhuanet.com/eng lish/special/2021-07/01/c_1310037332.htm

Yergin, Daniel. 1991. *The Prize: The Epic Quest for Oil, Money, and Power.* New York: Simon & Schuster.

  2011. *The Quest: Energy, Security and the Remaking of the Modern World.* New York: Penguin.

Young, Oran R. 2010. *International Dynamics: Emergent Patterns of International Environmental Governance.* Cambridge, MA: MIT Press.

Young, Oran, and Gail Osherenko, eds. 1993. *Polar Politics: Creating International Environmental Regimes.* Ithaca, NY: Cornell University Press.

Zadeh, Lofti A. 1965. "Fuzzy Sets." *Information and Control* 8(3): 338–353.

Zakaria, Fareed. 2020. "The New China Scare: Why America Shouldn't Panic about Its Latest Challenger." *Foreign Affairs* 99(1): 52–69.

  2024. "Taiwan: Unfinished Business—A Special Fareed Zakaria Special." CNN (Cable News Network), March 10. https://cnnpressroom.blogs.cnn .com/2024/03/08/taiwan-unfinished-business-a-fareed-zakaria-special-pre mieres-sunday-march-10-at-800pm-et-on-cnn-cnni/

Zelleke, Andy. 2020. "'Strategic Clarity' Won't Solve the United States' Taiwan Dilemma: An Open Commitment to Defend Taiwan Won't Mean Much Unless the U.S. Has the Certain Capacity to Do So," *The Diplomat*, October 2. https://thediplomat.com/2020/10/strategic-clar ity-wont-solve-the-united-states-taiwan-dilemma/

Zhang, Ketian. 2019. "Cautious Bully: Reputation, Resolve, and Beijing's Use of Coercion in the South China Sea." *International Security* 44(1): 117–159.

  2024. *China's Gambit: The Calculus of Coercion.* Cambridge: Cambridge University Press.

Index

Afghanistan War (2001–2021), 94, 147, 227, 234
agenda setting
  comparative studies on, 40, 42
  elements of, 73–75, 82
  issue definition influence on, 28
Alexandrova, Petya, 42
alliance status
  conditions for US interventions, 128, 138, 144–145
  Russo-Ukrainian War and, 145
Allison, Graham, 13, 51–52, 150, 161, 176, 197, 232
anti-US coalition
  factors in forming, 88, 103
  potential emergence of, ix, 10–11, 97, 103, 221–222
  risks from forming, 100
appeasement, rational vs. selective, 231–232
Australia
  agenda setting in, 42
  cohesion in, 148–149
  Quad membership, 110
authoritarian systems
  democratic systems vs., 42–46
  information distortion in, 44, 229
  policy disasters in, 45
  political security of leaders, 72
Axelrod, Robert, 7

Bacevich, Andrew, 193
balance of power, 195–212
  academic movement away from, 186
  balance of threat vs., 202, 210, 212
  classical realism views, 196–198, 210–211
  contradictions of, 83, 197–199
  disparity between distribution of benefits and power, 178–179, 198

misunderstandings and miscommunications, 211–212
  multiple connotations of, 183, 194–196, 208–209
  peace enhanced by, 89, 168, 196, 198
  revisionist vs. status quo states, 200–207, 209
  role in the world wars, 207–209
  sameness of states, 199–201, 209
  soft balancing, 88
balance of threat theory, 202, 210, 212
bandwagon effect
  factors in, 86–87
  momentum in, 87, 93, 105, 224
  from positive feedback, 24, 217, 231
bandwagoning
  classical realism views, 196
  defined, 83
  unraveling of, 96–97
Bartel, Larry, 86
Baumgartner, Frank, vii, 3–8, 12, 21–23, 25–26, 29, 32–36, 38, 40–41, 45, 51–54, 65–66, 68, 73, 82, 84–85, 152, 221–222, 225, 233
Bay of Pigs invasion (1961), 100, 116, 119, 139, 188
Beckley, Michael, 169, 179
Benjamin, Roger, 159
Berki, Tamás, 45
Bernstein, Richard, 147
Bethmann Hollweg, Theobald von, 171, 208
Bevan, Shaun, 42
Biden, Joseph
  China policies, 66, 68, 185
  defense of Indo-Pacific allies, 111–113
  election of, 66, 192
  Hamas–Israel War, 228

eastward expansion of, 61, 145, 172
Trump remarks on, 216
negative feedback, *See also* positive
feedback
in media attention, 36
stabilizing effects of, 23–25, 217–219
in US policymaking, 31–33
Netanyahu, Benjamin, 226
Nexon, Daniel, 196
Nixon, Richard, 58–60, 62–66, 76–78,
104, 142, 184, 219
North Korea, nuclear capability of,
100–102, *See also* Korean War
(1950–1953)
North, Robert, 162
nuclear power, issue redefinition of, 26,
29
nuclear weapons
capabilities of North Korea and Iran,
100–102
great powers use of, 102, 224
realist views of, 210
Ukraine's relinquishment of, 101,
210
US programs, 49, 102, 155
Nye, Joseph, 148

Obama, Barack, 66, 183, 187
oil price shocks, 94, 96
Olson, Mancur, 43, 160
OPEC (Organization of Petroleum-
Exporting Countries), 94, 96–97
Opium War, 175
Or, Nick Hin-Kin, 42
Organski, Kenneth, 167, 173, 197–198,
204
Osherenko, Gail, 79

Parsons, Wes, 164
participants, in the garbage can model,
See also political entrepreneurship
defined, 74
determinants of, 79, 87
interactions among model elements,
82, 104–105
OPEC oil price hikes, 96
UN seat for China, 90, 93–94
Peloponnesian War (431–404 BCE),
232–233
Pelosi, Nancy, 68, 109, 119

policy disasters, 44–46
policy image, defined, 26, *See also* issue
definition and redefinition
policy persistence
democracies vs. autocracies, 43
factors in, 222, 227
garbage can model explanation of,
82, 105
prevalence of, 23–26
self-entrapment in, 228
Sino-American relations influenced
by, 69–73
stick-slip dynamics, 38
policy venues
availability of, 75
defined, 30
interaction with issue definition, 28, 30
linkages among, 25
stability and instability driven by,
25–26
policymaking, *See also* garbage can
model of policymaking
costs of, 87
difficulty of predicting changes, 75,
79, 222, 229
episodic nature of, 3–8, 19, 75
maturation and momentum role,
90–94
positive feedback loops in, 82–90
serendipity in, 16, 74, 78, 82, 105,
222
varying sources of, 65
political entrepreneurship
forum shopping, 28, 65, 73, 98
issue redefinition in, 27–29
necessity of, 7, 18, 57, 75, 105
overview, 181–182
political narratives
construction of, 193, 212–216, 227
narrator reflected in, 189
revisionist vs. status quo tendencies,
206
Pompeo, Mike, 116, 191
positive feedback
destabilizing effects of, 24–25,
217–219
going with the winner and, 82–90,
217
momentum in, 56, 224, 231,
233–234

Printed by Integrated Books International,
United States of America